Spiritualism In Great Britain

Emma Hardinge Britten

Kessinger Publishing's Rare Reprints

Thousands of Scarce and Hard-to-Find Books on These and other Subjects!

- Americana
- Ancient Mysteries
- Animals
- Anthropology
- Architecture
- Arts
- Astrology
- Bibliographies
- Biographies & Memoirs
- Body, Mind & Spirit
- Business & Investing
- Children & Young Adult
- Collectibles
- Comparative Religions
- Crafts & Hobbies
- Earth Sciences
- Education
- Ephemera
- Fiction
- Folklore
- Geography
- Health & Diet
- History
- Hobbies & Leisure
- Humor
- Illustrated Books
- Language & Culture
- Law
- Life Sciences

- Literature
- Medicine & Pharmacy
- Metaphysical
- Music
- Mystery & Crime
- Mythology
- Natural History
- Outdoor & Nature
- Philosophy
- Poetry
- Political Science
- Science
- Psychiatry & Psychology
- Reference
- Religion & Spiritualism
- Rhetoric
- Sacred Books
- Science Fiction
- Science & Technology
- Self-Help
- Social Sciences
- Symbolism
- Theatre & Drama
- Theology
- Travel & Explorations
- War & Military
- Women
- Yoga
- *Plus Much More!*

We kindly invite you to view our catalog list at:
http://www.kessinger.net

Because this article has been extracted from a parent book, it may have non-pertinent text at the beginning or end of it.

Any blank pages following the article are necessary for our book production requirements. The article herein is complete.

Through teachings received also from individuals, who of all others, merited the name of OCCULT ADEPTS, the author has been led to consider that Occultism is in theory the revealment of that which was hidden, or the occult powers and potencies in the animate and inanimate realms of being; whilst Spiritualism is the demonstration of the same occult forces manifested from a super-mundane state of existence. The modern writers who have assumed for themselves the name of "Occultists," are not contented with this position.

Their interpretation of what and who "Spirits" are, and what is the work which this volume has been written to record, will be briefly described in our section on India; it must suffice for the present to say, that the author's definitions would appear in connection with the theories of "the Occultists," as worthless and shadowy as the spirits of whom we write appear, in comparison with the inconceivably *high* presences, or "144th embodiments" of exalted "egos," of whom the "Occultists" write. Eliphas Levi, without soaring into the extraordinary flights of revelation assumed to be authoritative by these same modern "Occultists" still occupies ground that takes no direct part with the spontaneous developments of spirit power manifested in the modern outpouring, nor yet with the simple formulæ of the spirit circle.

The day will come when true Occultism and "common place Spiritualism," will be recognized as being built upon earth and founded in man himself; leading to heaven, and culminating in the personality of angels.

In that day when theories shall be scientifically formulated from facts, and facts will not be scornfully derided to suit theories, Eliphas Levi and many another profound writer, whose words are now "Kabbala" to the multitude, will be recognized as the prophets of the grand Spiritual science of the future. Till then, it would be unphilosophical to give "that which is holy to the dogs."

CHAPTER XII.

SPIRITUALISM IN GREAT BRITAIN.

ONE of the chief difficulties which besets a writer who would attempt to give a faithful account of the Spiritual movement in Great Britain, is the very "embarrassment of riches" with which the subject is loaded, Spiritualistic experiences having become so universal that the author's requisition for evidence is met by an influx of responses which make the task of selection too herculean for the purposes of this volume. Still another subject of perplexity arises from the characteristic reserve of those with whom the phenomena of Spiritualism are very generally associated in this country.

In America, where the sources of popular power are derived from the people, Spiritualism may be found more generally represented by the rank and file of Society, than among the wealthier classes.

In Europe on the contrary, where the governing power centres in an hereditary and influential aristocracy, the people derive their opinions as they do their laws and fashions, from the ruling classes, and it is chiefly amongst these that Spiritualism flourishes.

It is not claimed that this wonderful movement is confined to any class in either hemisphere. It will be found in the hut, and the palace; in the mining camp, and the halls of legislation. Nevertheless its greatest prevalence is ever with the ruling power. Since then Spiritualism in Europe takes the deepest hold of those whose rank and station induces them to shrink from subjecting their personal experiences to public criticism, the author too frequently becomes the recipient of valuable testimony which cannot be made available, because the communicants insist on withholding their true names and addresses. "Miss E." and "Mrs. D.;" "Captain A." and "My Lord X. Y. Z." are impersonals, whom no one puts any confidence in. There is no satisfaction in offering such shadowy testimony to those who are asked to believe in occurrences of an unprecedented and often startling character. Resolving as we have done, not to demand credence for phenomenal incidents upon any testimony open to the charge of unreliability, we feel obliged to relegate an immense mass of interesting matter of this kind to the obscurity which unauthorised statements justly incur.

It would seem as if the Spiritual founders of the great outpouring had been experimenting with the forces at their command, and seeking to open up communion with the two worlds in many places, before they succeeded in systematizing the direct telegraphy which has marked the American phase of the movement.

Those who have perused the author's work entitled, "Modern American Spiritualism," will remember that a statement to this effect was made through the lips of an entranced subject magnetized by Dr. Hallock, of New York. If this hypothesis is admitted, it would account for the great prevalence of Spiritual phenomena which has marked this century in many parts of the world, prior to the disturbances in America known as "The Rochester Knockings." Thus it seems that Scientific Spirits, desirous of founding a Spiritual telegraph between the mortal and immortal realms of being, were instrumental in promoting the phenomena which occurred at Epworth Parsonage, in the family of John Wesley, and influencing Mesmer and his followers in the discovery of the life principle of magnetism.

The wonderful "preaching epidemic in Sweden;" the obsessions in Morzine; the uprising of Mormonism, Shakerism, the gift of tongues amongst the Irvingites, and the great revivals in Ireland, are all unmistakable fruits of the same mighty contagion of Spiritual forces, surging through an age specially prepared for their reception.

Let any candid student of Pneumatology peruse with attention the array of facts collected by Kerner in Germany, Cahagnet in France, and Mrs. Catherine Crowe in her English work, "The Night Side of Nature." Let him remember that these eminent writers contributed their vast mass of Spiritualistic testimony in advance of the "Rochester Knockings," and it will be impossible to evade the conclusion, that the widely separated lines of evidence all diverge from one powerful spiritual centre. Commending to our readers' attention Howitt's exhaustive "History of the Supernatural," the writings of R. D. Owen, Thomas Brevior, Kerner, Ennemoser, and Mrs. Catherine Crowe, for a wealth of detail not attainable in this work, we shall now lay before our readers some of those striking spiritual way marks which antedate the introduction of the modern spiritual telegraph in England.

The first representative case of spontaneous spiritual manifestations we select, occurred in the village of Sandford near Tiverton in Devonshire, about the year 1812. Quoting from an account published by the author some years ago, the particulars of which were derived partly from the newspaper reports of the time, but chiefly from the testimony of Mrs. Floyd—the author's venerable mother who was *an eye witness* of the scenes described, we call attention to the following details which we give in the language before published.

"It was about the year 1812 when my mother, then a young single lady, went with her parents to visit friends at the town of Tiverton, Devonshire.

"It was summer time, and during her first evening's residence she remarked, with surprise, the throng of private carriages which all seemed to be passing one way, and coming forth at one special time. Upon inquiry she learned that the object of this remarkable exodus was to proceed to a village some four or five miles distant, where a number of clergymen—of whom there were many residing in the town—together with the mayor and the principal physician of the place (both personal friends of my mother's family) were going to 'lay the ghost' which had, for a long time, haunted a certain old-fashioned residence in the village of Sandford. The 'trouble' which attached itself to this house, consisted in unaccountable noises, the ringing of bells, pattering of footsteps, lights proceeding from no human source, and other forms of preternatural disturbance.

"The house had been occupied for many years past by different tenants, none of whom had been able long to endure the terrors of their weird surroundings. Every effort made by the owner of the property to detect a mundane source for these annoyances had proved unavailing. At the period when my mother visited the neighbourhood, the house was tenanted by a family who had been induced to occupy it rent free, and who devoted the lower part to the business of a general shop.

"The presence of this family, however, seemed to have no effect, for the disturbances were as constant as ever. Even in open day passers-by could hear the knocking resounding 'like the tap of a shoemaker's hammer.' After nightfall the timid inhabitants of the village carefully avoided even the precincts of the place, whilst doctors, divines, politicians, and officers from the neighbouring garrison, assembled nightly to hold colloquies with the invisible tormentors.

"It seems that the order of these midnight conclaves was as follows. A large wooden table was placed in the centre of the room which the ghosts most commonly affected. Round this the assembled company would seat themselves, and question the rapper in much the same manner as we adopt in our modern investigations.

"For example: Several coins would be placed upon the table, and their number be indicated, *upon demand, and always correctly,* by knocks. At times the number of persons present, even their ages and professions, would be *correctly* told by signal raps. Had the sitters of seventy years ago been instructed how to anticipate the formula of the modern spirit circle, they could not have depicted its *modus operandi* more faithfully. Through the medium of certain signal raps, the sitters were always informed that the knocker was *a spirit, a female,* and one who had terminated an evil career by a violent death.

"Now although the united wisdom of a neighbourhood famous for its learning and piety pronounced through the press the solemn verdict, that 'a tremendous imposture existed *somewhere,*' yet for ten years, during which the house perpetually changed inhabitants, and was the subject of unceasing examination, the said '*imposture*' was never brought to light, nor could any mundane origin for the mysterious disturbance be detected.

"The mixture of ignorance and conservatism which prevailed amongst those who investigated this subject may be judged of from the following circumstances.

"Mr. Colton, a clergyman well known in the literary world as the author of 'Lacon' and other metaphysical works, had been a constant attendant upon the ghostly *séances,* and finally gave it as his opinion 'that the affair could never be cleared up on *mundane* grounds. No sooner was this statement circulated, than the journals of the day inferred, *that Mr. Colton must know something more of the causes than he chose to tell ; in fact, who knew but what the whole thing might have proceeded from him, as a clever ventriloquist ?* Not until Mr. Colton's departure for a foreign land, and the continuance of the hauntings, was the theory abandoned, that he, who dared to hint at a super-mundane origin of the mystery must himself be its source. Again, the magnates of Tiverton pitched upon a poor soldier of somewhat questionable character, who had returned from the war and was glad to share with his parents, the shelter of a place obtainable rent free, as the cause of the trouble. These wiseacres forgot that the disturbances had preceded the soldier's presence for two years ; however, in order to test the validity of their theory, they spirited him out of the village, and shipped him to a foreign land. But all was in vain. Neither the absence of the learned scholar nor the ignorant soldier affected the Sandford invisibles except—as if in mockery—to increase the force of their harassing demonstrations.

"The tenants who had been found bold enough to occupy the haunted mansion at the period when my mother's family came to visit Tiverton, were a poor shopkeeper with his wife and several children.

"Amongst the latter, a little girl of about ten years of age seemed to be the special theme of the ghost's malevolence.

"The child often complained of an *ugly old woman* whom she could see crouching in a corner of the room, making faces at her, and who would wake her up at night, and almost scare her into fits. One day this child was found lying dead upon the hearthstone. A coroner's inquest was held, and the verdict of the jury left it doubtful whether the poor little creature had been struck by lightning, died in a fit, or by the visitation of God. One thing was certain, namely, that the child had perished in the *haunted room*, and that she, above all the rest of the household, had been the victim of the ghost's malignity. A calamity of such a nature was too much even for the hardihood of the present tenant. He resolved upon an immediate removal, and would have put his determination into effect, had he not been delayed by the premature confinement of his wife, whose period of trial was hastened by the tragic circumstances of her little girl's decease.

"Pending the recovery of the sick woman, the physician, at whose house my mother and her family were temporary visitors, was called in to attend the woman. He was also requested to send a nurse competent to assist in such a case. Dr. Guffet, although well acquainted in his professional capacity with all the poor women of the neighbourhood, was unable to induce any one however necessitous to take service in the 'haunted house.'

"Having at length obtained a suitable attendant from a long distance off, the doctor flattered himself that his patient's case was progressing favourably. He soon found however that he was reckoning—in this instance at least, without *his ghost*—for it became evident that the stranger nurse was as much an object of the invisible's malignity as the deceased child had been.

"Having been put to sleep for convenience in the room where the child had so mysteriously died, she became the target for an incessant system of persecution. She was unable to obtain rest by day or night, and one morning when Doctor Guffet was summoned to attend her, he found her confined to her bed, from the effects of the severe beating she had received during the night from invisible hands. Her body was completely black with bruises, and these she testified before a magistrate, she had sustained from some invisible source which came and went without any known means of access to the chamber. The woman affirmed, that she felt a hand belabouring her, as if with a stone. The room was uncurtained, and the brightly shining moon made it as light as day. She testified upon oath in her examination, that no human being was in the room, nor could she discern a single creature near her. When at length her cries for help aroused the other inmates, and brought them to her room, the whole party heard a heavy bumping sound, as if something was falling off the bed, and moving of its own volition across the room, out at the door and down the stairs. The chief witness to the truth of this strange story was the doctor himself, who not only testified to the pitiable condition in which he found the poor nurse's body, but he added, 'the woman whom I sent to that house, hale, hearty, and stout, only a fortnight ago, is now an emaciated object, worn to a very shadow, and so distraught by fear that it would be murder to keep her there one hour longer.'

"The next incident which I have to record of this terrible abode, occurred at the sale of furniture which ensued, the very first hour that the mother of the family became convalescent.

"The auctioneer, who was related to Dr. Guffet, with whom my mother and her parents were visiting, informed them that as he was making an inventory of the goods, previous to the sale, he passed into the 'haunted chamber' about noon, and there found an old lady rummaging a wardrobe which stood partly open near the door. Deeming it one of the members of the family, although her dress pointed her out to be a person of some distinction, he proceeded with his work for some minutes, until he heard the voice of the landlord calling to him to come to dinner. Bowing to the old lady as he passed her, he stood at the door to see if she would go first; but as she continued her occupation without noticing him, he descended the stairs, and having taken the seat placed for him, proceeded with a courtesy peculiar to himself, to put another chair *for the lady whom he had noticed above.* On being questioned why he did so, explanations followed, and the family in haste ascended the stairs to see if any human being could really be found. All was in vain. Every nook and corner was searched without result, and when the auctioneer, at request, described the appearance of the strange visitor, it was universally admitted that the description corresponded exactly to the detestable vision which had tormented the poor deceased child.

"After these persons quitted the house it remained tenantless for many months. The noises could be heard for a considerable distance, and lights were seen flashing at the windows at all hours of the night.

"Workmen were employed to rip up the floors and pull down the walls, in the hope of discovering concealed springs and trap doors. All was to no purpose, however. During these researches, two windows at opposite ends of the long chamber—the principal scenes of the hauntings—were pierced by a bullet or missile of some kind, projected with such skill, that two perfectly round holes were found in corresponding panes of glass. The wind was felt of the passing missile, and the shiver of the glass heard by the workmen, yet nothing was seen, and as the room was on the second storey, without a ledge or the slightest foothold for any human being without, it might be inferred that the haunters desired to prove that no human agency could be at work in these manifestations. At length the sounds became so frightful that neither free tenants nor workmen would enter the place by day or night. It was ultimately abandoned, fell into decay, and what remained of it was pulled down. The papers of the time were full of reports, doubtless much exaggerated. Sages and scientists were alike baffled. Magistrates blustered and threatened, and several officers of the army, who had volunteered to sit up during the night, abandoned their watch, end refused again to enter such a 'veritable *Inferno*.'"

Remembering how many respectable witnesses testified to these facts,—how many years their continuance was a source of horror to a whole neighbourhood, and loss to the proprietor of a once splendid mansion, recollecting moreover, that one of the eye-witnesses is now living, and is a venerable lady incapable of falsehood, we have as good a right to admit this narrative into the category of historical records, as any well attested event of ancient or modern times.

We now turn to another form of haunting, selected from numerous other cases, because some of the witnesses are still living, and holding positions of the highest respectability. We refer to the unaccountable and persistent ringing of bells, which occurred in the house of Major Moor, a gentleman till lately residing at Great Bealing, near Woodbridge. These disturbances commenced on February 2nd, 1834, and continued at intervals with more or less violence till March 27th. The phenomena consisted of incessant ringing, sometimes of two or three, and not unfrequently of a whole row of nine bells at the same time—they rang day and night; at times when Major Moor, his servants, and friends, were facing them, when the doors were locked within, and the house was guarded without; when the wires of communication *were cut*, and nothing but the bells remained. The ceiling and walls were dented by the violence with which the bells were dashed against them, and despite the stringent measures taken to discover imposture or trick, this strange disturbance continued without evidence of human interference, for a period of fifty-three days. At the end of that time, it stopped as suddenly as it had originated, leaving its cause involved in impenetrable mystery. From a pamphlet published by Major Moor on this subject, entitled "Bealing Bells," also from some accounts printed in the Ipswich and other journals, we learn, that during the continuance of this persecution, Major Moor's investigations were assisted by several of his brother officers, some scientific gentlemen, and not a few clergymen who were attracted by the accounts which appeared in the papers of the day.

Amongst the persons who addressed letters to Major Moor, alleging that similar phenomena had occurred in their own houses, were families in

Cambridge, Ramsgate, London, Oxford, Windsor, Ipswich, and numerous other places. Mr. Wm. Felkin, Mayor of Nottingham, and Mr. Ashwell, a gentlemen of high standing in Chesterfield, gave accounts of the mysterious bell ringings occurring at their residences. But one of the most marked cases reported by Major Moor, in addition to his own experience, was that of Lieutenant Rivers, one of the officials of Greenwich Hospital. This witness stated that he had detailed thirty-seven watchers by day and night in the attempt to detect fraud in vain. He employed a bellhanger and his assistant to cut the wires of every bell in and about his premises, and then, in the face of the men and the presence of many neighbours who had come in to witness the wonder, the entire set of bells all over the house began ringing at once, and kept up incessant peals for several hours. The bells in some of the other officers' apartments in the Hospital were rung in the same way, and when Major Moor himself visited the place, he not only received the personal testimony of a large number of witnesses, but examined carefully the locality, and was made aware of the impossibility of the ringing being effected by any human agency.

The publicity which Major Moor gave to these circumstances, called forth a flood of testimony to events of a preternatural character, from various sections of the country. Then it appeared that bell-ringing was not the only form of disturbance prevailing. Hauntings not unlike in character those of the " Sandford Ghost," were reported from many quarters.

The Rev. Mr. Stewart, Incumbent of Sydensterne near Fakenham, Norfolk, wrote in a letter to Major Moor :—

"Our noises are of a graver character. Successions of rappings, groans, cries, sobs, heavy trampings, and thundering knocks in all the rooms and passages, have distressed us here for a period of nearly *nine* years, during the occupancy of my cure. They still continue, to the annoyance of my family, and the alarm of my servants. I am enabled to trace the existence of these disturbances during a period of sixty years past."

Mr. Stewart said that in 1833 and 1834, his predecessors in that house opened the doors to all respectable persons who desired to satisfy their curiosity or wished to investigate the hauntings, but he adds : "Their kindness was abused, their motives misinterpreted, and even their characters maligned. We therefore," he says, " shut *our* doors, and they remain hermetically sealed."

In closing these curious narratives it may not be amiss to give a few extracts from the records of a spirit circle which was held not long since, in which some parties present were commenting severely on the " unmeaning character of such manifestations as bell-ringing and knocking." At this juncture one of the communicating spirits interrupted the conversation with the following pertinent questions :—

" *Spirit*—Pray, sir, what do you do when you want to enter a house and find the door closed ?

" *Mortal*—Well ! If we really want to get in we knock or ring.

" *Spirit*—Then, don't you suppose it probable that those who have been knocking and ringing in your houses for the past half century are trying to get in too ?

" *Mortal*—Why, what can spirits want to get into our houses for ? Having left the earth, it seems strange that they should want to get back to it again.

" *Spirit*—Most of those who knock and ring in your houses have never left the earth, and would far rather get away from it than remain in it. But higher and wiser spirits wish to call the world's attention to the actual facts of spiritual existence, and the real conditions under which life beyond the grave is continued. Spirits of a very ethereal nature cannot affect material substances, and yet, in order to call the world's attention, and waken humanity up to what they have to say, they use the methods so familiar to yourselves—*they knock and ring ;* and those who cannot do this for themselves influence the earthbound spirits, who are magnetically chained to the scenes of their earthly misdeeds, to do this for them.

" *Mortal*—May we regard these hauntings, then, as transpiring under the direction of superintending spiritual wisdom ?

" *Spirit*—Everything in the universe outworks the conditions of the being that belong to its state, and providential wisdom avails itself of different states to convert evil into good, and evolve uses out of the worst of abuses. Ten thousand preachers on the human plane of existence could not demonstrate the fact of spiritual existence so conclusively as a spirit who rings a bell *in response* to a human voice, or *answers a question by knocks,* when no mortal is near to produce the sounds heard." *Verbum sap.*

As a final example of hauntings, especially of that kind which subsequently connected itself with the intelligence manifested at Spirit circles, we shall cite a history furnished to the author some years ago by a party of her personal friends, amongst whom was a gentleman of probity and scientific acumen, well remembered amongst dramatics writers and musicians, as Mr. Lenox Horne. This gentleman being in somewhat embarrassed circumstances about the year 1829, took up his abode temporarily in apartments offered to him at a very moderate rent in an old house near Hatton Garden, long since pulled down. At the period of which we write the house was large, the rooms spacious, especially one, supposed to have been a banqueting chamber, which Mr. Horne used as a music room. As all the lower chambers were either appropriated to the storing of goods, or rented to legal gentlemen as offices, there were no persons sleeping in the house except Mr. Horne and a porter, who occupied a small room on the ground floor. The building had long borne the reputation of being haunted ; it was fast falling to decay, and the former occupants of Mr. Horne's chambers were seldom known to remain long within the gloomy precincts. Report alleged that the place had once been the residence of Sir Christopher Hatton, and the weird reputation that attached to the antique domicile, connected itself with the magical practices attributed to his unfortunate lady.

Mr. Horne had tenanted these apartments some months before he was aware of the phenomena occurring within his own premises. At length he was apprised by Mr. March, a police officer with whom he was acquainted, that for several consecutive nights he and a number of persons invited to share his watch, had remarked that long after the hour when Mr. Horne was accustomed to retire to rest, the great banqueting room, which he had no means of lighting up, and therefore never entered except in daylight, could be seen from the court below *brilliantly illuminated.* Whilst acknowledging that he had often been disturbed by strange noises, odd music, loud laughter, and footsteps, for which he could not account, Mr. Horne—at once the most fearless and least superstitious of beings—strenuously combated the idea of the lights, and it was only when, after watching for several nights with March and his associates, he himself beheld every window of his own apartment, one that he had left closed, locked, and in total darkness, lit up as if by a multitude of gas jets, that he could be brought to believe in the story his friends narrated to him. On several succeeding occasions the same party beheld this spectacle repeated, and whilst some of their number remained below to watch that no intruder passed out from the one entrance of the house, the others would hasten to examine the apartment, to find it enveloped in thick darkness. One of the curious features of this appearance was, the invariability with which the lights disappeared from the eyes of the watchers below, at the moment when the apartment was opened by the searchers above. Only on one occasion was this rule reversed, and that was on a certain night in February, when a larger number of persons than usual had assembled in the court below to watch for the phantom lights.

They blazed out suddenly and in full radiance about one o'clock in the morning, when, after observing them for some five minutes, Mr. Horne, Mr. March, and a nobleman whose name we are not at liberty to mention, determined to ascend the stairs and open the door of the haunted room ; and as they did so they agreed to give the signal of a whistle to those in the court below. At the moment when Mr. Horne threw open the large door of the room in question, he and his companions were thunderstruck to perceive that it was full of company.

One of the three observers had given the signal agreed upon of the whistle which he held in his hand, as he gazed upon the extraordinary scene that met the eye. The vast company seemed to be in the act of dancing. They represented ladies and gentlemen, arrayed, not in the Elizabethan style attributed to the Hatton period of the mansion, but in the costume of the reign of Charles the Second, and the whole air seemed to be full of waving plumes, fluttering ribbons, and sparkling jewels. The three witnesses, who subsequently compared notes with each other, and found their own observations fully corroborated by those of the others, affirmed, that the particulars of the whole scene as above related were plainly, clearly defined, in addition to which, all three declared that every one of these splendidly attired revellers wore, or appeared to wear, *a mask, resembling some disgusting animal.*

Before the astounded witnesses could sufficiently collect their senses to take any action on what they saw, the lights began to pale and shimmer, the whole scene quivered, melted out slowly and gradually, as in a dissolving view, and at length, that is, in the space of a few minutes, the apartment was seemingly empty and in total darkness. The watchers below reported to those above, when at last they had sufficiently collected themselves to descend, that the lights were stationary for about five minutes after the whistle sounded, and disappeared *more gradually* than usual.

Immediately after this vision, the house became wholly uninhabitable even to Mr. Horne, and the two friends who volunteered to share his quarters with him.

Heavy poundings were often heard during the day, for which no account could be given. But these were nothing to the Saturnalia which ensued as soon as darkness had set in. Tramping of feet, clashing of arms, the clinking of glasses, the crash of broken china ; all the sounds attending drunken revels, rude brawls, and even murderous fights, were heard, at times with horrible distinctness. Low moans, wails, and bitter sobs, were still more frequent, and the rushing as of blasts of winds from unknown sources, was a frequent feature of these frightful disturbances.

The witnesses, and they were many, represented their experiences to their friends only to encounter the usual sneer of incredulity and scornful derision. Two or three clergymen volunteered to offer prayers, and one zealous Catholic went through the formulæ of exorcism in the possessed mansion ; but always to encounter such a storm of blows, laughter, and hideously derisive sounds, as drove them in horror from the place, a retreat in which they were shortly imitated by the tenants, who never after

7

recurred to their painful experiences without a feeling of deep awe, solemnity, and an earnest entreaty that their narration should not be met with the ordinary methods of rude denial, and insulting jest.

Despite what he had already witnessed, Mr. Horne had no knowledge of, or belief in, the reputed modern Spiritual manifestations, the spread of which, since the year 1848, he had noticed but never investigated.

About the year 1853, being invited to spend the evening with some musical friends residing in Holloway, London, Mr. Horne was there introduced to Madame Albert, a French lady who was accompanied by her little daughter, a child of some eleven years of age. During the evening, the hostess proposed that they should try the the experiment of "table turning," which was at that time, the technical expression used for evoking Spiritual manifestations. Madame Albert had it seemed become developed for mediumistic powers, whilst little "Josephine," was reported to be a fine somnambulist or trance medium. When the *séance* was first proposed, Mr. Horne laughingly alleged his entire ignorance of the subject, but at once placed himself *in position* at the table, under the direction of the attendant Sybils, "to see what would come of it." No sooner were the party seated, than Mdlle. Josephine seizing the pencil and paper which had been placed on the table, wrote in an incredibly short space of time, in a large bold hand, the following communication, addressed "To Mr. Lenox Horne," a name which the child up to that moment had never heard. The writing was given in English, a language, it must be remembered, of which the little medium was entirely ignorant.

"You say you know nothing of spiritual existence or the soul's power to return to earth. Oh, my friend! Why will you reject the light that has already dawned upon you? In your own house, you have heard the sounds, and seen the sights, which bore witness to the presence of human spirits. Have you forgotten the phantom dancers, whom you and your companions thought wore animal masks? Those dancers were my companions in vice and wickedness. They and I lived amidst scenes of revelry too shameful to be detailed. We were associates of the frivolous *roué*, that occupied the throne of England,—Charles the Second,—and in the house where you found shelter, we often used to hold such revels as demons alone could take pleasure in. When we became spirits, the base passions with which our lives on earth were animated, became so engraved upon our spirits, that all who looked upon us from a higher plane, beheld us transfigured into the semblance of the animals whose natures we partook of. Shocking as this disclosure of our true natures may be, it haply may help future generations to account for the idea of the doctrine of the transmigration of souls. Unhappily, that doctrine is not true. We might be happier as the animals whose limited instincts we represent, but oh, unhappy that we are! we are at once the human beings we ever were, with the additional humiliation of knowing that we take to others the semblance of the lower creatures, whose passions we have imitated. Friend Horne! Our hell is, *not to pass into other states*, but to live in *our own*, and by the knowledge of what we have made ourselves, to grow into higher conditions. You thought we wore masks. Alas! We had only dropped them, and exchanged the mask of seeming for the face of reality. In the spirit world, all its inhabitants are known for what they are, and the soul's loves take the shape of angelic beauty, or brutish ugliness, according to the tendencies of the life within. On the night when you beheld our revels, we were obliged, by the law of our being, to go through the earthly scenes which we had taken too much delight in. On earth such revels were our heaven; in the spheres they are our hell. Their enforced enactment was part of our penance; but thank God! I have seen the errors of the past, and henceforward I am atoning for it, and living my wasted life over again. I am on the road of progress, and even this humiliating confession will help me forward, and aid me to become stronger to save others and myself from the vices, the memories of which still cling to me like a garment. Farewell! My earthly mission is done; there will be no more haunting spirits in the old house in Hatton Garden."

The signature to this singular communication was, "One who was known in the day and time of Charles Stuart as the finest woman of her age—Lady Castlemaine."

Appended to Mr. Horne's manuscript, entrusted to the author some years ago with a view of publication, were the following words :—

"Great Heaven! If this be indeed a true picture of the life hereafter, should it not make us afraid of doing wrong? But, above all, what a wicked and soul-destroying delusion has been the clerical farce of salvation by a vicarious atonement!—L. H."

CHAPTER XIII.

EARLY SPIRITUALISM IN GREAT BRITAIN (CONTINUED).

REPRESENTATIVE CASES CONSIDERED.

THE circumstances of the following narrative, although they have been frequently referred to in other publications, are too nearly related to the early history of Spiritualism in Great Britain to be omitted. They bear, moreover, so closely upon the hypothesis that wise Spirits have been experimenting during this century in many directions, with a view of establishing telegraphic communications between the two worlds, that our present recital seems peculiarly apposite to this portion of the work.

It seems that a young girl of about 13 years of age, the daughter of Mr. John Jobson, a resident of Bishop Wearmouth, near Sunderland, sometime during the year 1839 became the subject of a severe but inexplicable illness.

Mary Jobson had been a strong healthy girl up to the period named, when she suddenly seemed to collapse under an attack which confined her to her bed for over seven months, during which she became blind, deaf, and dumb. From time to time numerous physicians were called in, by whose directions the poor patient was subjected to all the penalties of the "heroic" system of treatment.

Her case was described as "an abscess on the brain," but whatever the malady might have been, it was obviously increased by the applications resorted to by her medical attendants.

Soon after the most serious features of this case became developed, it was remarked that the whole house, and especially the sick girl's chamber, resounded with unaccountable sounds, consisting of heavy poundings, pattering of feet, the ringing of bells, and the clashing of metallic substances.

As the girl's disease progressed in violence, these disturbances grew more marked; there were times however when they changed to soft and delightful music which centred in the invalid's chamber, yet resounded through every part of the dwelling. Sometimes it would seem as if a vast crowd of people were ascending the stairs and thronging into the room. *Even the wind that might be occasioned by passing bodies was felt*, when no one but the ordinary attendants were visible. During the progress of these phenomena, the tones of a human voice were frequently heard protesting against the application of leeches and blisters, and recommending mild herb drinks, which, when tried, invariably alleviated the poor patient's sufferings. On one occasion when several members of the family, together with Drs. Clanny and Embleton, were present, this voice spoke clearly and said; "Your appliances will never benefit, but materially injure the girl. She will recover, but by no human means." On several occasions the glasses containing medicines, together with blisters and leeches, were snatched out of the attendant's hands, and thrown to distant parts of the room. Not unfrequently a crooning tone was heard, as of a mother soothing a sick child, and the poor girl's hair was put back and smoothed by tender invisible hands, Dr. Beattie who witnessed many of these scenes, affirms, that it would be impossible either to describe or forget, the angelic expression of the invalid's face at the time when the manifestations of invisible presence were most evident.

About the sixth month of this strange drama, the ceiling of the room in which Mary Jobson lay, was suddenly found adorned with a beautifully painted representation of the sun, moon, and stars.

The father of the patient—who from the first had been determinately hostile to the invisible actors, alleging that they were " demons," and the cause of his child's sickness—no sooner perceived this fresh proof of spiritual agency, than he proceeded to obliterate the paintings with a thick coat of whitewash. His work was in vain however, for the obnoxious paintings re-appeared as soon as the whitewash was dry, only fading out when the child's recovery was established.

On June 22nd, 1840, Mary Jobson regained her speech, hearing, and sight, as suddenly as she had lost them. Her strength too returned, and in a few days, without any apparent cause for the change, she was entirely restored to her usual health and spirits. For several weeks the occasional sounds of music, voices, knockings, and the movement of bodies continued, but these phenomena ultimately ceased, and have never since returned.

The chief witnesses to this wonderful history were the girl's parents, numerous friends and neighbours; Doctors Embleton and Beattie; also Dr. Drury, Messrs. Torboch and Ward, eminent surgeons, and Dr. Reid Clanny, F.R.S., physician in ordinary to the Duke of Sussex, and at the time of these occurrences, senior physician of the Sunderland Infirmary.

Dr. Reid Clanny, who was not professionally called in to attend the child, became informed of her case through the reports that were in circulation concerning it. Like a true and candid scientist, this gentleman, heedless of all the wild rumours that reached him, called on the parents, and subsequently followed up the case with the closest scrutiny, often witnessing the phenomena described, and satisfying himself according to his own published statement, " that the power—come from whence it may—was not only kind and beneficent, but that it manifested all the tokens of human intelligence, and was better able to prescribe remedies and delineate the course of the disease than any of the attendant physicians."

These admissions were made in an account of the case which Dr. Clanny published in pamphlet form, and though he staked his reputation upon the truth of his statements, and cited the testimony of numerous respectable witnesses, including Doctors Drury, Embleton, Ward, and Torboch, his fearless and timely publication was met by the scoff of the press, the ridicule of those scientists *who had not witnessed the phenomena described*, and the special denunciation of the learned and pious.

The pamphlet, nevertheless, was eagerly bought up, and a second edition soon called for. In this Dr. Clanny bravely maintained his position, adding the following earnest words from Mr. Torboch, one of the surgeons who followed the case throughout :—

"I have had lengthened and serious conversations at different times with nearly all the persons who have borne testimony to this miraculous case, and I am well assured they are religious and trustworthy, and, moreover, that they have faithfully discharged their duty in this important affair between God and man."

Since the above account was written the author has been favoured with a perusal of Dr. Clanny's pamphlet, from which the following few additional details are gathered. After commenting on the peculiarity of the voice heard speaking in Mary's chamber, Dr. Clanny says :—

"The phenomena of human voices speaking, did not seem to be special to the sick girl's chamber. Mrs. Elizabeth Gauntlett, a schoolmistress, was suddenly startled by hearing a voice crying to her, 'Mary Jobson, one of your scholars, is ill ; go and see her, it will be good for you.' This person, the child's school teacher, did not know where she lived, but finding the address, she went as directed, and was called by the voice in a loud tone, audible to all those in the house, to come upstairs. On her second visit, delightful music filled the room, and was heard by sixteen persons.

"The voice often declared the child did not suffer, her spirit being away, and her body being sustained by guardian spirits. These voices told many things of distant persons and scenes which came true.

"Before the girl lost her speech she affirmed that she was often visited by ' a divine being who looked like a man, only exceedingly heavenly and beautiful.' Mr. Joseph Slagg, and Mrs. Margaret Watson, friends of the family, who often visited the sick girl, alleged that each of them had at different times beheld the same divine apparition, and had been assured by it that the girl would recover. On several occasions ' the voice' desired that water should be sprinkled on the floor, and when the sceptical father refused compliance, water from some unknown source fell in showers around the witnesses.

"On the 22nd of June, when the poor child seemed to be in the last extremity, the family assembled round her bed united in prayer that God would be pleased to take her and terminate her sufferings. At five o'clock in the afternoon *the voice* cried out, ' Prepare the girl's clothes, and let every one leave the room except the baby.' This was a little child of two years and a half old, who was playing about near the window. When the family at length most reluctantly obeyed, they remained outside the closed door for fifteen minutes ; they then heard a voice calling out, " Come in," and when they entered they found Mary quite well, sitting in a chair with the baby on her knee, smiling and happy."

The report adds :—

"Up to this time, January 30th, 1841, no relapse has taken place, and Mary Jobson seems as well as girls of her age ordinarily are."

Dr. Drury, Dr. Clanny, and Mr. Torboch all assert that many persons of rank and some ministers of the Established Church visited Mary Jobson, and unreservedly testified to the truth of Dr. Clanny's published report.

Few seekers into the evidences which cluster around the history of Spiritualism in England will forget the law suit instituted by a Mr. Webster, the proprietor of a house at Trinity, Edinburgh, for damages done to his property by Captain Molesworth, a gentleman, who with his family, rented Mr. Webster's house, and was accused of causing extensive dilapidations therein, by his attempts to discover the secret of the terrible hauntings which beset the place.

Captain Molesworth entered upon possession of the house in question in June, 1835. Shortly after this, one of his daughters died, leaving a sister of about thirteen years old. This young lady soon after fell into ill health, took to her bed, and after some months of a strange and unaccountable illness, died.

It was generally asserted that the cruel suspicions and harassing investigations, that followed upon the disturbances, the principal scene of which was the poor invalid's chamber, did more to hasten her decease, than either the phenomena, or the course of the disease. In this case as in that of Mary Jobson, delightful music, and audible human voices from unknown and invisible sources were constantly heard around Miss Molesworth's bed.

In other parts of the house, heavy poundings, loud enough to be heard in the street, together with groans, cries, footsteps, and rustlings, were of frequent occurrence.

The sleepers were awakened at night by the beds being heaved up, and rappings, which would respond by given signals to questions asked by the family.

In Mrs. Catherine Crowe's "Night Side of Nature," it is stated, that carpenters, masons, city officials, justices of the peace, and the officers of the regiment quartered at Leith who were friends of Captain Molesworth, all came to aid in his investigations, in the hope of detecting imposture, or exorcising his tormentors, in vain.

Cordons of guards were stationed round the house by day and night, whilst the poor invalid, whose room seemed to be the chief centre of the hauntings, was not only carefully watched, but even tied up in a bag, and subjected to all sorts of harassing annoyances to make sure that she had no hand in producing the disturbances.

Absurd and vexatious as these suspicions were, they were soon put to flight by the suffering girl's decease. Meantime, the evidence called forth by the trial for damages done to Mr. Webster's house, conclusively enough proved to the world the supramundane character of the hauntings, and the impossibility of any human agency accounting for them.

The case of Elizabeth Squirrel, the vision seeress ; of the haunted house at Willington—still in possession of its spiritual occupants, as the latest reports from Newcastle testify—together with many hundreds of well-attested instances of hauntings, ghost seeing, visions, wraiths, and divers other forms of Spiritual manifestations, occurring in Great Britain during this, and the preceding century, have been so minutely described in the works already alluded to, that it would be unnecessary to add to the examples already cited.

In reviewing the narratives thus presented, there will invariably appear to be many striking points of resemblance amongst them. For instance ; they will most generally be found to represent the spirits of human beings, and to manifest human intelligence. Invisible though they may be to mortal eyes—except in rare instances—the actors seem to take cognizance of persons and things in the material world ; to hear speech addressed to them, and to respond intelligently by signal sounds or motions.

In some cases—as in that of the "Sandford ghost"—the invisible presence seems to be malign and mischievous—in others, as illustrated by the bell-ringing at Great Bealing, the demonstrations appear to be simply meaningless and silly.

Intelligence, skill, and kindness, marked the action of the invisible presence that attended Mary Jobson, and lessons of deep import and suggestion grew out of the hauntings detailed by Mr. Lenox Horne.

Could all Spiritual manifestations have been thoroughly sifted, and direct question and answer have taken the place of the foolish exorcisms, threats, and denunciations, with which these hauntings were formerly received, might they not have been explained upon the same hypotheses which are revealed to humanity in the open communion that now exists between the Spiritual and natural worlds?

By these we learn, that haunting spirits are magnetically fettered to the scene of their earthly crimes ; that the sounds and sights heard and seen in such places, are projected from the spirit world into the earth's atmosphere by unhappy spirits; the remembrance of their former evil deeds becoming their hell, in which they are compelled to re-enact the deeds that continually recur to their minds.

Other spirits of a higher grade with better intentions, and better guidance, ring and knock to attract attention, and compel enquiry; and still again others, whose love for humanity prompts them to become the guardian spirits of dear relatives still remaining on earth, endeavour to make their watch and word known, as in the cases of Mary Jobson and Matilda Molesworth, by acts of beneficence and tokens of tender ministration.

Could every demonstration of Spiritual presence, whether it comes in the form of haunting or loving ministry, be thoroughly investigated, whilst its phenomena would unquestionably afford to mankind the indication of Spiritual laws now unknown, it would also resolve itself into such strictly human intelligence, that we should marvel how we could have ever relegated it to the dreary horrors of a weird supernaturalism.

Mr. S. C. Hall, the venerable editor of the *Art Journal,* was the first writer we believe who contributed to the literature of Spiritualism the well-known narrative of the spirit calling himself "Gaspar."

This denizen of the other world seemed compelled, in his first attempts to communicate with earth, to manifest his presence by the usual array of terrifying sounds and movements which accompany supernatural agencies ; in process of time however he was enabled to converse with the family to whom he was attracted, through the methods of ordinary human speech. For over three years this Spirit took part in the daily life, interests, and welfare of his human friends; talking with them, advising, and counselling them, with all the wisdom and affection of a beloved member of their household, and when at last he left them, in pursuance of some Spiritual conditions which, as he alleged, would aid his progress, but deprive him of the power to hold further audible intercourse with them, they felt "as if they had lost their best friend," and could hardly be reconciled to his absence.

Nothing can more conclusively prove that the darkest shadows of "Supernaturalism" have become dissipated, and given place to light and reason, than the present open communion with the Spirit world. In this, we recognize the men, women, and children of this world over again ; the good ascending into angel-hood, the indifferent still lingering on the threshold of the earth, with which their affections have been all too closely interwoven,—and the evil-minded, either exhibiting the first monitions of remorse which impel them forward on the path of progress, or the same hardened adherence to criminal tendencies which await the softening influences of penitence, to lead them into the way of reform.

The great American Seer A. J. Davis, describes in one of his works, a visit he made to the bedside of a man, suffering under an aggravated attack of *delirium tremens.*

On entering the room, Mr. Davis beheld the apparition of a beautiful female Spirit standing at the foot of the bed, scattering visionary flowers over the coverlid, and endeavouring by magnetic passes of her fair hands, to soothe the sufferer's fever-haunted condition.

On describing this celestial visitant to the family present, she was at once recognized as a departed relative, whose pure life corresponded to her angelic appearance. It seemed however that the spiritual perceptions of the unfortunate patient were sufficiently awakened to be conscious of. *the presence*, although not of its beneficent character, for in the midst of his frantic ravings, he was perpetually complaining of a *demon, who stood at the foot of his bed, stinging him with thorns, and throwing off fire from her hands. He often appealed to those around, asking if they could not see this demon, whose frightful appearance filled him with horror.* Is not the delirium of ignorance and superstition just as capable of transforming angels into demons, as the delirium of drunkenness?

We must now invite the reader to consider in some detail, the signifi-:ance of four well-known movements, each of which, by the wide-spread influence they have exercised over their votaries, demands recognition and earnest attention from the students of psychological philosophy. These are Mormonism; Shakerism, the sect known as Irvingites, and the Irish Revivals; of course the two former, although largely recruited from British sources, belong to the history of American Spiritualism. Neither of these movements may be commended to public acceptance, for their beneficial influence upon mankind.

But, though the CUI BONO of the subject is not the point with which the facts of history are called upon to deal, it will become self-evident to thoughtful students, that there is something wonderfully significant in the lessons which these singular and exceptional movements teach us. For example; Mormonism, which originated through the Spiritual Mediumship of Joseph Smith, illustrates with overwhelming force the depravity into which human beings may be plunged, by seeking authority for their religious beliefs, in the days of ancient barbarism; and setting up for modern example, the old Jehovah system, which not only sanctioned, but even enjoined the horrors of relentless warfare, and the infamies of Polygamy.

On the other hand, we have the religion of Anne Lee, the spiritually-inspired founder of Shakerism, rushing into that opposite extreme of excessive asceticism, which, if Shaker life and practice could prevail over the earth, would depopulate it in a single generation.

Both these movements owe their origin to spiritually-inspired founders; both are advent footprints in the wilderness of modern materialism; but whilst Mormonism illustrates the futility of looking to the past, to find authority for our religious beliefs, Shakerism equally proves the imbecility of attempting to inaugurate in the earthly present, a system of asceticism which only belongs to our condition as pure spirits, in the future.

THE IRVINGITES.

THE third movement to which allusion was made above, is the wonderful Pentecostal outpouring which fell on certain members of a church presided over by the Rev. Edward Irving, from whom the affected persons were called by the name of "Irvingites." The following brief summary of this remarkable demonstration, is gathered chiefly from the history of Edward Irving by Mrs. Oliphant, published in Mr. Thomas Shorter's excellent account of Spiritual manifestations, entitled "The Two Worlds," and a small volume on "The Revivals," written by W. M. Wilkinson, Esq., solicitor, of Lincoln's Inn, London.

The latter in introducing his subject says :—

"Of Mr. Irving himself, it is only necessary to say that he believed and preached that the Church might and ought to have a restoration of the divine gifts which are promised in the gospels, and that the not having such, was a sign of its low state and was in fact its condemnation.

"Whatever may be thought of his theory, he was a great and good man, as all who knew him testify.

"Carlyle, who knew and loved him, says of him—'He was the freest, brotherliest, bravest human soul mine ever came in contact with.

"'I call him on the whole the best man I have ever, after trial enough, found in this world, or ever hope to find.'"

One thing is certain, that panegyrists and detractors alike, attribute to Mr. Irving a character of singular purity and rectitude, whilst it is universally admitted, that his eloquence, and the marvellous power he exerted over his immense and fashionable congregations, were as remarkable even before the Spiritual outpouring with which his name is associated, as any phenomena which occurred during that wonderful visitation.

It was in the magnificent church in Regent Square, erected at a cost of fifteen thousand pounds expressly for Mr. Irving—then the most popular preacher in London—that the outpouring of "the gift of tongues" occurred.

It seems that the first manifestation of this singular power, commenced in Port Glasgow sometime in 1830.

Mr. Irving, a Scotchman by birth, had commenced his ministerial career in Glasgow, and as the reputed demonstrations were of the character which he himself alleged the Church of Christ should possess, he became strongly interested in the tidings that reached him, and forthwith sent one of the elders of his own church to enquire into, and report upon the matter.

The following extracts are condensed from Mr. Irving's own narrative of the "gift of tongues," published in *Fraser's Magazine* (vol. iv.), in which is embodied the report of the agent above alluded to. The latter, writing to his Pastor, Mr. Irving, says :—

"About this time (1830), in the death-bed experiences of certain holy persons, there appeared many and very wonderful instances of the power of God's Spirit, both in the way of discernment and utterance. *They were able to know the condition of God's people at a distance.* In one instance, *the countenance shone with a glorious brightness, as if it had been the face of an angel ;* they spoke much of a bright dawn about to arise in the Church ; and one of them, just before death, signified that he had received *the knowledge of the thing about to be manifested.* . . .

"In March, 1830, on the evening of the Lord's Day, the gift of speaking with tongues was restored to the Church. The handmaiden of the Lord, of whom He made choice on that night to manifest forth in her His glory, had been long afflicted with a disease which the medical men pronounced to be a decline. It was on the Lord's Day, and one of her sisters, along with a female friend who had come to the house for that end, had been spending the whole day in fasting and prayer before God, with *a special respect to the restoration of the gifts.* They had come up in the evening to the sick chamber of their sister, and, along with one or two others of the household, were engaged in prayer, when the Holy Ghost came with mighty power upon the sick woman as she lay in her weakness, and *constrained her to speak at great length, and with superhuman strength, in an unknown tongue,* to the astonishment of all who heard. She has told me that this first seizure of the Spirit was the strongest she ever had ; and that it was in some degree necessary it should have been so, otherwise she would not have dared to give way to it.

"The editor of the *Morning Watch* * writes : 'We have seen eight different individuals who have been eye-witnesses of these manifestations, and who are unanimous in their testimony to the *supernatural, holy, and influential energy of what they there witnessed.*' We subjoin the testimony of one of these, Mr. John B. Cardale, who is now the head of the church. He was specially sent by Mr. Irving to make enquiry, with five others, into these alleged tongues, and he thus gives their observations :—'During our stay, four individuals received the gift of tongues. The tongues spoken by all the several persons who had received the gift are perfectly distinct in themselves and from each other. *J. M'D. speaks two tongues, both easily discernible from each other.* J. M'D. exercises his

---

* A periodical established mainly as an organ of the Irvingites.

gift more frequently than any of the others ; and I have heard him speak for twenty minutes together, with all the energy *of voice and action of an orator addressing an audience.* The language which he uttered is full and harmonious, containing many Greek and Latin radicals, and with inflexions resembling those of the Greek language. The only time I ever had a serious doubt whether the unknown sounds which I heard on these occasions were parts of a language, was *when Mr. M'D.'s servant spoke during the first evening.* When she spoke on subsequent occasions it was invariably in one tongue, which was not only perfectly distinct from the sounds she uttered at the first meeting, but was satisfactorily established, to my conviction, to be a language.

"'One of the persons thus gifted we employed as our servant while at Port Glasgow. She is a remarkably quiet, steady, phlegmatic person, entirely devoid of forwardness or enthusiasm, and with very little to say for herself in the ordinary way. The language which she spoke was as distinct as the others, and it was quite evident the language spoken at one time, was identical with that spoken at another time.

"'*The chanting or singing was also very remarkable.* J. M'D.'s ordinary voice is in singing, harsh and unpleasing ; but when thus singing in the Spirit, the tones are perfectly harmonious. On the morning after the day on which Mrs. —— received the gift of tongues, I heard her singing stanzas with the alternate lines rhyming. The tune was at first slow, but she became more and more rapid in her utterance, until at last, syllable followed syllable as rapidly as was possible, and yet each syllable distinctly enunciated.

"'These persons, while uttering the unknown sounds, as also while speaking in the Spirit in their own language, have every appearance of being under supernatural direction. The manner and voice are different from what they are on ordinary occasions.

"'Their whole deportment *gives an impression not to be conveyed in words, that their organs are made use of by supernatural power.* M. M'D. one morning, having, in consequence of a severe cold, so entirely lost the use of her voice as to be unable to speak out of a whisper, yet, on a sudden, commenced, and from ten a.m. to two p.m. continued speaking in a loud voice—sometimes in intercessory prayer in the Spirit, sometimes in denouncing the coming judgments, *and occasionally speaking in an unknown tongue*— and at the end of that time she relapsed exactly into her former state.'

" When this messenger returned to London with his tidings, it was to find *the tongues of flame sitting on his own wife and daughters.* Still, not rashly, nor arrogantly, was the marvel proclaimed to the world. For some time, only in private meetings was the gift invited to manifest itself.' There, philological learning pronounced the utterances something more than jargon, and observation failed to detect imposture. Prayer-meetings were then held every morning at the church in Regent-square, and were numerously attended. At these meetings, exhortations would be uttered in the 'tongue' by one person, and the interpretation chanted in English by another. Warnings and predictions were sometimes given. On Sunday morning, October 16th, a '*sister*' (*Miss Hall*) *burst forth in the open congregation with an utterance in the tongue.* I calmed the 1,500 or 2,000 people who had risen in alarm, bade the sister console herself—for she had struggled with the power that had possession of her, and hastened her into the vestry of the church, there to give it speech—and expounded to the congregation the 14th chap. of the First Epistle to the Corinthians, as explanatory of the occurrence. In the evening *a 'brother' produced even greater excitement than the morning speaker ;* and in the course of the week all London was talking of this new phase. The 'unknown tongues' continued in the church, and other 'utterances in the Spirit' were also given ; and remarkable cases of healing by spiritual power occurred.

" Those who speak in the tongue always declare 'that the words uttered in English are as much by power supernatural as the words uttered in the language unknown.' But no one hearing and observing the utterance could for a moment doubt it, inasmuch as the whole utterance, from the beginning to the end of it, *is with a power, and strength, and fulness, and sometimes rapidity of voice* altogether different from that of the person's ordinary utterance in any mood ; and I would say, both in its form and in its effects upon a simple mind, *evidently supernatural. There is a power in the voice to thrill the heart and overawe the spirit after a manner which I have never seen.*"

Besides "the tongues," the gift of healing became manifested in the church, and the power extended to other congregations.

At Liverpool and Baldock in Hertfordshire, manifestations similar in character to those of the churches in Port Glasgow and Regent Square, became openly displayed.

Mr. Irving at the earnest solicitation of many interested persons, wrote accounts of the manifestations which were published in *Fraser's Magazine* (vols. iv. and v.) ; he also contributed largely to the columns of the *Morning Watch*, a quarterly magazine in which the facts and philosophy of the strange movement were freely discussed.

Mr. Irving very highly commends the manner and forms of this " divine speech," and by abundant and earnest reasonings, endeavoured to show that it was a renewal of Apostolic gifts and powers. After some two years continuance of these manifestations, certain members of Mr. Irving's congregation began to utter loud complaints of the disorders that had arisen, the result of which was, that a charge of heresy was ultimately preferred against him.

At the trial that ensued " an utterance in power" came from Mr. David Dow, charging those who were faithful to arise and depart, whereupon Mr. Irving and Mr. Dow made their way out of church, and sentence against the pastor was formally pronounced.

Besides this ruinous division in the excellent and amiable clergyman's congregation, there were other causes of disunion at work with the Revivalists themselves, which militated against the subject, and tended to bring it into ill odour with the world. The principal causes of this division originated with Mr. Robert Baxter, once an enthusiastic subject of the lingual gift, and subsequently a disbeliever in the divine origin of the power which he himself had manifested.

This secession from the Irvingite ranks, was announced by Mr. Baxter himself in a tract which he published entitled, *A narrative of facts characterizing the supernatural manifestations in the members of Mr. Irving's congregation, and other individuals in England and Scotland, and formerly in the writer himself.*

As no description of the subject can depict it in the same vivid light that it borrows from the testimony of witnesses and participators, we shall give the following quotations from Mr. Baxter's pamphlet as the best illustration on record of " the power," and a subsequent condition of disenchantment.

Mr. Baxter says, writing of himself sometimes in the third person, and again in the first :—

" He had heard many particulars of the extraordinary manifestations which had occurred at Port Glasgow, and thought that there were sufficient grounds in Scripture to warrant a fair investigation of them. Being called up to London in August, 1831, he 'had a strong desire to attend the prayer-meetings which were then privately held by those who spoke in the power and who sought for the gifts.' Having obtained an introduction, he attended, and heard 'the utterances,' both in the unknown and in the English tongue. In the latter there was, he says, 'a cutting rebuke to all who were present, and applicable to my own state of mind in particular. *In the midst of the feeling of awe and reverence which this produced, I was myself seized upon by the power ; and in much struggling against it, was made to cry out, and myself to give forth a confession of my own sin in the matter for which we were rebuked.* There was in me at the time of the utterance, very great excitement, and yet I was distinctly conscious of a power acting upon me beyond excitement.'

" From this period, for the space of five months, I had no utterances in public ; though when engaged alone in private prayer, *the power would come down upon me, and cause me to pray with strong crying and tears for the state of the church.* On one occasion, whilst in my study, endeavouring to lift up my soul in prayer, the power came upon me, and I found myself lifted up in soul to God, and by a constraint I cannot describe I was made to speak a prayer that the Lord would deliver me from fleshly weakness, and graciously bestow upon me the gifts of his Spirit. This prayer was so loud, that I put my handkerchief to my mouth to stop the sound, that I might not alarm the house. When I had reached the last word, the power died off me, and I was left as before, save in amazement at what had passed.

"In January, 1832, when I again visited the brethren in London, the gifts in Mr. Irving's church were now being exercised in the public congregation. The day following my arrival, being called upon by the pastor to read, I opened upon the prophet Malachi, and read the fourth chapter. As I read, the power came upon me, and I was made to read in the power. My voice, raised far beyond its natural pitch, *with constrained repetition of parts,* and with the same inward uplifting which at the presence of the power I had always before experienced. When I knelt down to pray, *I was carried out to pray in the power* for the presence and blessing of God in the midst of the church; in all this I had great joy and peace, without any of the strugglings which had attended my former utterances in the power.

"On the Sunday following, the power came in the form of revelation and opening of scripture; and as I read, the opening of it was just as light flitting across the mind. A passage would be opened in the clearest manner, until portion after portion having been opened, and an interpretation given *which I not only had never thought of, but which was at variance with my previous systematic construction of it.*

"If it were convenient here to make particular mention of men's names, I could name you many, who of late years have received such strange preservations, even against the common course of nature, that might convince an Atheist of the finger of God therein.

"*It hath been my own case more than once, twice, or ten times.* When means have all failed and the highest art has sentenced me hopeless, I have been relieved by the prevalence of fervent prayer."

During the prevalence of "the power," a large number of seemingly miraculous cases of healing occurred with those upon whom the spiritual gifts were poured out. Among the most notable was the cure of a Miss Macdonald, an invalid of many years standing, who was entirely restored to health, by the touch, prayer, and command to "arise and walk," of her brother James, one of the Port Glasgow subjects of the "supernatural power." This same man, after raising his sister from the sick bed to which she had been confined for years, addressed a letter to a dear friend, a Miss Mary Campbell, who had just been given up to die by the doctors. In this letter, James Macdonald informed the sick lady, she must instantly arise and go forth to testify for the Lord. Without the least help, "the *dying girl*" arose, dressed herself, walked down to the meeting-room, and entered upon a career which lasted for many months as a prophetess of the new church.

Mrs. Oliphant in her life of Irving, also mentions a sister of Mary Campbell's—Isabella, who was cured in the same way and with the same results.

Still more renowned was the case of Miss Fancourt, the daughter of a clergyman, who for eight years had been a helpless cripple, and whom her father's congregation had been accustomed to see carried to church in the arms of attendants and laid on her back in her pew during the service. The wonderful cure of Miss Fancourt was effected *in a single minute* by the prayers of an eminent subject of the gifts, Mr. Greaves. As the cure has been reported at length in numerous religious as well as secular publications, we must close our notice of it with a brief extract from a letter written by the lady's father, the Rev. T. Fancourt, to the *Christian Observer,* of November, 1831:—

"Her backbone, which was *curved* before, is now perfectly straight, and her collar-bones are quite equal, whereas one of them was previously much enlarged. It is four years since she walked at all, and then it was but for a short time with the assistance of a stick, and subject to a pain in her hip. She now walks stoutly and free from all pain."

It is almost unnecessary to add, that whilst the fact of these, and many other equally marvellous cures could not be disputed, the invariable tone of explanation adopted by the religious journals was, that "the cures were wholly wrought by the name of Jesus;" and "faith in the Lord Christ," &c., &c. These religious writers then, as now, forgot to explain why the millions of earnest Christians that have been done to death and tortured barbarously by other Christians, during the ages of Christian warfare and persecution, were neither saved from death at the stake, or mutilation, by faith in the name of Christ. John Huss, Latimer, Ridley, Joan of Arc, and tens of thousands of devout Christians, have called upon the name of their Lord in their hour of anguish in vain. If the prayer of faith was all that was necessary to save from death and agony, why were the Misses Campbell and Miss Fancourt cured, and ten thousand Christian martyrs unregarded? An equally pertinent question arises in reference to the thousands of cures which have transpired amongst the modern Spiritualists, many of which are recorded in their literature, and some few referred to in this volume. The prayer of faith in these instances is wanting, and the name of Christ is seldom or ever used. Can our Christian friends explain the *modus operandi* of these anti-Christian healing exploits? Even Mr. Baxter, after abandoning the Christian solution of his problematical state, does not deny the facts of healing of which he was an eye-witness, and a subject himself. Can the "Satanic" theory upon which this eminent witness falls back, cover the ground of Spiritual healing as well as the name of Christ? If so, can our Christian friends explain the difference of the power, and the superiority of one source over the other?

As the limitations of our space will permit of no more extended notice of this remarkable movement, nor of the vast multitude of witnesses whose testimony was rendered to the facts of healing as well as of tongues, we must conclude with the following brief extract from the life of Edward Irving by Mr. Wilks, one of his admiring followers.

This writer, after detailing the circumstances of Mr. Irving's trial, and final withdrawal from the church, concludes with the following touching remarks :—

"His public work was over. His flesh became wan ; his raven hair hoary as with extreme age. His eye gleamed with an unquiet light, and the hectic spot on his pale cheek betrayed the fire burning at his heart. On December the 8th, 1834, he passed to that rest for which his weary spirit longed. The last words he was heard to utter were 'If I die I die unto the Lord. Living and dying I am the Lord's.'"

It would be needless to pursue in farther detail the course of the *Catholic Apostolic Church*, an organization which claims the noble-minded and devoted Edward Irving as its founder, although it neither adopts his name, nor conserves "the power" which made that name during four short years a milestone on the highway of immortality.

Numerous records of kindred powers are to be found in the history of Spiritualism, but those which distinguished the uprising at Port Glasgow, and the Irvingites in London, undoubtedly owe a large share of their world-wide renown to the talents, eloquence, and unspotted life of the brave and devoted gentleman who gave all he was, and all he had, even *to his very life*, to uphold the truth and divinity of the mighty outpouring with which his name is associated.

It is one of the triumphs as well as the consolations of Spiritualism, to be assured, that Edward Irving still lives, and though removed from the scenes of earthly trial in which his pure life was consumed, "he being dead, yet speaketh !"

CHAPTER XIV.

EARLY SPIRITUALISM IN GREAT BRITAIN (CONTINUED).

THE IRISH REVIVALS.

THE fourth and last great movement of a Pentecostal character to which we can call attention as occurring during the present century, has been named "The Irish Revival," and though we have no direct account of its unfoldment before 1857—nine years after the commencement of "Modern Spiritualism" in America, the scenes of the Irish drama were so distant from and unconnected with other European centres wherein "spirit circles" were generally held, and the people upon whom "the power" fell, were so far removed in rank and national isolation from the cultured classes amongst whom Spiritualism in Great Britain for the most part took root, that there does not seem even a possibility of tracing any connexion between the two movements, unless we admit the hypothesis of a universal outpouring of the Spirit all over the world and one moving in psychological currents of influence from all points of the compass.

In commencing our necessarily brief review of the Irish Revivals, we must give some account of the place as well as the persons with whom they originated, and this we do in the words of William Arthur, A.M., a learned gentleman who published several voluminous tracts on this subject.

After speaking of the colonies of Protestants from England and Scotland who peopled Ulster, and whose descendants form now its main population Mr. Arthur says :—

"The people are notoriously cool, practical, money-making, strong-willed, and fond of disputation.

"None of the popular religious delusions which took effect in other places found their way into Ulster. Spiritual life was low, but the exaggerated crimes which prevailed in Romish parts of the land were rare. Still many forms of vice were very prevalent. *Drunkenness raged like a plague ; swearing, cockfighting, gambling, and large numbers of illegitimate births, formed its natural train.* A policeman on the streets of Belfast told us that he had lived in Ahoghill for two years, and that it was the 'worst wee place in the world.' On a day when a funeral took place, he said, there was so much drinking and fighting, that the lock-up was always full ; and on a fair day you could not go many yards without hearing drunken men cursing the Pope.

"The origin of the present movement is clearly traced to Connor, a parish seven miles long, peopled by small farmers, weavers, and linen manufacturers, nearly all Presbyterians, mixed only with a handful of Church people, and scarcely any Roman Catholics.

"There was a young man residing at Ballymena, a few miles away, who was zealous for religion after his manner, and stood in his own eyes as a Christian. But he heard a lady from England conversing with some young women, and describing true conversion. Her words reached the heart of the young man. He sought the inward and holy power of religion, and found clear and joyful acceptance with his Father in heaven. Full of this new happiness, he returned to his own parish.

"In the month of September, 1857, *he and three other young men joined together in secret fellowship, to pray for God's special blessing on the people around them.*

"Three months later what is called 'The Spring Communion' came. The parish had been more or less filled with tidings of the prayers that were being offered, and of the happy conversions which had taken place. Their minister had been preaching *on the subject of a great revival*, and telling what the Lord was doing for his vineyard in America, with a strong desire for the like at home. The services of the Communion were crowned with unwonted influence. Life, inquiry, deep convictions. strong crying and tears—these became the familiar tidings of that favoured parish. Prayer meetings sprang up on every hand, and wonderful was it to the staid Presbyterian folk to hear, out of the lips of the unlearned and the ignorant, out of the mouths of babes and sucklings in religion, *prayers of deep import and heavenly power."*

After many fervent expressions of thankfulness for the conversions effected as above shown, Mr. Arthur goes on to say :—

"At a prayer meeting in the meeting-house there were about three hundred persons. All were unexcited, though earnest. At the call of the minister, a young man, one of the recent converts, read a portion of Scripture, and delivered a short exhortation. Then the minister called on them to *spend a little time in silent prayer.* At first it seemed as if the moments would pass in deep silence ; but after a while, *breathings began to be heard, low, subdued, but earnest—no voice, no tone, no words ; but a breathing throughout the place, as if each one apart was breathing out the soul to God. That strange sound rose and came quicker till it almost rushed, and the place seemed all astir with suppressed but outbursting prayer."*

Very different results soon grew out of these peaceful "unexcited" prayer meetings, as the reader will perceive if, passing over a few pages filled with descriptions of similar scenes and individual experiences, he takes up the thread of Mr. Arthur's narrative in June, 1859, two years later than the first "conversion" alluded to. We resume our extracts at the following point of advance :—

"One who had felt the joy of pardoning love filling his own soul, and opening in his breast a little heaven, longed to see his mother, who lived in a neighbouring parish. He got one of his comrades *to join him in earnest prayer for her conversion.* After this, he went home to see if prayer had had any effect, and, to his joy and wonder, found that *just while they had been praying, deep conviction had fallen upon his mother's soul ;* she had sought mercy, and was now rejoicing in hope of the glory of God. This triumph of prayer was no sooner won than came the question, Where was his brother ? *Away at a cockfight.* Thither he followed him : there he found him, and, seizing him, he said, 'I have a message for you from the Lord Jesus.' This went to his heart ; he too fled for refuge to the open arms of the crucified Redeemer. His burden fell off, joy and peace took possession of his soul, and he rushed away to his minister, exclaiming, 'I am saved ! I am saved !'

"Converts from Connor then came to tell the people of Ahoghill what the Lord had done for their souls. It was a strange thing to hear weavers, and stone-breakers, and butchers, and others unskilled in speech, pouring forth reverent and thoughtful prayers. It was more wonderful still to hear them tell how the Lord had sent his arrows through their souls.

"'You ask,' cries a convert, 'if you did find mercy, how you would know it ? *Ah, you would know it very well, you would feel it.'* And there his argument ended. But something was in these new-born souls—*which went further than ten thousand arguments.* The power of the blessed Spirit attended them. *And then began those overwhelming affections of body and mind together,* which have resounded through the world, and made the Ulster Revival notorious to the religious and the curious alike.

"In an opposite direction to Ahoghill lies the town of Ballyclare. There, one fair day, a slater coming home to dinner, was told by his wife that *there was a man in the fair who had lost his reason ;* for on the 'fair hill,' in his cart, he was praying aloud, and crying for mercy to his soul. The man went to see, and found it even so : it was a man from the neighbourhood of Broughshane, where the Revival had now begun ; and, as he came into the fair, such deep conviction of sin seized upon him, that he cared not for the eye of the crowd or the course of business, but felt he was going down into the gulf ; and he cried, 'Lord, save, I perish !' *There was something in the cry which went to the soul of the slater,* who had come to see the man 'out of his mind.' He felt, It is time for me to seek mercy too.

"And, as if the Lord had said, 'Return to thine house, and show what great things the Lord had done unto thee,' he did return, and told his tale of redeeming love, *and speedily the holy flame was lighted up in Ballyclare.*

" At Hyde Park, a village a few miles from Belfast, I had the happiness of witnessing a wonderful work of revival, and, on inquiry as to its origin, found it traced to a lad from Ballyclare. He told how the Lord had converted him, and seeing a boy impressed by it, fell upon his neck, and 'the affection of this boy seemed to break down the hearts of the people.' How slight a cause is followed by wonderful effects, when a mighty power of the Spirit operates !

" *After nearly two years the first converts are steadfast, and the original seat of the revival more and more alive.* Only within the last two months has it attracted public notice ; but in that time it has spread like fire, among country districts, market towns, and considerable cities. From Belfast to Coleraine, I have been permitted to see its effects, with wonder and deep adoration. I never read of anything equal at once in extent and transforming power, and hereafter it will be my endeavour to trace the work through some of those stages in which, instead of the tranquil and gradual progress which marked its early course, it burst forth with such manifestations as filled the newspapers, and became the all-absorbing topic of the country."

As Mr. Arthur's views of revival practices are evidently dictated more in the spirit of orthodox sympathy with the actors than that of philosophic and deliberate investigation, we now turn to the testimony of a still more impartial collator of revival incidents, in the person of Dr. Massie, a writer of eminence, whose excellent account of the Irish Revivals is thus rendered in Mr. W. M. Wilkinson's volume on this subject before alluded to. Dr. Massie says :—

" We may remark that the first noticeable cases of decided impression appeared in Ballymena, on the morning of Monday, the 16th of May ; and, up till noon of the following Wednesday, the entire number was about thirty. These cases occurred chiefly in streets of an inferior description, and among the lower classes of the population. It would be impossible to ascertain the exact number so visited within the town—for cases are now to be found in every street, among all classes of the people. We know of one house wherein seven persons were impressed in the usual mysterious manner in the course of a single evening ; and the total number in Ballymena alone cannot be reckoned at less than three hundred. On the evening of Thursday, the 19th instant, the public excitement, particularly in Springwell Street, was intense ; and we visited that locality for the express purpose of witnessing and reporting upon the phenomena. On one portion of the street we found an assemblage of at least two thousand people engaged in services of prayer and praise under the leadership of laymen, six or seven houses elsewhere in the same street were crowded with people in every spot where standing room could be obtained. The doors, and in some cases the windows, were open, and besieged by a throng of all classes anxious to hear the proceedings within. These houses we found to be the homes of ' stricken ' parties, who were then labouring under the influence of the shock in sundry stages of its operation. Some were in a state of very great weakness and partial stupor ; some were dreadfully excited, calling upon God for mercy, with an earnestness of which no intelligent investigator could doubt the reality for a single moment ;. some were uttering exclamations of despairing agony ; others were pouring forth accents of heart-touching and adoring gratitude. In all cases they were surrounded by crowds of friends or comforters. They were prayed over, in some cases by a single leader, in others by several persons at the same moment, the stricken person sometimes uniting with them *in language of glowing and continuous eloquence,* and at other times by interjectional exclamations of doubt, hope, faith, or joy unspeakable. During the earlier paroxysms the sufferers generally experienced considerable relief *from sacred music ;* and hence the devotional exercises were frequently varied by the singing of psalms, in which all who were within hearing appeared to join most cordially. This description of the proceedings in one house may be regarded as applicable to all the others—for we visited them all, and were favoured with opportunities for investigation in seventeen different cases.

" In the course of the evening we had an opportunity of witnessing cases of ' impression ' in the earlier stages, the scene at one of which we shall attempt to describe. Having made our way up a narrow staircase, crowded with anxious listeners, we entered a small apartment in which about twenty people of both sexes were grouped in various attitudes of deep attention or devotion. A neatly-attired young woman, apparently about twenty-two years of age, had been stricken an hour previously, and was supported in the arms of an elderly female, who was seated upon a low stool. The person impressed, appeared to be in a state of partial stupor, from which she was occasionally roused into a feeling of mental agony, depicted in heart-rending expressions of the countenance, and deep, low wailings of terrible despair. *Her face was deadly pale*, and her eyelids closed, except when partially raised by a convulsive paroxysm, *and even then no part of the eye was visible, except a narrow line of white.* Her pulse was intermittent and feverish, and her face and hands covered with perspiration. Occasionally she extended her arms with an action as if groping in the air, and at other times they were elevated high overhead, the hands clasped, and her features rigidly fixed into an expression of supplication, of which no language could convey an adequate idea. Her utterance was interjectional and incoherent, mingled with sobs, moans, and agonizing expressions of despair, like the following :—'Is there no hope?' 'Oh, my heart, my heart!' 'Pardon, pardon!' 'Oh, Jesus, save me!' 'Oh, God, have mercy!' Beside this poor girl two men were standing and praying aloud alternately.

"In other portions of the room *hands were clasped, and tears silently streaming from many an eye*, but our attention was irresistibly attracted to the movements of a young woman, evidently of the lower classes, who had been 'stricken' two days previously, but had now recovered, and was bending over the sufferer with emotions exhibiting the deepest and most affectionate solicitude. She told her of Jesus, who was ever willing to save ; she repeated passages of Scripture that spoke of hope and consolation to the penitent ; and then burst forth into *a lengthened and apparently impulsive prayer*, well expressed and perfectly intelligent, but chiefly interjectional.

"Now, it may be asked, who was this earnest suppliant for peace and consolation to the afflicted sufferer? Four days previous to the evening of which we write, she was a reckless and, apparently, God-forsaken young woman—*a common street prostitute in Ballymena!* Before we left the scene which we had thus attempted to describe, the impressed person had obtained considerable relief, and, at intervals, we observed that her lips were silently moving, as if in inward prayer.

"In the meantime *the movement was progressing with rapidity in every district of the surrounding country.* Soon after breakfast hour on Saturday morning, six or seven young women became suddenly affected with all the usual symptoms, while engaged at work in the spinning factory at Raceview. Intense excitement immediately ensued, *the alarm soon became general*, and within an hour twenty or thirty people of both sexes were found prostrate. The business of the entire establishment was interrupted, and, as a matter of necessity, the factory was closed at twelve o'clock. It was re-opened on Monday, but nearly half the ordinary number of hands were absent, and we understand that the business of Ballygarvy bleachworks has been seriously impeded, owing to a similar course. About six o'clock on the evening of Sunday week, a congregation, numbering fully four thousand people, assembled in the open air, in front of the Presbyterian Church at Broughshane, where services were conducted by the Rev. Mr. Robinson and a number of Revival converts from other localities. Numerous and strongly-marked cases of sudden 'conviction' occurred among the audience, and several persons were carried into the church, from which place they were not in a condition for removal till midnight. The total number of persons affected on that occasion has been estimated at more than one hundred. On the same evening open-air prayer-meetings were held at Cullybackey and Straid. At Carniney, about a mile from Ballymena, the assemblage numbered fully two thousand, and they separated into large groups, for each of which there was a speaker. Numerous impressions occurred, and some of the parties so affected were removed from the ground on cars, followed, in some cases, by ranks of people singing psalms."

"Dr. Massie gives the following extracts from a Ballymena correspondent : 'Last night, at a prayer meeting in Wellington Street Church, so crowded that the doors and windows were surrounded by a multitude who could not obtain admission, scenes occurred which bowed the heart with awe and solemn fear, as if the invisible world was opening to view. Attempts have been made to describe such scenes, but no one can describe them, they must be witnessed. During the time that Mr. Shaw was speaking, a person labouring under strong convictions of sin was carried out into the session-room. He was a person who had had convictions before, but on this occasion they returned in a manner most distressing to witness. He was a strong, middle-aged man ; but in the mysterious, half-conscious state in which he was, his soul actually seemed to the beholders as the battle-ground between the powers of light and darkness, filling his body with agony unutterable. His cries for mercy, for salvation from Satan, and from his former sins, at first inarticulate, but at last so loud as to be heard over the body of the house—his clasped hands, as he knelt in prayer, with his face turned upwards, his eyes shut, every vein swelled almost to bursting, and the perspiration streaming down his face—his becoming calmer while listening to singing, and at last the torrents of tears running down his face, as he asked the 116th Psalm to be sung, showed the agonizing conflict that had been going on. Would that sceptics and those at a distance would at least suspend judgment until they saw one such case as this! I would venture to say that if they had stood over that man in his agony and listened to his unutterable groanings for pardon and for peace,

8

if not convinced themselves, they would speak of the present movement, not with sneers or mockery, but with solemn and reverential awe. Further, with respect to this man, he has shown one of the best tests of sincerity, in giving up a lucrative business, when first convinced of sin, about three weeks ago. He feels, as many now do, that a Christian and a whiskey-seller are not compatible terms. During the time that this man was suffering so much last night, others, *all children, were brought in, or were seized with convictions in the room.* The same cries for mercy, for deliverance from Satan, were repeated. During this scene in the session-room, the vast crowd in the church, led by one of the ministers, were praying, great numbers of them audibly, for those under convictions.'"

"On the 18th of June, the *Observer* of Ballymena remarks—'In the town and neighbourhood of Ballymena the mysterious influence continues in unabated operation; and numerous cases, accompanied by all the wonderful phenomena so frequently described, are occurring daily. At the Presbyterian church, the congregation was so numerous on Sunday last, that many persons were unable to obtain admittance, and four or five new cases of "conviction" occurred during public worship. In the evening an immense concourse of the community assembled for united prayer in a grass park to the west of the Galgorm Road. All the churches in Ballymena would not have contained the number present; and the spectacle was one of the most solemn we have ever witnessed.

"'The services were opened by the Rev. S. J. Moore; after which addresses followed in succession from four or five lay converts. Their language was characterized by the unpolished but effective eloquence of nature, for they were thoroughly *in earnest.* Several strongly-marked cases of sudden conviction occurred, while these exhortations were in progress; but the parties had been carried to a remote corner of the enclosure. The services were brought to a conclusion by the Rev. Mr. Moore; but the audience *did not separate,* for strange and most exciting scenes immediately ensued. Suddenly one person, and then another, and another, in rapid succession, *fell to the ground with piercing cries of mental agony. The mysterious influence was at work.* It spread still further among the assemblage; and within half-an-hour we found not fewer than twenty human beings stretched upon the grass, exhibiting emotions, both of soul and body, sufficient to appal the stoutest heart. In all cases it appeared as if *every fibre of the heart, and every muscle of the body were wrung with some excruciating torture.* Then followed loud cries for the Redeemer's mercy, expressed in tones of anguish which no imagination can conceive or pen describe.

"'By some intelligent investigators it is believed that just in proportion to the fairness or immorality of previous character the visitation is more or less severe. *The correctness of that opinion is liable to considerable doubt;* but we know that, from whatever cause, there *is* a great variety in the extent of suffering. Some cases are comparatively mild. But the majority of the cases of this evening were among the *severest* that we ever witnessed—and we have now seen hundreds of them. In general, the stricken parties were carried out from the pressure of the thronging multitude, to localities where they became objects of solicitude to smaller groups in other portions of the enclosure. At about half-past ten o'clock we reckoned nine circles or assemblages of this nature, in a single one of which *we found eleven prostrate penitents, smitten to the heart, and fervently supplicating God, for Christ's sake, to pardon their iniquities.*

"'Over these parties, pious bystanders or some of the converted offered prayer. Other circles laboured to console the sufferers by singing appropriate hymns or psalms. In one of the circles we noticed a case of terrible severity, one in which visions of unspeakable horror must have been pictured to the imagination of the unhappy sufferer. A young woman lay extended at full length, her eyes closed, her hands clasped and elevated, and *her body curved in a spasm so violent that it appeared to rest, arch-like, upon her heels and the back portion of her head.* In that position she lay without speech or motion for several minutes. Suddenly she uttered a terrific scream, and tore handfuls of hair from her uncovered head. Extending her open hands in a repelling attitude of the most appalling terror, she exclaimed, "Oh that fearful pit!—Lord Jesus save me!" "I am a sinner, a most unworthy sinner—but oh, Lord, take *him* away, take *him* away!" "Oh, Saviour of sinners, *remove him from my sight!*" During this paroxysm three strong men were hardly able to restrain her. She extended her arms on either side, clutching spasmodically at the grass, shuddering with terror, and shrinking from some fearful inward vision; but she ultimately fell back exhausted, nerveless, and apparently insensible. How long she remained in that condition we are unable to say; but we understand that she was treated with Christian sympathy, and removed from the field in safety before midnight.

"'This was an extreme case—not without parallel, but certainly the most frightful that we have ever witnessed. We may remark that, three days afterwards, that woman was visited by a Christian friend, who had been a witness of her agony. He found her weak in body, but her mind was thoroughly composed. She was a new creature. *The light of peace and love was beaming from her countenance, and joy reflected in her eyes* as she told him of her perfect reconciliation with God, and her unwavering faith in the Redeemer. Now we do not pretend to explain the moving *cause* of these mysterious convictions; but we feel bound to say that such have been the *results in every case brought under our notice during the last two months.* In that respect there is not the slightest perceptible distinction in the influence, whether upon the old or the young, the rich or the poor, the learned or the unlearned. Whether the agonies are brief or lengthened, moderate or severe, the *effect* is invariably the same—the fruit is love, peace, joy, temperance, and humility. Some of the "impressed" recovered ability to walk, but the greater number were supported by their friends, or carried away, and the ground was entirely vacated about half-past eleven o'clock.'"

Painful as it is to narrate, and call upon common-sense readers to follow these narratives, it is imperatively necessary that the philosophic student of psychology should trace out the workings of the wonderful modern Spiritual outpouring, in all its various phases. It is not an uninteresting subject of consideration moreover, to observe how the same influx operating upon different grades of religious thinkers, is estimated by the ruling powers of modern society. When an ignorant and half-savage multitude screams and writhes, and, in convulsive agonies, only to be paralleled in the cells of Bedlam, howls forth supplications "that God will pardon them" for *imaginary crimes*, the clergy fold their hands, look reverently on, and cry, "Behold the work of the Lord!" When a broken-hearted mother listens to the telegraphic signals which assure her the child she mourns as lost, still lives and blooms in Paradise, and she dries her tears, and calmly goes forth to proclaim in modest and eloquent terms, the fact of immortality demonstrated—that same clergy holds up its hands in holy horror, and cries, "Behold the work of Satan!"

It is time that a discerning public should have the opportunity of pronouncing judgment upon both sides of these pictures, and of comparing the theologic with the Spiritual influences prevailing during the psychological upheavals of this century.

With this view we shall present a few more examples of the celebrated Revival movement in Ireland.

A Belfast paper, speaking of Messrs. Ewart's mill, Crumlin Road, says:—

"On the morning of Tuesday, in one of the departments of a manufacturing concern, which employs a vast number of workers, male and female, nearly twenty girls were struck down, each in an instant, at their work, several becoming apparently insensible at once, and others uttering agonizing cries for mercy. The scene produced the greatest excitement throughout the entire works, and not a little alarm. Cars were provided for those who could not otherwise be removed to their homes, and the rest were assisted out of the premises, and taken to their respective places of abode. Orders were given that the workrooms should be closed for the day; *but some additional cases of visitation occurred even as the young women were leaving the place and passing down stairs.* Some of those attacked, have not yet been able to return to work. In most cases, on reaching home, the persons affected, or their friends, *sought spiritual, and some of them medical advice*; and when prayer had been offered up, in a majority of instances, speedy relief both from physical and mental suffering appeared to be produced. Several of the young women, we have been informed, have found peace, and a number are earnestly seeking it in prayer."

"The Rev. J. O'Brien, writing to the *Dublin Express*, says:—
"'Mrs. Connor has been one of the most striking cases I have seen. Her bodily affection was very severe. She screamed so as to be heard a quarter of a mile off. She said "she had felt heavy for some days, *and had to hold up her heart*," putting her hands to her *stomach.* She was still in a very weak state. Her husband, who had been a man of very bad character, had been converted also, but was now able to return to his work, and spent all his spare time in trying to convert others.'"

"'He speaks of another who "complained of a *burning from her throat down to the bottom of her heart*, and said that none but God could do her any good.'"

"The editor of the *Ballymena Observer* writes:—

"'We went to Ballyclare last night to attend a revival prayer-meeting, and, truly, I cannot understand it. I can only say that "it is the Lord's doing, and marvellous in our eyes." The scene when we arrived baffles all description. Imagine a large meadow, with an immense multitude of people in all attitudes—some praying, weeping, and crying for mercy ; others lying in utter helplessness, only able to utter feebly their entreaties for pardon, surrounded by groups of friends and strangers, all interceding for them, and urging them to call on Christ ; and again, *others with their faces beaming with a more than earthly light,* listening to the speaker, with rapture, eloquently praising God ; fathers and mothers, *tender children and strong men, the infant of a few years, and the grey-haired woman, all equally struck,* all equally earnest and eloquent. I saw stalwart men led away as if they were helpless children ; and during the singing of one of the Psalms, a man beside us suddenly burst out into the most terrific cries, running round and round in circles in such a wild manner that it was dangerous to be in his way—when his cries changed suddenly into calls on the name of Jesus, and in a few minutes, after the most awful suffering, *he fell, unable to stand or even speak.* The public-houses are empty, all through the town. There is a prayer-meeting in almost every second house. Groups about the streets are praying or conversing on the all-engrossing topic. Public works are stopped in consequence of this strange and awful manifestation. All places are alike ; people are struck down while following their daily avocations, resting on their beds, or traversing the streets. Among the people the visitation is sudden. The prayers and supplications for mercy by and for the afflicted are, oh, how awfully solemn and earnest ! *From being one of the wildest towns in the neighbourhood, Ballyclare has become one of the most religious.*'"

"Dr. Carson, of Coleraine, who has written an excellent pamphlet on the Physical side of the Manifestations, gives the following :—

"'A poor child, I think about *seven or eight years of age,* came to my house one night at a late hour, and asked to see Mrs. Carson, who had gone to her bedroom. The interview was readily granted. The child became affected. Her imploring and heart-rending cries for mercy, for she said *she was a sinner on the brink of Hell,* were so absolutely distressing that I had to leave the house for a time, as I could not bear to listen to the melancholy tones of her infant voice. The expressions of deep despair on her countenance could not be imitated by the best actor I ever saw on the stage. It was a dreadful scene. In a few hours, the poor child got the most perfect relief, and her countenance appeared almost superhuman with delight. She then began to pray, and her prayer would have melted the heart of a rock. It was so powerful, so fluent, and so full of thought, that it almost looked like inspiration in a child so very young.'"

"The Rev. Dr. Spence, of the Poultry Chapel, giving the results of his personal experience, says :—

"'I saw by the countenance of many of them that they were conscious of an unusual joy. I spoke to several of them individually about their spiritual change and their Christian hope. In some cases I could find *no intelligent foundation for their joy beyond the simple fact that they had been "struck," and by-and-by had found happiness ;* but in other cases I found the most profound sense of sinfulness, and the most loving reliance on the Lord. I endeavoured, when I was brought into contact with those who had been "struck," to test in every case the character of the change which had been experienced. The result was various. Sometimes I could find *no solid scriptural basis for the transition from sadness to joy ;* often, on the other hand, was my own soul refreshed by the simple narrative of a deepening sense of personal unworthiness, and a growing experience of the Saviour's grace. There may be ground, however, to fear that in not a few cases *feeling alone had to do with the change.*'"

"Dr. Massie relates of 'M. Napoleon Roussel, who came to see the revival, that he was full of mistrust, and that he had decided "to surrender his judgment only to evidence, to let no one know his intention of publishing." He describes the physical crisis much as I saw it ; in general consisting 'in wringing of the hands, raising the arms, moving the limbs, *or holding the stomach in the hands,* in a state of violent despair, or at least of great excitement under a sense of sin.'"

"The Rev. Mr. Tocock writes :—

"'I was requested to come to a young boy, in a most frightful state, *stricken in a moment, and fearfully distracted, throwing out his arms, and kicking with his feet, and dancing and shaking in great agitation.* I told him to be a little calmer, for *he would displease the Lord by his conduct ;* urged him to look to Jesus, and to pray for pardon ; engaged with him in prayer, he repeating the words ; then we sung, and being aided by *two young converts,* he came to Jesus, and found peace very soon afterwards.'"

"From Ballibay it is written :—

"'The church ministers are beginning to join us. Twenty-five fell in one church *along with the minister.* In another church, there is *a hundred of the congregation and the minister* converted.'"

"The Rev. Mr. Steel, of Dalry, describing a meeting at Glengarnock, says :—

"'About ten o'clock, a person rose and said that we ought to kneel and engage in prayer. A working man then rose, and, with a heart like to burst, poured out a most earnest prayer to Almighty God. At the close of the prayer, the whole meeting seemed to be moved by an invisible power. Here and there were persons crying out for mercy, and strong men crying in such a manner as I had never heard before. I have seen persons suffering under various stages of cholera—I have seen much agony in my day, but never such a sight as this.'"

"The *Ballymena Observer*, describing similar cases, says :—

"'On Sunday evening last, an assemblage numbering 2,000 people, *many of them from Ballymena*, congregated at a prayer meeting in the open air near Kilconriola. The third speaker had nearly concluded his exhortations, when a case of sudden impression, with all the ordinary symptoms, occurred among the audience. The patient was a young woman of the neighbourhood, who had been slightly affected some evenings before, at a meeting near Carncoagh. *Some excitement immediately ensued, and other cases followed in rapid succession. Within half an hour fully twenty people of the audience were laid prostrate ;* some of them utterly helpless, and for a time unable to utter anything but incoherent expressions of bodily pain and mental agony. The excitement now became intense, and the scene that ensued baffles all power of description.'"

"Mr. Wilkinson, on p. 91 of his volume, 'The Revivals,' says :—'Let us read the following, which we quote from the *Ballymena Observer :*—

"''The most extraordinary event of that evening occurred in the case of a *mere child, only seven years of age ;* a poor barefooted girl, cleanly but indifferently clothed. Without the slightest appearance of any previous agitation, she was struck prostrate in a single moment. For a time *her body was found to be perfectly rigid*, and her face colourless. On partial recovery she clasped her hands, and, looking up, exclaimed in low accents, "Lord Jesus, have mercy upon me, and bring me to the foot of thy cross !" For a considerable time she continued to repeat—but in an undertone, " Jesus !" " Jesus !" " Jesus !" Her fascinated and soul-absorbing look was fixed, far away beyond all spheres ; *and the mild, unclouded spiritual light of that unwavering gaze into the heavens* will never be forgotten by those who witnessed it. We certainly never saw any condition *so manifestly preternatural ;* nor any result so nearly approaching to a practical illustration of the poet's beautiful, though fanciful, idea of the "Angel's whisper to a slumbering baby." The trance-like attitude of body, and the rapt expression of her eye, appeared to favour the supposition that *a world of glory, invisible to other mortals, had been unveiled to her inner sight, and that, for a temporary period, she had been admitted to communion with the spirits of the just made perfect.* We understand that the girl was restored to nearly her ordinary condition in about an hour. Phenomena analogous to the foregoing came under our personal observation at a house in Alexander Street, in the afternoon of Tuesday last— and it is worthy of special notice that the party affected had *never been at any of the revival meetings.* We there found an interesting girl, *less than eight years of age,* and we ascertained that her general character is that of a shy, intelligent, and truthful child— that she is a pupil in the infant department of Guy's free school. When we first saw her she was extended upon a pallet, and slowly recovering from a *somnambulic trance,* into which she had been instantaneously stricken about five hours previously when in the act of preparation for school. For some time subsequently to the visitation, her eyes were fixed on vacancy, her hands clasped, and her lips moving as in silent prayer. Her arms were frequently elevated, as if to grasp some object immediately in view ; and, on one occasion, she clasped her father's hands, and pointing upward, motioned him to look and pray. At another time she called upon the bystanders to raise her up, in order that she might take hold of some glorious object presented to her imagination. On recovery from this state, she insisted that *she had been in the company of superhuman beings in a world of light and blessedness ; and, to the utter amazement of her parents, she affirmed that she had there intuitively recognized her infant brother, who had died eleven months after his birth, and five years before she was born !'"

"The following remarkable case is given in a Coleraine paper about the same time. It occurred at Kilconriola :—

"'The person affected was a married woman, of middle age. She appeared to be greatly *excited and feverish ; her pulse was quick, there was a hectic tinge upon the cheeks, her eyes were bloodshot, and her face was streaming with perspiration,* and for the space of fifty-six hours she was unable to taste anything but water. After the first four hours of racking pain and incessant cries for mercy, she remained prostrate for nearly three days in the condition which we have described. During the prostration of this woman her house was visited by hundreds of the neighbouring people. *She had never been taught to read or pray, and was unable to distinguish one letter of the alphabet from another,* yet she prayed with intense fervency, and exhorted the people to repentance with astonishing fluency and accuracy of speech. This case, like many others, was accompanied by visionary scenes — *illusions, certainly, but of a very extraordinary character.* Among other things she maintained that *a Bible, traced in characters of light, was open before her, and that, although unable to read, a spiritual power had endowed her with capacity to comprehend the meaning of every word in it.* It is an undoubted fact that *she repeated with literal accuracy, and as if reading from the volume, a very large number of quotations from the Old and New Testament,* applying them in an appropriate manner in connection with the prayers wherein she was engaged ! but these perceptions gradually faded in her progress towards recovery, and entirely disappeared on restoration to her ordinary health.' "

"The Rev. J. Marrable narrates the following, as occurring under his own eyes :—

" ' I was particularly struck with the following case : N. C., not eighteen years of age, *was in the act of holding a conversation with an invisible Being whom she called an "angel."* I shall not attempt to describe this scene, or the words she uttered ; but when, in about half an hour, she awoke out of the trance, to see many faces looking in amazement at her, *with tears flowing from all eyes,* her tongue, which could scarcely articulate plainly before, became loosened, and *in the most eloquent manner she addressed all present* on the subject of salvation, with an expression of holy joy and gratitude *beaming in her intelligent countenance.* She continued for several minutes in such eloquent strains that all present were compelled to admit that they had *never seen or heard anything like it before. I would myself have gone a thousand miles to see this one case, and did not think it possible that the human countenance could be lit up with so sweet and happy an expression of delight.*' "

"Dr. Massie introduces the following narrative in these words :—

" ' On Monday evening we called to visit a little girl in the Commons, called M. E. R. (aged fourteen), who had been labouring under conviction for some days previous. We found her in a melancholy, depressed state, and after conversing with her for a little, we intimated that we would engage in singing and prayer before leaving her. While singing, she fell speechless at our feet, when it was evident to all that she had been deprived of both speech and sight ; her mind, however, was active as ever, and her sense of hearing unimpaired. During the forenoon, Drs. Macaldie and Clarke visited her, and expressed their opinion that none could heal her but the Physician of souls. Later in the day, the dispensary doctor visited her, and endeavoured to restore her by applying remedies to the body, but without effect. About half-past three in the afternoon of the next day, we again visited her, and sung, " Lo ! He comes with clouds descending," and ere this hymn was finished, her tongue was loosed, he reyes we reopened, and she joined us in praising God. This was about four o'clock on the evening of Tuesday—she having been eighteen hours deprived of sight and speech.' "

"Dr. Massie proceeds :—

" ' In compliance with numerous applications upon the subject, we proceed to notice other recent phases of manifestation not less astonishing. Two young unmarried women (whom we shall call Jane, aged eighteen, and Ellen, aged twenty-three) reside at a locality about two miles distant from Ballymena, and within three hundred yards of each other. Both were apparently in good health ; and about a month ago they were stricken with " conviction," accompanied by agonies of conscience and nervous excitement. It would appear, that a species of sympathy became established between them in such a manner, that whatever affected the one party was sure to exercise a corresponding influence upon the other. On Monday, about two o'clock in the afternoon, Ellen, whilst busily engaged at work in her own house, suddenly exclaimed that Jane had become ill—said that *her mind told her so, and that she must go and visit her.* With that intent she left the house ; and on entering that of her companion, found that she had just fallen into a trance— deaf, dumb, and motionless. Within a minute afterwards, Ellen had fallen upon the floor *in a precisely similar condition, and both remained in that state and position for fully three hours.* Both recovered *at the same moment,* and immediately on their recovery they were separated ; Ellen being forthwith taken to her own house, where she fell upon her knees, and was engaged in prayer for half an hour. To the great surprise of her relatives, she then affirmed that, precisely at four o'clock on the following evening, she would become deaf, dumb, blind, and without power of motion in one side of her body, for the space of six hours, and that she should be restored to her natural condition at ten o'clock. On being asked how she could know that she would be visited in such a manner, she replied, " I cannot explain how I know it ; but my mind tells me that it will surely be as I have said." Every effort was made to remove the impression from the mind of the party thus affected ; and care was taken that Jane should *have no information of what had been predicted in reference to her companion.* Ellen continued at her ordinary work, and apparently in her usual health, throughout the forenoon of Tuesday ; and the hand of the house clock was secretly put back fifteen minutes in the course of the day. Precisely at the moment when the clock indicated that it wanted a quarter to four, but when the real time *was fifteen minutes later,* Ellen's arms dropped, her eyes closed, and she fell from her chair without speech or motion, and in a state of absolute insensibility! She was carefully laid upon a bed; and on examination it was found that the joints of her right arm and leg were perfectly immovable, and rigid as iron. The excitement among the people of the house was naturally very great; but it was doubled in intensity when intelligence arrived that *Jane had fallen into a state exactly resembling that of Ellen, precisely at the same moment that Ellen had been thus affected.*

"'In this abnormal condition both women remained for a period of six hours, and both awoke to consciousness, and in the full possession of all their faculties, *precisely at the same moment.* At five minutes before ten, Ellen's rigid arm regained its natural condition, and she was observed to raise her hand and lay it gently across her breast; but up till the stroke of the predicted hour, no other change became perceptible. Before the remaining strokes of ten had sounded from the clock, she was fully awake; and her first exclamation, amid a house then crowded with anxious visitors, was, "Christ is my Saviour! He is all and in all!" It may appear incredible, but the fact is established beyond all controversy, that *these identical words were the first* uttered by Jane in her own house three hundred yards distant, as she awoke to consciousness *at the same moment!*'"

Dr. Massie relates with great minutiæ of detail, many additional cases of a similar character to those already given, together with instances in which the "stricken ones," both male and female, were poor ignorant people— some of them *very young children,*—servants, and workmen,—who could *neither read nor write,* yet, these persons in their "trances," did intelligently read out consecutive verses, and sometimes whole chapters of the Bible, and exhort, pray, and sing, with a fervency and eloquence, not to be equalled by the best cultured ministers of religion. The last cases which we can cite are as follows:—

"The Rev. R. Gemmell, after saying, 'With regard to the bodily manifestations, I can give no opinion, nor do I like to hear any opinion, as I believe no man can give any satisfactory explanation,' gives the following:—

"'A young lad about sixteen years of age was struck down in his own house. It took four strong men to hold him, to prevent him from dashing his brains out on the floor. He continued in this state for several hours. When he recovered, he had *lost the power of one of his sides, and was unable to utter a word distinctly.* The third day after, I visited him, about three o'clock; he was still in the same state, but, to my utter astonishment, when standing at the door at seven o'clock, he came running forward, and shook hands with me, and said, "O Sir, I am now quite well!"'"

"Dr. Massie says:—

"'One fearful case was specified to me of an infatuated scoffer, who professed to fall down as an awakened and stricken sinner, while a companion, as depraved, ran to request the attendance of a servant of God. When they came to the spot where the feigned penitent was lying, they found him dead.'"

"The Rev. Mr. Moore says:—

"'In my own congregation five or six cases—and some of them very painful—have occurred. We hear occasionally *of dreams and visions—the mere drapery of the work, and the effect of its deep and intense reality*—but though beautiful and interesting in themselves, such things are not made much of here, *and the less the better.*'"

"At Paisley, in September, similar cases were frequent. The Rev. Mr. Macgregor says:—

"'Among the young women affected, two were for a time deaf and dumb, and while in this state, their countenances indicated, from their expression, the most joyous happiness. Many of them had been *dreaming dreams and seeing visions.* It was the case that, *wherever the revivals had arisen, they had dreams and visions,* and they were to be regarded as evidence of the outpouring of the Holy Spirit.'"

"The Rev. Hugh Hunter writes:—

"'It is now nearly five weeks since the Lord's work commenced in good earnest in this neighbourhood. It was going on amazingly in the neighbouring county of Antrim. Every day brought new tales of *trances, sleeps, visions, dreams and miracles; such as, that persons who never knew a letter of the alphabet when awake could read the Bible distinctly, sing psalms and hymns, preach, and pray with ease, eloquence, and fluency.*'"

"The Rev. J. Whitsitt, of Drum, Monaghan, writes to a friend:—

"'It was true the report which you heard. At one of our meetings for prayer, at which there were a number of convictions, a dark cloud formed on the ceiling, and, in the course of a few minutes, a number of forms burst out. One in particular was of human appearance, which passed and repassed across all the lights, and descended to the pew in which a young woman was rejoicing. The appearance lasted for three minutes, or more, produced no terror, but joy, especially among the converts. All present did not see it. Perhaps 300 saw it, and can testify to the reality. I cannot tell what it was; the substance is in heaven, and will not be visible until the time when "every eye shall see Him."'"

CHAPTER XV.

SPIRITUALISM IN GREAT BRITAIN (CONTINUED).

SUMMARY OF CONFLICTING OPINIONS CONCERNING THE IRISH REVIVALS.

IT cannot be supposed that the mighty wave which had surged over the "stricken" subjects of the Irish Revival, could pass away without calling forth an immense array of diverse opinions from various leading minds, concerning the origin and significance of the wonderful movement.

As a general rule the attempts to find an adequate cause for the marvels which flooded the land, during the Revival frenzy, may be classified thus :—

1. The work proceeds from "the Devil."
2. From the Holy Ghost.
3. From interested and artful professional Revival preachers.
4. From mesmerism, hysteria, and other unknown physical agents.

About the time when the Irish Revivals were at their height, some scenes of a kindred character, though conducted on a more limited scale, and promptly checked by the officiating ministers of the time, were proceeding in some of the rural districts of England, and amongst the lowest of the East-end ragged schools of the metropolis. An able writer in the London *Sunday Times* thus comments on scenes of this character, of which he claims to have been an eye-witness in a ragged school in St. Giles' on the preceding Sunday.

"Here are one hundred and fifty ragged, ill-fed, uneducated little boys and girls, from six to fourteen, kept until after ten at night to listen to a 'deeply impressive' account of the doings in Ireland, in all their agonising details. Was there no mercy in the heart of the speaker? No sense of childhood's weakness? No thought of the Divine Justice? And there they were rolling upon the floor, crying out until two in the morning about their sins. Great God! how art thou insulted. Their sins! Why surely, if God arose in His anger it would be, not to crush down and agonise these little friendless, hungry, orphaned children, only six years old, who cannot comprehend the meaning of such subjects, but *He would rise against the high and the mighty*, the men of wealth and statesman power, who, through neglecting their duty, have left these little ones to become the victims of hunger and cold, and hence also the victims of our hard laws, and, to them, cruel institutions. Comments upon such mockery and cruelty are needless."

And again :—"I am not dealing unjustly in thus speaking. I see the poor little girl crying in the Irish churchyard; I see the young women rolling in agony upon the Irish meadows; I see the ignorant men, the hysterical women, and the fear-struck children in the Irish churches, with horrible anxiety pictured upon their terror-stricken countenances; and I see the poor little boys and girls in the St. Giles' refuge rolling upon the floor, their young hearts filled with fear through the story of Irish madness which, without stint or mercy, had been poured into their ears. Yes, I see all this, and more than this—more than can now be told ; and then, while listening to the wild screams which burst from the agonized hearts of an ignorant and frenzied people, I hear also, and blended with the screams, the voices of the ' holy men '—voices of the leaders and teachers in our spiritual Israel—raised as in thanksgiving to God for all this agony, which, either in their blindness or through their hypocrisy, they dare to call ' His great mercy.' I hear them pray that the same ' blessing ' may be granted unto us ; and, from all this, what is it possible to conclude other than that, if they are in earnest, then are they blind also ? but, whether earnest or not, they are endeavouring to inflict upon England one of the heaviest curses that could descend upon a people whose ancestors won freedom alike on the fields of civil and ecclesiastical conflict.''

Mr. Wilkinson, in his excellent work on "The Irish Revivals," says :—

"Archdeacon Stopford of Meath is the champion of the physical mode of accounting for the Revival, whose arguments are the best poised, and sufficiently comprehend those of others having the same views. He does not, however, fail to see ' much good in the movement.' He says, ' Even a stranger cannot fail to be struck with the earnest concern about religion which appears to pervade the people ; as I listened to a street preacher—the best sermon which I heard in Belfast—it was impossible not to be impressed with the earnest and reverent expression of countenance in all the working men and lads who gathered round, perhaps one hundred and fifty in number ; faces so earnest I never saw before in any congregation. From house to house I saw much of the same feeling.' "

The question of hysteria has been so widely canvassed, that it is worth while to present the argument as it appears in one of Dr. Carson's excellent letters. Dr. Carson says :—

"I see a good deal of time and labour have been spent in *asserting*, over and over again, that the physical manifestations are neither more nor less than hysteria. Were it not that the public might be misled by the plausible and ostentatious statements which have been put forward on the subject, I would not think of occupying time with its consideration.

"There is no reason why the country should be free from hysterical cases now, more than at any other time. Hence, as might be anticipated, *some cases of hysteria are to be met with in every district where the Revival has appeared.* But the man who will confine his observations to these cases, or confound them with the Revival manifestations, has but a poor capacity for the observation of facts. The fact is, *the Revival and hysteria have scarcely any symptoms in common.* Any person in the Revival district may easily convince himself of this fact by turning to the article ' Hysteria,' in the first work on the ' Practice of Medicine' he can lay his hands on. To enter fully into the distinguishing marks of these two affections would extend this letter to an unreasonable length ; but there are two or three features which require to be noticed, and which are capable of being judged by all parties. . . . Hysteria is *almost entirely confined to the female sex.* It is very common in the female, but so *extremely* rare in the male, that the late Dr. Hooper, and the present Dr. Watson, of London, in their immense practice, have seen only *three cases* each, which they could at all compare to hysteria, and these cases occurred in debilitated subjects. . . . In regard to the Revival, it occurs chiefly amongst the lower and middle classes of society, who are obliged to earn their subsistence by their daily labour. It is to be found as readily amongst the hardy inhabitants of country parishes and moun-tain districts, as in towns and cities. If all ages are included, there are very nearly as many males affected by it as females. I have seen and known of an immense number of instances in which *the strongest, the stoutest, most vigorous, healthy, and lion-hearted men in the country have been struck down like children,* and have called, with the most agonising entreaties, for mercy for their souls. How could all this be hysteria ? "

Dr. Watson, an eminent medical practitioner of London, who spent some time in personally examining the condition of many of the Revivalists, arrives at the conclusion that the principal source of the movement is a *physical*, though unknown agent, and his views are given in the following remarks :—

"I now fearlessly state, that, in my opinion, *there is a physical, as well as a spiritual, agent concerned in the Revival.* There does not appear to me to be any other rational way of accounting for the facts. Whatever I may have been disposed to think at first, I am now fully satisfied the symptoms of a Revival case do not correspond to the effects which are manifested as the result of mere mental impressions. The unearthly tone of subdued entreaties, and the partial prostration of muscular power in the individual affected, are very different from the wild screams, and convulsive paroxysms, which arise from sudden mental anguish; and we cannot consistently refer them to a sudden view of spiritual danger, *because the same sudden view of spiritual matters has been revealed to thousands of individuals of different constitutions, at different periods of the history of the world, without producing the like results.*

"The explanation by mere mental impressions will not satisfy a close thinker in regard to them. There must be a special physical agent concerned.

"This view is greatly strengthened by the way in which the Revival has travelled. *It has followed a steady, gradual, and uninterruped course from parish to parish, and district to district. It has travelled almost like a wave.* Again, it was observed that the most illiterate convert, *who had himself been physically affected, had far more power in producing the manifestations in the audience, than the most eloquent speaker who could address them.* There did not seem to be any proportion between the words uttered by the speakers and the results produced. It looked more like a physical effect produced *by individual on individual than anything else.*

"The idea of exclusive spirituality in the Revival would involve us in endless difficulties, which can all be avoided by the simple idea of the double agency. If we do not adopt this view, what are we to do with those *cases of deafness, dumbness, blindness, extraordinary visions, and prophesying,* which have occurred in some localities? They are not either directly or indirectly the effects of the Holy Spirit. They are entirely owing to the effects of the physical agent on the brain and nervous system.

"In regard to the nature of the physical agent, I have no hesitation in acknowledging my utter ignorance. I know of nothing to correspond exactly with it in the whole range of philosophy.

"No person but the man who has witnessed them could have any idea of the awful effects produced by a number of Revival cases. A scene like the one which took place on the night in which the new hall in Coleraine was first filled with these cases has, perhaps, never been equalled in the world. It was so like the day of judgment, when sinners would be calling on the mountains and the rocks to hide them from the storm of God's wrath, that it struck terror to the heart of the most hardened and obdurate sinner."

As the Evangelical views of the causes operating to produce these Revivals, have already been sufficiently hinted at to make the reader aware that a large number of Ministers of the Gospel attributed the above movement to the direct action of the "Holy Ghost," it only remains to call attention to the very suspicious way in which those peculiar demonstrations were received, which in the form of trances, dreams, visions, and prophecies, seemed to be all too dangerously allied to the *bête noir* of every denomination, namely modern Spiritualism, a development which might well have been unknown to the poor illiterate subjects of the Irish Revivals, but which was by no means *either new or strange* to the better-informed Doctors, Lawyers, Divines, &c., &c., who watched the Spiritual epidemic of the unmanageable Irish Revivals.

Mr. W. M. Wilkinson opens up this question with significant force when he says :—

"What are we to think of that class of phenomena, of which there are so many instances, in which the converts have fallen into swoons and trances, and into those peculiar states of the organism in which they have seen and described visions of angels and devils—of heaven and of hell—and which were so common, 'that almost every girl now struck in Belfast had visions, and would be greatly disappointed if she had not.' 'There are also very many astonishing statements and events which, some years ago, and in other circumstances, would have been called clairvoyance by those who believed that there was such a mode of obtaining knowledge.' Others, again, who could not read a word in their ordinary state, had a faculty or power, when in this wondrous state, of perceiving in letters of light, and reading whole pages from the Bible; others of seeing things and persons at distances beyond the ken of natural eyes. . . .

"Now, how it has come about we know not, but these phenomenal aspects of the Revival have brought down upon it, its bitterest opponents, and in view of them, the whole movement has been characterised by some religious critics as the direct work of Satan, and by the more sceptical as a work of imposture, or as the product of diseased imagination. Here, again, it is to be noted, that at first there are not so many words used against the calm and quiet part of the awakening; but when it came to pass that its subjects were seers and seeresses no words are strong enough for its condemnation."

Again, Mr. Wilkinson in commenting on the *pyschical* aspect of this movement, and the various phenomena (far too numerous to admit of farther description) which corresponded with the manifestations of Spiritualism, says :—

"In attempting to gather up facts of this nature at a distance from the places of their occurrence we find, of all those who could not in fairness omit noticing them, there is not one who gives them a kindly welcome. Several suppress them altogether, the others have to apologize for them in the best way they can.

"The excellent Minister at Connor, when in the great excitement of prostrations and ecstatic phenomena, some similar cases were threatened amongst his flock, set his face against them altogether. Others are blamed for not having followed his plan, which had the good effect of preventing them. We shall see that they were amenable to this treatment, and it is a suggestive fact for our consideration.

"In the early days of the excitement arising from these cases, some were made public through the newspapers, and there are others to be found in some of the narratives, but every day they become more difficult of access, as mention of them is seldom made, and it is only from occasional glimpses that we see how common they were—so common, indeed, that they occurred in the majority of the stricken cases, and those who did not have visions, or some of the other extraordinary phenomena accompanying their prostration, complained of the deficiency of the Holy Spirit, and feared that their conversion was not complete. . . .

"We could have wished that these cases had been as fully stated and as largely investigated as the others, for they form a chapter in the book of man that is worthy the most serious and earnest consideration."

We have already extended the notices of this singular movement to so great a length, that we turn, though most reluctantly, from the many suggestive arguments adduced by the author of "The Revival" to show that a great magnetic wave, contagious as magnetism ever is in its effects, world-wide in its centres of evolution, and purely spiritual in its source, underlies these Irish Revivals, just as surely as it does the doings of the *Polter Gheist* in Germany, the manifestations of clairvoyance in France, or the *Rochester Knockings* in America.

Who can doubt that if this Revival had occurred on Mahometan ground, the visionists would have seen Houris and paradises; screamed for Mahomet, and sought through him reconciliation with Allah? Occurring in a land, the very atmosphere of which was saturated with Calvinistic ideas, and governed by a Calvinistic priesthood, the great magnetic influx which poured into the hearts and minds of a naturally impulsive and susceptible race of people, inevitably partook of the dominant religious idea; and this was so strengthened by the powerful influence of Revival preachers, that it was only now and then that angel faces could look through the theological veil of terror, in which the peasantry were enshrouded, or in rare cases, that true Spiritual mediumship could be unfolded, and triumph over the unreasoning ecstasies of religious gloom and mystery.

The sunbeam which gives life to the rose and lights up the blue eye of the violet, quickens the heap of corruption into the life of the foul reptile, and stinging insect. The sun of spiritual existence shines on the just and the unjust, and *quickens, but creates nothing*.

Thus we may realise by careful research into the fanaticisms of the Irvingites, the abominations of Mormonism, the unnatural asceticisms of Shakerism, and the frenzied agonies of Irish Revivalism that "all are but parts of one stupendous whole"—*differences of administration, but the same spirit working in all.*

CHAPTER XVI.

SPIRITUALISM IN GREAT BRITAIN.—SECOND PERIOD.

IN searching amongst the scattered records of Spiritual manifestations in England, the historian cannot fail to come to the conclusion that there are two well-defined sources of power which antedated in point of time the introduction of that systematic mode of telegraphy practised by the American mediums who commenced to visit this country in 1852.

The first of these was the very general outpouring of Spiritual manifestations noted in preceding chapters, and occurring in the form of haunting isolated phenomena, and Religious Revivals.

The second was Animal Magnetism, which, by preparing the world for the study of occult phenomena, and unfolding in many organisms the potencies of clairvoyance and other Spiritual endowments, paved the way for the more pronounced and comprehensive demonstrations of Spiritual Mediumship.

From the year 1820 to 1840, numerous gentlemen of learning and high social standing, openly avowed themselves disciples of Mesmeric philosophy, and practised with success healing by Animal Magnetism.

As experiments of this character were very often productive of clairvoyance, prevision, trance speaking, and even Spiritual seership, a wide spreading interest began to arise concerning these mysterious potencies. About the year 1851, a Mesmeric Infirmary was established in Wimpole Street, of which Drs. Elliotson, Ashburner, Wilson, Haddock, Mrs. De Morgan, and numerous other ladies and gentlemen became patrons and supporters. In this institution, patients were treated by magnetic processes, and in many instances cures were effected of cases deemed hopeless by the ordinary methods of medical practice.

For some years previous to the formation of this establishment, the advocates of Mesmeric philosophy had conducted an excellent periodical entitled the *Zoist*, in which hundreds of notable experiments were recorded, and the phenomena as well as the facts of magnetic practices were carefully detailed.

In view of the persistence with which the columns of the secular journals are open to all manner of communications antagonistic to new discoveries, and new ideas, and closed against their advocates, the publication of the *Zoist* which was continued for many years, and supported by an able staff of editors and contributors, will be understood to have been the principal means of widening the sphere of knowledge on occult subjects, and preserving many valuable records which would otherwise have been lost to the world.

In the initiatory numbers of this journal, Dr. Elliotson, one of its earliest and most distinguished supporters, alleges, that Mesmerism as a recognised "science," was first established in England in 1828, through the influence of an Irish gentleman, a Mr. Chevenix, who after a long residence in Paris, where he had witnessed, and personally assisted at a number of experiments, finally began to practise on his own account in Ireland, where he found a fine field for his operations amongst the susceptible peasantry of that country.

Drs. McKay, Peacock, Cotter, Gooch; Mr. Smith, surgeon to the Coldstream Guards; Professor Gregory of Edinburgh, Drs. Elliotson and Ashburner of London, Dr. John Wilson, physician at Middlesex Hospital, and many gentlemen of equal standing in their profession, who had avowed themselves advocates of Mesmeric practices, succeeded, both in creating a wide-spread public interest in their philosophy, and in awakening the most relentless spirit of antagonism from those who thought proper to range themselves on the opposite side of the question.

To those who realise with the author, that Mesmerism has been—humanly speaking—the corner-stone upon which the Temple of Spiritualism was upreared, the following notice of some of the curious experiments recorded in the early numbers of the *Zoist*, will be of interest.

Dr. Ashburner, in reviewing a pamphlet written by Dr. John Wilson of Middlesex Hospital entitled, "Trials of Animal Magnetism on the Brute Creation," says :—

"Dr. Wilson successfully magnetized fish, birds, and savage beasts. I was with him on one occasion at the Surrey Zoological Gardens while honest Mr. Cross was proprietor of the menagerie. The great male elephant was put into a deep sleep by the strenuous and energetic passes of my colleague. The keeper told me, 'The Doctor off with his coat, wrought like a Trojan, and got the old animal into a sound sleep and no mistake.'

"Mr. Cross had a very savage and irascible hyena. Dr. Wilson mesmerised him, and it was amusing to see the delight of the fierce creature at the Doctor's approach."

In the pages of the *Zoist* will be found an answer to the sneer with which those readers will peruse the above-named experiments who—having found their efforts to stamp out unwelcome facts ineffectual—proceed to depreciate their value by the imbecile query, "What is the use of it?" The *use* of Mesmerism is shown, even in the early stage of the movement of which we are writing, by the facts that the Mesmerisers recorded; namely; well attested cures of typhus fever in its last and most hopeless stages; consumption, dropsy, bronchitis, all manner of nervous disorders, besides many surgical cases.

Amongst the latter, is described the perfect cure of a woman, employed in the Hospital at Hoddesden, superintended by the celebrated writer Mrs. Ellis,—who was suffering from a severe case of ovarian tumour, for which in fact she was on the point of submitting to a dangerous and doubtful operation. Dr. Ashburner hearing of her dilemma, persuaded her to try Mesmerism, through the instrumentality of which, she became entirely cured. Several other instances of a similar kind are recorded in the *Zoist*, including one, of *malignant cancer*,—a cure so thoroughly well proved, and of such a remarkable character, that we would refer the curious reader to its full details, which may be found given by Dr. Elliotson in the 6th volume of the *Zoist*, page 213. Mesmeric practices received a strong impulse, especially in the unfoldment of remarkable psychological powers, in the year 1849, by the visit to England of two renowned French clairvoyants, Messrs. Alexis Didier, and Marcellet.

Through numerous experiments conducted with these gentlemen, the Magnetizers were enabled to prove, not only that disease could be cured, but that mental power of a highly exalted and wonderful character could be evolved in the magnetic sleep.

The French clairvoyants were adepts in the examination of obscure diseases, in tracing lost, hidden, and distant objects, also in the faculty of mind reading.

The powers thus displayed in the magnetic sleep, were found to be more general than had hitherto been supposed; hence, clairvoyance, in addition to the healing faculty, became another horn of the dilemma with which the materialistic opponents of the new philosophy found themselves compelled to do battle.

To the voluminous writings of Mr. Henry Thompson, Professor Gregory, Mrs. De Morgan, Drs. Barth, Dixon, Elliotson, Ashburner, and Haddock, Mr. Joseph Hands, and above all, to the experiences of Drs. Deleuze and Eisdale, in India, we must refer the readers, desirous to acquaint themselves in farther detail, concerning the origin, practices, and results of Mesmerism in Great Britain.

Quite recently—that is, at the present date of writing—the practice of Mesmerism, whether as a curative process, or an agent for the unfoldment of marvellous psychologic powers, has received a most favourable impulse from the writings, lectures, and private practice of Miss Chandos Leigh Hunt (now Mrs. Wallace), a lady who has thoroughly and philosophically mastered as much of the subject as can at present be known or experimented with. In a scholarly and exhaustive treatise written by this lady on the Science and Art of Organic Magnetism,* the powers and possibilities of this wonderful mesmeric force are admirably described, and the immense range of operations, both curative and psychologic, which the talented authoress delineates, renders it now, as heretofore, a reproach to the age, that no philanthropic as well as philosophic associations should be formed for the study of the stupendous principles suggested by Mrs. Wallace's writings, and practically taught by her, to all who are interested enough to put vague theory into the form of demonstrable proof.

Another valuable work treating of the results, though not of the *modus operandi* of Mesmerism, is Mrs. De Morgan's work, written quite early in the advent of the Spiritual movement, entitled, "From Matter to Spirit." Our learned authoress says :—

"Every wonderful effect produced by mesmerism, has since found its explanation or its counterpart in the spiritual phenomena, so that had unseen powers been working for our instruction, they could not have taken a better method of giving the needful elementary knowledge, than by making us acquainted with the processes and results of mesmerism."

Mrs. De Morgan in illustrating the statement given above, cites numerous examples, amongst others, the following experience, recorded by Dr. Jacob Dixon in his published manual, entitled "Hygienic Medicine." This author says :—

"Persons in some of the highest mesmeric states, appear to have gained an insight into the world of spirit. Of this I had striking experiences *long before* the time of raps, seeing mediums, and mysteries of the present day.

"Although I had too many instances of earthly clairvoyance to remain sceptical in that direction, yet I held all belief in intercourse with spirits to be a delusion. This scepticism was first shaken by the following occurrence.

---

* *Private Practical Instructions in the Science and Art of Organic Magnetism.* By Miss Chandos Leigh Hunt. Philanthropic Reform Publishing Office, 2, Oxford Mansion, Oxford Circus, London, W.

"Being invited to see a young lady in a clairvoyant state, in which she professed to see and converse with spiritual beings, I entered the room after she had been put in the mesmeric state, whilst my name was not even mentioned or my presence known. . . . At length my friends asked, whether she could look for any spirit for the party sitting beside her. She would try. I mentioned two names without giving age, sex, or relationship to myself.

"She then said: '*I am now in a garden quite full of flowers. There is a group of children. . . . Two come out of the group. The girl is the oldest. They are ten and eight years' old.*' She then described perfectly every feature of the two children I had asked for, dwelling with animation on their beautiful appearance and surroundings. The ages she mentioned, however, were much in advance of the reality.

"When I remarked this she said : '*They say that I see them as they are now, you must remember, that they have been here some time.*'"

The writer adds—

"It then appeared that the **ages she mentioned** would have been exactly correct had the two remained on earth."

In the year 1851, there was a society organised in England for the purpose of collecting and examining evidence into the alleged facts of " Supernaturalism." In relation to this society, called in the usual tone of popular derision, " The Ghost Club," Mr. Robt. Dale Owen in his exhaustive work, " Footfalls on the Boundary of Another World," speaks as follows :—

"A society was formed in the latter part of the year 1851 at Cambridge, by certain members of the University, for the purpose of instituting, as their circular expresses it, 'a serious and earnest enquiry into the nature of the phenomena vaguely called supernatural.' The society included some of the most distinguished members of the University, most of them clergymen and fellows of Trinity College, and almost all of them men who had graduated with the highest honours.

"The names of the more active amongst them were kindly furnished to me by the son of a British peer, himself one of the leading members.

"To him also I am indebted for a copy of the printed circular of the Society, an able and temperate document, which will be found at length in the Appendix.* "

Mr. Owen adds in a footnote to page 34 :—

"The Society popularly known as 'The Ghost Club,' attracted a good deal of attention outside its own circle. Its nature and object came to my knowledge through the Bishop of ——, who took an interest in its proceedings, and bestirred himself to obtain contributions to its records."

Although we may often encounter in future chapters some of the individual members of this association of investigators, our notice of their combined researches must terminate here, hence we deem it not entirely out of place to anticipate by a few years the effect which those researches must have produced upon some at least of its members, when we give as the addenda to the subject, the following extracts from the London *Spiritualist* newspaper, dated April 11th, 1879 :—

"AN ADDRESS BY MR. JAMES CAMPBELL.—Mr. J. A. Campbell, President of the Cambridge University Society for Psychological Investigation, will read a paper next Monday week, April 21st, at one of Mrs. Makdougall Gregory's evening receptions. There will be a large and influential gathering of Spiritualists and non-Spiritualists, the latter of whom will have an opportunity of learning that Spiritualism is not what it is represented to be by daily newspapers. The title of Mr. Campbell's address will be, 'The Record of the Seers concerning the Great Change.'"

* *Appendix. Note A.* " Footfalls on the Boundary of another World." By R. D. Owen.

In the *Spiritualist* of the same date, is an address from Mr. Campbell entitled :—THE HISTORY OF THE MOVEMENT KNOWN AS MODERN SPIRITUALISM, AND THE FACTS AND THEORIES CONNECTED WITH IT, *by J. A. Campbell ; President of the Cambridge University Society for Psychological Investigation.* Mr. Campbell's speech, although a most excellent one, would only anticipate statements which the progress of the history itself must unfold—but its presentation some twenty years or more after the formation of the society of which he was and we believe is still the honoured President, is noticed now to show that the subject has not proved an evanescent one, or unworthy the consideration of eminent and learned scholars during a period of nearly a quarter of a century.

CHAPTER XVII.

SPIRITUALISM IN GREAT BRITAIN.

SECOND PERIOD (CONTINUED).

AMERICAN SPIRIT MEDIUMS IN ENGLAND.

HITHERTO our history of the Spiritual movement in Great Britain has followed the waymarks made by an invisible host in the production of spontaneous and unsought phenomena. We must now proceed to consider those results which grew out of the invocatory processes of the Spirit circle, and the agency of acknowledged Spirit Mediumship.

Long before the rumour reached England of the American disturbances called the "Rochester Knockings," the practices of "table turning" by what was supposed to be *will power*, were quite popular in many a fashionable circle. That these curious evidences of an unknown force had any connection with the agency of "disembodied spirits" never seemed to enter the imagination of "table turning" *experts*, until the advent in England of Mrs. Hayden, an American lady, who came to this country on a professional tour, in company with her husband and a business agent—as an avowed *medium for communications between earth and the world of disembodied spirits.*

Very shortly after the advent of the "Rochester Knockings" in New York State, America, Mrs. Hayden, the wife of a respectable journalist, found herself the subject of the same strange rappings connected with intelligence, which distinguished the earliest American Mediums. Having been induced to sit for the public as a professional Medium, Mrs. Hayden was visited by a Mr. Stone, an English gentleman on a tour through the United States.

Mr. Stone received such striking tests of Spirit presence through Mrs. Hayden's mediumship, that in 1852 he persuaded her to accompany him to England, never doubting that his own countrymen would become as much interested in the results of her marvellous gifts as he himself had been.

In all the accounts published of early Spiritualism in England, Mrs. Hayden is mentioned as *the Medium* who first introduced the American system of communicating with Spirits through the alphabet and rappings, and strange as it may appear to thoughtful minds that any human beings could do otherwise than hail with delight a system of telegraphy which restored to the mourner his beloved dead, and converted the mere hope of immortality into demonstrated proof, it is nevertheless an historical fact, that an avowed Medium for Spiritual communications no sooner appeared on the scene, than the leaders of the press, pulpit and college, levelled against her a storm of ribaldry, persecution and insult, alike disgraceful to themselves, and humiliating to the boasted liberalism and scientific acumen of their age. From the author's personal knowledge of Mrs. Hayden, she is convinced that her gentle womanly spirit must have been deeply pained, and the harmony of mind so essential to the production of good psychological results constantly destroyed, by the cruel and insulting treatment she received at the hands of many of those who came, pretending to be investigators, but in reality burning to thwart her, and laying traps to falsify the truths of which Mrs. Hayden professed to be the instrument. Sensitively alive—as all mediumistic persons are—to the animus of her visitors, she could feel, and often writhed under, the crushing force of the antagonism brought to bear upon her, without—at that time—knowing how to repel or resist it.

In those early days of the movement, the Mediums had neither the advantage of experience nor precedent in such embarrassing circumstances. Oppressed as they were by the opposing force which was purposely arrayed against them, their distress of mind only served to complicate the mental inharmony of the surroundings, and make it most difficult for Spirits to construct those delicate psychologic batteries, upon which the success of the communion depends.

We all acknowledge that the most carefully prepared and chemically adapted elements are necessary to evolve the force of electricity, and promote a perfect result from the formation of a battery, yet we overlook the fact, that the mental and spiritual telegraph must work through laws just as absolute, and whilst men ruthlessly invade those laws and destroy the equilibrium under which that battery works, they triumphantly regard failure as an evidence that no such battery was in existence at all.

We not only know better now, but with all that tendency to exaggeration which marks the crises of man's ignorance and fanaticism, too many Spiritualists of the present day rush into the opposite extreme, and endeavour to palliate the most daring frauds, by pretending that sceptical minds and antagonistic forces have *compelled* detected impostors to prepare masks and other paraphernalia to personate spirits, when *injurious conditions prevented their materializing,* &c., &c. That the real truth lies between the extremes of antagonism on the one hand, and wilful imposture on the other, none can doubt. In Mrs. Hayden's time, there is good reason to believe that the occasional failures which occurred at her circles, were the result of cunningly prepared traps to involve the inexperienced medium in contradictory statements, and when once the would-be detectives thought they had succeeded in these notable plots, the columns of the public journals were filled with triumphant accounts of "the entire collapse of the Spirit rapping delusion."

As an illustration both of the spirit of the times, and the manifest injury to Mediumship, which determined antagonism can exercise, we give a few

9

extracts from a little work which the writer has wisely bequeathed to posterity in an *anonymous* form. Doubtless "he builded wiser than he knew," and whilst his evil record serves the purpose of preserving both sides of the shield of history, he is spared the disgrace of sending down his name to posterity, branded with the tokens of folly his writings display.

The title of the work is "Spirit Rapping in England and America," and the author after a derisive and perverted account of the American manifestations, goes on to detail the incidents of a *séance* which he professes to have held with Mrs. Hayden shortly after her arrival in London in 1852.

Let the reader picture to himself the poor Medium, leaving the pleasant homes of New England, and establishing herself in the proverbially cold and cheerless shelter of a London lodging-house, in the "pea soup" atmosphere of a London November, and amongst a people not, *at that time*, particularly in favour of "*Yankee speculators.*"

Sneering scoffers of the "gent" order, as described by the late witty writer, Albert Smith; insolent aristocrats seeking for a new sensation and dividing their interest between wrenching off door-knockers at night, and Yankee Spirit rappers" by day; glib press men bound to supply a *funny* item, and not caring if the fun is made out of the souls of their ancestors, so long as they were employed to indite journalistic satire against an unpopular thing—these were amongst the daily visitors of the poor foreigner, whose power to satisfy their demands depended upon the most peaceful and harmonious conditions of mind and body. When we add to this, that the Medium herself was as much a tyro in the means of producing successful manifestations, as those who sought her, the marvel is that any Spirit short of a Mephistopheles or Lucifer, could be enabled to rap out names and dates correctly at all. If the reader has fully possessed himself of the conditions under which the first Spiritual telegraphic messages were produced in London, he need not be surprised at the results obtained, as narrated in the anonymous work which we are now about to quote. After a great deal of circumlocution of an unimportant character, the reader is informed that the visitors were "Brown" and "Thompson;" names no doubt meant to imply that they were assumed to mask two very *illustrious personages*. After all sorts of derisive remarks about the Medium's lodging and surroundings, these *gentlemen* proceeded to hold a *séance*, of which the following extract is a specimen :—

"At length, getting too weary of the scene to pursue it farther, 'I wish,' said Brown, 'to ask some questions concerning the future ; can the spirits answer them without your knowing what they are ?' 'If they cannot, they will be silent,' said the medium, 'sometimes they do so. Try.' 'As they are questions which I should not like to ask in public, will they see them written on paper ?' 'O yes.' Brown wrote down very clearly : 'Shall I soon be married ?' 'Will the spirits answer this question ?' Rat-tat-tat. 'Is "yes" the answer ?' Rat-tat-tat. 'How many children shall I have ?' was written next, Brown saying 'This is a question that must be answered in numbers. Does the spirit see it ?' Rat-tat-tat. 'Can it answer me ?' Rat-tat-tat. And so the spirit answered by the usual process, 'One hundred and thirty-six.' When the 1 was obtained, and then the 3 to go next to it, and then the 6 to go after that, the rapid growth of Brown's family amused Thompson, and the imminent carrying on of the sum into thousands was prevented by his ill-timed mirth. The production of children by Brown stopped, therefore, prematurely, at the number of one hundred and thirty-six.

"The medium, who always asked whether the answers fitted, and who did not clearly know whether she might not be succeeding vastly, although she evidently felt a little puzzled by the sense that she was not doing so well as might be expected, was now re-assured by the reverent tone in which the too explosive Thompson asked whether the spirits of his sisters were in the room. His only sister being in vigorous health, he did not expect her ghost ; but it was there, and very prompt to answer him. How long had she been dead ? Two years.

"So the dreary labour was continued ; but we cannot fatigue our readers with the whole monotony of a sitting that was not enlivened by one happy guess."

"Brown" cursorily remarks, among other contemptuous comments on this scene, that Mr. Stone, the party who had undertaken the management of the *séances*, enquired if they were satisfied, *and offered if otherwise to give another séance free*, to which the said Brown only adds in his gracious way, "But we had seen enough," and so there was nothing more to do than to show up the whole thing as "a humbug, through the medium of the press."

The late Judge Edmonds, of New York, assured the author, that he did not dare to make up his mind definitively upon so unprecedented, and important a subject, until he had attended at least one hundred circles, and seen some fifty Mediums for various forms of Spiritual power. "It was through such methods of investigation as these," said this learned jurist, "that I at length became convinced of the fact that the soul of man is immortal, can and does communicate, and that we are even now standing in the dawn of a great and wonderful day of Spiritual science. This knowledge so invaluable, and opening up possibilities so unlimited, is surely worth more than the cost of one hundred hours out of any man's life, however *exigéant* the demands upon his time may be."

"But Judge Edmonds was a crazy Spiritualist," answers Brown. "Thompson and I spent one hour with a *mejium*, and found it all false ; what are *his* hundred hours' experiences compared to our one ? "

Shortly after this, a favourable report appeared in the *Leader*, in which a party of ladies and gentlemen who had engaged Mrs. Hayden to attend in their own house, bore testimony to her entire honesty, the excellence of the tests they had received, and the utter impossibility of her agency in producing either the sounds, movements, or intelligence ; whereupon certain gentlemen of the press, who seemed to have made it their special duty "to explode the thing," proceeded to the accomplishment of their creditable work in the way recorded as follows. "Mr. Lewes," the *Leader's* editor, or representative, was the party from whom the annexed report proceeded. He says, in the work on "Spirit Rapping," above alluded to :—

"Before I had witnessed these 'astounding phenomena,' I had formed an hypothesis of the whole process, which turned out to be accurate. It did *not* seem in the least surprising to me that the questioner should be correctly answered, even when asking questions mentally, of which no living soul but his own knew the answer. I invariably said : 'The cause of your delusion is that you direct your attention to the *thing said*, and not to the *way in which it is said*. Whatever the trick may be, it will be just as easy to answer a question of one kind as of another—the nature of the question has nothing to do with it. If you ask where your grandfather died, his death being a mystery to the whole world, the answer is as easy as if you ask where Napoleon died ; because as it is *you* who really give the answer, not the medium, what you have in your mind is what will turn out to be the answer. You assure me solemnly that you do not tell the medium anything ; I declare unequivocally that you *do*. It is the same in cases of clairvoyance : you tell all, and fancy you are told. You do not tell it in so many words, but unconsciously you are made to communicate the very thing you believe is communicated to you.' . . .

"I had formed an hypothesis, and according to that hypothesis I framed certain traps into which the medium would infallibly fall if my supposition were correct ; the hypothesis and the traps I explained to certain friends *before* the experiment was made, and the result not only fully confirmed expectation, but showed what was certainly not anticipated—viz., that the trick was a miserably poor one.

"Our party comprised Mr. and Mrs. Masters, Sir William, Mr. Purcell, and myself (for obvious reasons, the names given are fictitious, except my own). It was after dinner, and we were smoking our cigars, when the footman announced that Mrs. Hayden was in the drawing-room. We soon joined her there, and found her talking to Mrs. Masters about the 'spirits, in the most easy, familiar way—indeed, she always spoke of them without awe, but with implicit confidence—as if they had been pet monkeys. The conversation soon became general, as we formed a circle round the table. It of course turned upon the 'Manifestations,' and Mrs. Hayden was copious in anecdotes (adroitly mingled with aristocratic and well-known names) of the surprising success which had attended her. At last, the rappings having announced that the ghosts were impatient to do something for the money paid, we took our cards, on which the letters of the alphabet, and the numerals from one to ten, were printed, and the *séance* began.

"Sir William was the first. He thought of one dead. On asking whether the person he was then thinking of was present, an alacrity in rapping assured him of the fact. He took his card ; the raps were distinct ; but the letters were all wrong. He tried another spirit—again the letters indicated were wrong. He tried a third, but a third time nothing came right. I was beginning to get anxious lest repeated failures should alarm the medium, and make her give some evasive excuse ; so I suggested that Mr. Masters should try. He tried—but with the same desperate ill success. It was now my turn. Let me pause here to remark that both Sir William and Mr. Masters were determined to give no clue whatever—they remained purely passive, awaiting a result ; they passed their pencils along the alphabet with such terrible uniformity that the medium was reduced to vague guessing, and of course in each guess it was thirty-five to one against her. This was what I had anticipated ; but it was only negative evidence, and I was to elicit something positive.

"I thought of a relative of mine, and said aloud, 'I should like to know if she is present.' Rapping answered 'Yes.' Observe, the person I thought of was a real person— I was planning no trap this time, because the experiment was to be every way conclusive. I passed my pencil equally along the alphabet without once lingering, until after I had passed the letter J, with which her name began. Finding that I was not to have the *real* name, I thought I would try if I could not make the raps answer where I pleased. I chose N Raps came ; N was written down. What name, thought I, shall it be ? Naomi or Nancy ? Before I had finally settled, my pencil had passed A, and as I saw E, I determined E should be the letter, and E was indicated. N E, of course, would do for Nelly, and Nelly was spelled ! Then came the surname, which ought to have begun with H ; but as my pencil did not linger at H, on we passed until we came to S, which was indicated without any intention on my part. I had then to invent some name beginning with S, which was not done at once, from the very *embarras de richesses ;* however, I thought O would do, and O was indicated ; then R ; and after that I resolved the name should be Sorel. It is unnecessary to follow further thus in detail my first trial ; enough if I add, that Nelly Sorel informed me she died in 1855, leaving six children, two of whom were boys, the eldest fourteen—every answer being ludicrously wrong, but declared by me to be 'astonishing,' which declaration was accepted in perfect faith by the medium, who thought she had got one good, credulous listener, at all events. That was my object—to make her fall into my trap it was necessary she should believe I was her dupe.

"As far as my hypothesis went, it was confirmed by this conversation. I knew that it was the questioner who supplied the answer, and I made the answer turn out whatever I pleased—not, be it remembered, having that answer originally in my mind, so as to admit of any pretended 'thought reading'—but framing the answer according to the caprice of the moment, and invariably receiving the answer I had resolved on. Now you have only to replace *acted* credulity by *real* credulity, and the trick is explained. What I did consciously, the credulous do unconsciously. I spelled the words, so do they. The medium knows nothing ; she guesses according to the indications you give, and only guesses right when you give right indications ; therefore, if you ask what you and you alone can answer, she will answer it only on the supposition that you indicate by your manner what the answer is. But if any doubt lingers in your mind, let this my second trial suffice.

"To show how completely the answers are made at random, when no clue is given, but only a 'yes' or 'no' is required, here are four questions I wrote on a piece of paper, and the answers I received :—

"'Had the ghost of Hamlet's father seventeen noses ?' Yes.

"'Had Semiramis ?' Yes.

"'Was Pontius Pilate an American ?' No.

"'Was he a leading tragedian ?' Yes.

"I thought Mr. Purcell would have had a stroke of apoplexy, when I showed him these questions ; how he restrained the convulsion of laughter is a mystery !

"Let me not forget, that when Mr. Purcell called up a spirit, the answers were tolerably correct, not quite, but still near enough to be curious to one unsuspicious ; he confessed afterwards, however, that he had semi-consciously *assisted* the medium ; but, in his second conversation, he called up the spirit of an old family servant, who, at an advanced age, married an elderly woman, and who subsequently drowned himself. These were the questions and answers as written down :—

" ' Does James miss his children ?'   Yes.   (Never had any.)

" ' How many had he ?'   Yes.

" ' How many boys ?'   Yes.

" ' What did he die of ?'   *Wafer.*

"To explain this 'wafer,' it may be observed, that Mr. Purcell meant the death to be called water on the chest, which was his fallacious hint by way of an explanation of drowning ; and, when he said aloud that the word was incorrectly spelled *wafer,* whereas it ought to have been 'water on the chest,' Mrs. Hayden pointed triumphantly to the accuracy, 'Only one letter wrong, you see ; *wafer* instead of *water !*' and she referred to this several times in the course of the evening.

"I have not half exhausted my stock of questions and answers written down at the time ; but the foregoing will surely suffice ; and, should they be deemed inconclusive, perhaps *this* one will close the question. As I had been so very successful in getting correct answers, and was evidently regarded by the spirits with singular partiality, they never declining to answer any question I put, it occurred to me to write this question on my paper, which I showed to Mr. Purcell :—

" ' *Is Mrs. Hayden an impostor ?*'

"An unequivocating *Yes,* was the answer ; and, to make assurance doubly sure, Mr. Purcell affected not to hear that answer ; so we repeated the question, and again were assured that she *was* an impostor. This was the most satisfactory answer of the evening, and I felt very sorry that the medium was a woman—not a man, to whom I could have said, 'I asked the spirits if you were an impostor, and you hear them declare you to be one.' For I must plainly say, that a more ignoble imposture than this spirit manifestation never came before me—and that was the opinion of the whole party. It is easy for the reader to convince himself of this by a similar process."

"In the following number of the *Leader* the editor observed : 'Iconoclasts are generally welcomed with abuse from devotees. Entering the temples of superstition and charlatanism, they smite the hideous idols from their pedestals, amidst the howlings of indignant worshippers. It was to be expected, therefore, that in exposing the imposture of spirit manifestations which America has shipped for our gullible market, we should have to bear hard words and worse insinuations from indignant dupes ; and what we expected we have received.'

" ' Dr. Ashburner, for example, has felt himself personally insulted, and has written an insulting letter, complaining of the "flippant" treatment this "very sacred subject" received at our hands, but as he opposes our experimental *proof* by nothing stronger than his own emphatic assertion, he cannot expect those who reason, to attach much weight to mere declarations.' "

The portion of Dr. Ashburner's letter above alluded to, quoted by the veracious editor of the *Leader*, reads as follows :—

"Sex ought to have protected her from injury if you *gentlemen* of the press have no regard to the hospitable feelings due to one of your own cloth, for Mrs. Hayden is the wife of a former editor and proprietor of a journal in Boston, having a most extensive circulation in New England. I declare to you that Mrs. Hayden is no impostor, and he who has the daring to come to an opposite conclusion must do so at the peril of his character for truth. I defy Mr. Lewes or any one else to prove the acts of imposition or fraud in the phenomena that require the presence of such a medium as Mrs. Hayden for their development. I have calmly, deliberately, and very cautiously studied this subject. It may please superficial thinkers to treat it as they long treated Mesmerism and clair-voyance. The fire from the *Zoist,* the researches of Baron Von Reichenbach, Mr. Rutter's important discovery of the magnetescope, have settled, for posterity, the questions scouted by the twaddling physiologists of this generation. A battle is to be fought for the new manifestations. I have no hesitation in saying that, much as I have seen of Mesmerism and of clairvoyance—grand as were my anticipations of the vast amount of good to accrue to the human race, in medical and physical improvement, from the expansion given to them by the cultivation of their extensive relations—all sink into shade and comparative insignificance, in the contemplation of those consequences which must result from the spirit manifestations. This is a very serious truth, and must and will force its way. Animal magnetism and its consequences appeared marvellous to petty minds. The spirit manifestations have, in the last three weeks, produced *miracles,* and many more will, ere long, astound the would-be considered philosophers, who may continue to deny and sneer at the most obvious facts.   I am, Sir, your obedient servant,

"York Place, March 14th, 1853."   "JOHN ASHBURNER

No reformers who have attempted to present a new idea to the world, and been compelled to run the gauntlet of ignorance and prejudice, will fail to acknowledge that antagonism is as necessary to ultimate success, as ready acceptance.

So did it prove in the case of Spiritualism and "the American Medium." The attacks upon her so deliberately planned, carried out with utter disregard to all psychological influence, and subsequently so rudely and inhospitably trumpeted abroad as the blow which was for ever to crush out of existence the supernaturalism of thousands of years, had the effect which *wise invisible wire pullers might possibly have foreseen.* It called into print a perfect flood of testimony of a totally opposite character, and so far from crushing out the "delusion" by one fell swoop of the editorial pen, it became a hydra-headed messenger of an established Spirit telegraphy, to thousands of persons, who would otherwise have never known of its existence.

From multitudes of letters which poured in from every quarter in favour of the truth of the manifestations, letters which the press were at that time compelled to place side by side with the opposing testimony, we select the following as specimens of what calm deliberative minds were—even in that early day—impelled to think of the newly-developed telegraphy. Both the following letters were printed in the *Leader*, in connection with reiterated charges on the part of the editor, against "the fraudulent practices of the American Medium."

"Sir,—Having observed in your journal of the 5th instant a statement respecting the alleged spirit manifestations, from a correspondent who appears to have but partially investigated the matter, I take the liberty of transmitting to you a few additional particulars.

"I, upon the first occasion, called the spirit of an old servant—the experiment was unsatisfactory; I then attempted to help him, but got on with difficulty; had I had the inclination, I feel confident answers could have been obtained equally absurd as those your correspondent prides himself with having so ingeniously succeeded in obtaining.

"I, however, did not throw discredit on, or treat with scorn, the experience of others; I, therefore, determined to try again the next evening, believing that the failure rested either in myself or some other unknown cause. I called the spirits of two of my own nearest relations, who might naturally be supposed to be more intimately connected with myself; they both presented themselves, giving proofs of their identity which could never have occurred to me to seek. I tested them in various ways. I was also anxious to ascertain whether by willing strongly, and dwelling upon wrong letters, I could obtain false answers, but failed to influence them in any way whatever, whether the alphabet was placed upon, or concealed under, the table, and at each of the several successive interviews the *rapport* appears to be more thoroughly established; whether I ask questions audibly or mentally, concise and clear answers are given, excepting in some few instances when no reply can be obtained.

"So far as the moving of the table is concerned, I obtained my request, during the second interview, in so satisfactory a manner, that I consider time may be more profitably employed than in seeking a repetition of it; it moved out of reach of Mrs. Hayden, and soon after suddenly regained its former position; it also moved upon its axis in a peculiarly smooth, gliding manner; not the top only, but the whole table, as I particularly observed, commencing with an almost invisible motion until it gained a rapid pace, and stopped suddenly. I immediately endeavoured myself to produce a similar motion, but was unable.

"I will conclude by stating, that I have reason to consider Mrs. Hayden to be a lady possessed of courage, but, having a delicate and sensitive mind, any insults directed against her, whether personally or through the medium of the press, may be likely to have a tendency to disarrange and interrupt that subtle and mysterious agency so intimately connected with our higher nature. May I venture to recommend those who determine to investigate for themselves, to refrain from publishing the crude ideas of one hour's experience, especially should they arrive at conclusions opposite to those of the thousands who have been making the subject their earnest and constant study during the past five years? I am, sir, your obedient servant,

"March 21, 1853." "C. F. I.*

---

* Sir Charles Isham.

Another letter makes us acquainted with a novel mode of Spirit writing by medium intervention :—

"Sir,—Permit me, if you conveniently can, the opportunity of affording Mr. Lewes a peg on which to hang a few shreds of additional comments, in defence of his 'hypothesis' relative to the spirit-rapping 'imposture.' Mr. Lewes does not hesitate to impute, by anticipation, imposture to others, nor to '*act*' an imposture himself ; why should ' the spirits' be denied their revenge upon him ? Are there no wags out of the body as well as in it ? Are we to dictate to the wag above how he is to treat the wag below ?

"But, further, Mr. Lewes's hypothesis does not cover the whole facts of the phenomena. It does in no way explain the unexceptionably attested cases, recorded in the American literature on the subject, and in the records of private investigation, into which the vulgar notion of imposture, besides being excluded by the very nature of the occurrences described, is, on other grounds, wholly inadmissible. How, for instance, does it apply to the following case ?—A pair of scissors is held, by the points, by a 'medium,' over a sheet of writing-paper. One of the persons present drops a pencil into the thumb-hole of the scissors. Presently, the pencil stands apart from the steel, begins to move, and the hand of the medium is carried across the paper, and the signature of a person known to be dead appears ! The father, or other near relative of the person is present, and, from some peculiarity in it, disputes the genuineness of the signature. The recent letters of the person are appealed to, and there the very same peculiarity is found, and the exact correspondence of the two signatures demonstrated.

"This case is reported in Horace Greeley's paper, the *Tribune,* and he vouches for the honour and capacity of his correspondent, who gives the original letter of the father or relative of the alleged spirit writer. I mention it from memory, but am certain the main facts of the record are as stated.   "A.*

"Liverpool, March 21, 1852."

The next sword that was aimed against the new faith was drawn from an unexpected quarter, namely, by the hand of Dr. Elliotson, one of the most prominent writers in the *Zoist,* and a gentleman whose extensive experiences in mesmeric and psychologic phenomena suggested the expectation, that he would be prompt to welcome a phase of power so nearly related to many of the mental revealments that must have come under his own observation.

We do not pause upon the stern and relentless acts of warfare which this gentleman directed against the American Medium, nor is it necessary to say that his adherence to the ranks of the opponents was all the more eagerly welcomed by them, because they had anticipated from Dr. Elliotson's antecedents, a totally different result. It is a far pleasanter task to the author to record, instead of the harsh diatribes published in the *Zoist* by this ever faithful soldier of what he believed to be the truth, a delightful interview which she enjoyed with this venerable gentleman when, nearly sixteen years after the period now under consideration, Dr. Ashburner invited the author to call with him upon an aged and infirm gentleman unable himself to go through the ceremony of the first call, but who, as a *warm and devoted Spiritualist of many years standing, was all anxiety to welcome and converse with Mrs. Emma Hardinge, or any of the well-known American Mediums of the holy faith.*

This "aged and infirm gentleman" was Dr. Elliotson, once the bitter foe, now the warm adherent of Spiritualism, a faith which the venerable gentleman cherished as the brightest revelation that had ever been vouchsafed to him, and one which finally smoothed the *dark passage* to the life beyond and made his transition, a scene of triumphant faith and joyful anticipation.

---

* Mr. Andrew Leighton.

CHAPTER XVIII.

SPIRITUALISM IN GREAT BRITAIN (CONTINUED).

BESIDES the *Leader, Zoist,* and *Household Words*, the columns of several of the London journals began to be filled with *pro* and *con* articles on the subject of Spiritualism, soon after Mrs. Hayden's visit had opened up that topic as a theme of public discussion. Amongst other leading papers in which each side of the vexed question was allowed a fair representation, was the *Critic*, a journal to which Mr. Spicer, the well-known author of " Sights and Sounds," contributed a series of articles on the subject of Spiritualism, from which we give the following excerpts : —

"As Sir Charles Isham has already given his public testimony to the facts witnessed by himself, I need not hesitate to say that I received from him, and other members of his family (including the rector of a parish in Nottinghamshire), the most explicit and positive assurance that they all, together with several others, heard these mysterious sounds at Lamport Hall,* in a perfectly private family circle (neither Mrs. Hayden nor any other *professional* medium being present). They all assured me that there could be no mistake or delusion about it. The rector alluded to also mentioned several satisfactory tests to which he had subjected Mrs. Hayden's spirits---receiving correct answers, through another gentleman present (who held the alphabet), to questions which nobody present could have known by any ordinary mode. I have also received letters from a gentleman of the very highest reputation and authority in the scientific world, and with whose writings and character my Cambridge studies have long ago made me familiar, as those of the most cautious reasoner whom I know.† He is professor of mathematics in a well-known college ; is recognised as one of the first mathematicians in England ; and is pre-eminent for the profound and cautious scrutiny of principles and reasonings which characterises his writings. . . . Well, thus he writes to me :—

" ' Those who can set it down as easily explicable by imposture, are among the easiest believers I know—if they know anything of such facts as I know from a plurality of witnesses to each.'

" The founder of Socialism—the celebrated Robert Owen—has been converted by these rappings, to a belief in a spiritual world, and a future state. He has published a manifesto to that effect. I met him one day last week at Mrs. Hayden's, and heard from his own lips the statement of several of the facts which had produced this conviction in him. This, of itself, is a curious fact, which I presume even the sapient writer of the *Zoist* will not deny. 2nd. The excitement on the subject in the United States, having already existed nearly *five years*, is so far from subsiding or dying away, that it is increasing and spreading wider and faster every day. Only a month or two ago, a Dr. Tyng, one of the episcopal clergy in New York, preached a sermon, at the usual time and place, warning his congregation to have nothing to do with these spirits. The preacher did not for a moment pretend to deny or doubt the facts ; but, like the Rev. Hugh M'Neile in this country with regard to Mesmerism, he considered them of Satanic origin.

" The thing has scarcely begun in England as yet ; but already, within the few months since Mr. and Mrs. Hayden arrived in London, it has spread like wild-fire, and I have good reason for saying that the excitement is only commencing. Persons who at first treated the whole affair as a contemptible imposture, on witnessing these strange things for themselves, become first startled and astonished, then rush blindly into all sorts of mad conclusions—as for instance, that it is all the work of the devil, or (in the opposite degree) that it is a new revelation from Heaven. . . . That it is not imposture I feel perfectly

---

* Lamport Hall, Northampton. Seat of Sir Chas. Isham.
† Professor De Morgan.

and fully convinced. In addition to the tests, etc., above named, I had a long conversation in private with both Mr. and Mrs. Hayden, separately, and everything they said bore the marks of sincerity and good faith. Of course this is no evidence to other people, but it is to me. If there is any deception, they are as much deceived as any of their dupes.

"A word or two as to its being a money-exhibition. In the first place, there are, to my certain knowledge, several persons who are mediums in private life, who, so far from making it public and getting money by it, are only too anxious to keep it quiet; but, of course, such things cannot be altogether hushed up. Of these, one at least is a lady of rank (whose name I could give, if necessary), and others are in a position which renders all such charges as imposture and money-exhibitions perfectly out of the question.

"In the present state of public opinion, however, nobody cares to avow their belief in these sort of things, unless they have a particular wish to be set down by their friends as lunatics, or are desirous of profiting by it in a pecuniary way. But even these are not *fairly* dealt with, I think. Mr. Hayden held a respectable position in America as editor of a newspaper of good repute and circulation; and if he and Mrs. H. believed (as they state) that it was advisable to come over and make these things known here, why should they not be paid for their time and trouble? But this, of course, has nothing to do with the main point—'Are these rappings what they profess to be—the work of spirits?'"

The "manifesto" of Robert Owen, referred to in the foregoing communication, says :—

"I have patiently, with first impressions against the truthfulness of these manifestations, investigated their history, and the proceedings connected with them in the United States—have read the most authentic works for and against them; and although I long continued to doubt, and thought the whole a delusion, *I have been compelled to come to a very different conclusion.*" "While conversing with Mrs. Hayden, and while we were both standing before the fire, suddenly raps were heard on a table at some distance from us, no one being near it. I was surprised; and as the raps continued and appeared to indicate a strong desire to attract attention, I asked what was the meaning of the sounds. Mrs. Hayden said they were spirits anxious to communicate with some one, and she would inquire who they were. They replied to her by the alphabet that they were friends of mine, who were desirous to communicate with me. Mrs. Hayden then gave me the alphabet and pencil, and I found, according to *their own statements*, that the spirits were those of my mother and father. I tested their truth by various questions, and their answers, all correct, surprised me exceedingly." "In *mixed societies* with *conflicting minds*, I have seen very *confused answers* given; but I believe, in all these cases, the errors have arisen from the state of mind of the inquirer."

It would be impossible in this merely compendious notice of Spiritual progress in Great Britain, to pursue the course of Mr. Owen's investigations in farther detail; suffice it to say, they were followed out in the most thorough, calm, and deliberate spirit of enquiry.

Mr. Owen lived to realize many corroborative proofs of Spirit intercourse from other sources than Mrs. Hayden's Mediumship, and in his last days was often heard to declare, the sum of his whole life-long endeavour to bless and improve the condition of his fellow men, paled before that mighty illumination which brought, to him, but especially to earth's toiling martyrs, the assurance of immortality, and the certainty of reunion with all we have loved and lost on earth, "in another and a better world."

Very shortly after the advent of Mrs. Hayden in England, the public were privileged to witness another phase of Spirit power in the person of Miss Emma Frances Jay, a young lady who had quite recently become developed as a trance medium in America, in fact the first phenomenon of this kind that had as yet appeared upon the public rostrum.

Miss Jay's Mediumship consisted of speaking with extraordinary eloquence on metaphysical subjects. She also concluded her addresses by singing; both words and music being improvisations of remarkable beauty and sweetness.

These exhibitions, although singularly interesting, did not furnish the indisputable proof of a Spiritual origin for which the sceptics of the time were seeking; nevertheless, the wonderful improvisations poured forth by this gifted young sybil, might have convinced any experienced psychologist, that she was controlled by some power far transcending her normal capacity.

After a few months spent amongst the aristocratic circles of England, wherein Miss Jay's interesting phase of Mediumship rendered her the centre of universal admiration, she returned to America, and as Mrs. Bullene soon became one of the most popular *speakers* of the American rostrum.

But the great era in English Spiritualism, from which may be dated unnumbered conversions, was inaugurated by the visit of Mr. D. D. Home, who though of European birth, was brought up by relatives in America, from which circumstance he was at first generally spoken of as an "American Medium." As Mr. Home's wonderful gifts have exercised an unbounded influence upon European society, and his whole career forms an epoch in human history—the effect of which can never be blotted out, we must claim the privilege of dwelling somewhat minutely upon his first introduction to England, and although his own published biography, together with a whole encyclopædia of press notices, are already before the world, the history of the Spiritual movement in Europe would be inexplicable, were we to omit due notice of so important a link in the chain of cause and effect as Mr. Home, and his marvellous Mediumistic career. It has been alleged that Mr. Home came to England in the spring of 1855 for the benefit of his health, which, his friends deemed as a last, but almost hopeless chance, might be restored by an European trip. He was at this time about twenty-two years of age; had been studying for the medical profession, and though already celebrated in New England for his wonderful medial powers, he would have devoted himself entirely to the practice of medicine, had not the development of consumptive tendencies, compelled him to comply with the wishes of his friends, and seek health in entire relaxation from his professional studies.

Mr. Home never practised his Mediumship professionally. He seldom, if ever, sat in dark circles; never refused to submit to any tests demanded of him; was very careful not to sit in any such positions as to warrant the idea that he exercised any personal effort in producing the manifestations, often drawing away from contact with the table, whilst a large amount of the most remarkable phenomena produced in his presence occurred without the agency of tables at all. He never refused to submit to personal examinations, to prove that he carried no concealed apparatus before the commencement of his *séances,* and in every word and act, manifested a spirit of candour and sincerity, which none but the most prejudiced and illiberal bigots could have misconstrued.

We have already given some account of Mr. Home's wonderful Mediumistic endowments in our French section, and the reader will find further illustrations of this gentleman's marvellous gifts in the reports of *séances* in succeeding pages; it need only be added that Mr. Home's witnesses range from monarchs, princes, statesmen, scientists, and potentates, down to the professional and private grades of life, and throughout them all, it is impossible to find any proven account of fraud, or deception.

It was this marvellous phenomenal being that came in the year 1855 to visit London, and became a guest of Mr. and Mrs. Cox, the noble-hearted proprietors of a fashionable hotel in Jermyn Street, St. James'. Amongst the many distinguished personages that Mr. Home met at Mr. Cox's was the late Lord Brougham, who having became greatly interested in the marvellous phenomena exhibited through the young American, asked permission to bring his friend Sir David Brewster to witness the new and mysterious power.

As the correspondence which grew out of this, and a second visit which Sir David paid Mr. Home, when the latter became a guest of Mr. Rymer at Ealing, exercised a manifest influence upon the progress of Spiritualism in England in divers ways, at the risk of inflicting upon our readers, passages which have already attained to a wide-spread notoriety, we must here give a few extracts that will present a summary of the case in question.

It would seem that the correspondence arose from the circumstance of the *séance* being reported in an American paper, from whence it was copied into the London *Morning Advertiser*, and this called forth from Sir David Brewster the following remarks, from which we only excise some unimportant preliminary words addressed to the editor.

" To the Editor of the Morning Advertiser.

"Sir,—It is quite true as stated by Mr. Home, that I wrote an article in the *North British Review* in which I have denounced 'table-moving and spirit-rapping' in the strongest terms, and it is also true that I saw at Cox's Hotel, in company with Lord Brougham, and at Ealing, in company with Mrs. Trollope, several mechanical effects which I was unable to explain. But though I could not account for all these effects, I never thought of ascribing them to spirits stalking beneath the drapery of the table, and I saw enough to satisfy myself that they could all be produced by human hands and feet, and to prove to others that some of them at least, had such an origin."

The letter concludes with a strong adjuration to Mr. Home to announce himself as the *Wizard of the West* instead of "insulting religion, common-sense, &c., by ascribing his power to the *sacred dead.*"

To this epistle immediately succeeded the following answers from Mr. Cox and Mr. Benjamin Coleman. Mr. Cox, who had been present during Sir David's first investigation, after alluding to his surprise at the letter in the *Advertiser*, and quoting several of its allegations, says :—

"Without unnecessarily alluding to what I understand you saw at the house of an equally-disinterested investigator—for be it remembered all who have received Mr. Home in this country *are above suspicion*, and desire to arrive only at the truth—I beg to recall to your memory what took place at my house when Lord Brougham and you did me the favour to accept my invitation, and I will appeal to your candour to say whether there was a *possibility* of the various acts being effected by the hands or feet of anyone present.

"I have a distinct recollection of the astonishment which both Lord Brougham and yourself expressed, and your emphatic exclamation to me—'*Sir, this upsets the philosophy of fifty years.*'

"If the subject be beyond your powers of reasonable explanation, leave it to others ; for it is not just or generous to raise the cry of *imposture*, in a matter you cannot explain, taking advantage of your character to place humbler men in a false position, by allowing the world to think they were by ignorance or design parties to so gross and impudent a fraud.

"I am, Sir David,
"Your obedient servant,

"Cox's Hotel, Jermyn Street, October 4, 1855."   WILLIAM COX."

Mr. Benjamin Coleman—a gentleman of wealth and high social standing—one who subsequently figured largely in the Spiritual movement and against whose honesty, integrity, and acumen as a keen observer, even Sir David Brewster could bring no allegation, next takes up the cudgels by addressing a letter to the *Morning Advertiser*, to the following effect :—

"Sir,— Sir David Brewster has addressed a letter to you, attributing the phenomena which he witnessed in the presence of Mr. Home, to mechanical agency.

"Sir David, although he had at least two interviews, and was invited to further investigation, failed to discover the mechanism by which these marvels were produced.

"I am one of a hundred, who have recently witnessed these manifestations at the house of a friend, and I am sure that they were neither effected by trick, nor were we under a delusion. . . . I was as much astonished at what I saw in Mr. Home's presence as any man, and when I found that Sir David Brewster had been a witness of similar phenomena, I called upon Sir David, and in the course of conversation he said, that what he and Lord Brougham saw, was marvellous, quite unaccountable.

"I then asked him ; 'Do you think these things were produced by trick ?'

" 'No, certainly not,' was his reply.

" 'Is it delusion, think you ?'

" 'No, that is out of the question.'

" 'Then what is it ?'

"To which he replied, 'I don't know, but Spirit is the last *thing I will give in to.*'

"Sir David then told me what he and Lord Brougham had witnessed : 'The table— a large dinner table—moved about in the most extraordinary manner, and amongst other things, an accordion was conveyed by an invisible agency to his hand, and then to Lord Brougham's, in which, held by his Lordship's right hand, apart from any person, it *played an air throughout.*' Mr. Coleman adds : 'Is it reasonable—astounding as the fact may be—to attribute such a performance to mechanical agency beyond detection, or that it should have been effected by Mr. Home's foot ?' "

After the perusal of this letter, Sir David published an answer, either denying *in toto* Mr. Coleman's statements, or shuffling out of them in the following way. After alluding to the conversation which Mr. Coleman had with him at the Athenæum Club, he says :—

"I may once for all admit, that both Lord Brougham and myself acknowledged that we were puzzled with *Mr. Home's performances, and could not account for them.*

"Neither of us profess to be expounders of conundrums, whether verbal or mechanical, but if we had been permitted to take a peep beneath the drapery of Mr. Cox's table, we should have been spared the mortification of this confession."

As specimens of the form of denials which Sir David gave to the allegations of Mr. Coleman, the following items may serve :—

"When *all our hands were upon the table,* noises were heard ; rappings in abundance, and when we rose up, the table actually rose, *as appeared to me,* from the ground. This result I do not pretend to explain, but rather than believe that spirits made the noises, I will conjecture that the raps were produced by Mr. Home's toes—or as Dr. Schiff has shown, '*by the repeated displacement of the tendon of the peroneus longus muscle, in the sheath in which it slides behind the external malleolus,* and rather than believe that spirits raised the table, I will conjecture, that it was done by the agency of Mr. Home's feet which were always below it."

It seems sad, nothing short of humiliating indeed, to find a man like Sir David Brewster—one who, as a scientist himself, should have been the first to give a hospitable welcome to a set of phenomena which involved so many hitherto unknown phases of science, as sounds and motions by invisible agency—driven to such rude uncourteous denials, or evasions unworthy of his character either as a gentleman or a man of learning, in order to dispose of facts which transcended the sum of *his* belief, and *his* knowledge.

The whole correspondence however—which we may add was pursued on both sides of the question, in the same spirit as the above,—was shortly after summed up, at least as far as the impartial portion of the public were concerned — by a letter from Mr. T. A. Trollope, a gentleman whose position in the literary and social world is quite as pronounced as that of Sir David Brewster himself. It was addressed to Mr. J. S. Rymer of *Ealing*, and was afterwards published in the papers in connection with the entire correspondence. It is as follows :—

"Florence, October 23, 1855.

"My dear Sir,—I have read with much regret the letters from Sir David Brewster printed in the *Morning Advertiser*, to which you have called my attention ; and although it is extremely painful for me to come out from my tranquil obscurity into the noise and wholly inconclusive bickerings of paper warfare, it is impossible for me when called on, to refuse my testimony to facts of which I was a witness.

"Sir David writes—that when he was present together with Lord Brougham and Mr. Cox at Cox's Hotel—it was *not* true that a large dining-table was moved about in a most extraordinary manner. Further on he states that—'the table was covered with copious drapery *beneath which nobody was allowed to look.*' These italics are Sir David's.*

"I declare that at *your* house at Ealing, on an evening subsequent to Sir David's meeting with Mr. Home at Cox's Hotel, in the presence of Sir David, myself, and of other persons, a large and very heavy dining-table *was* moved about in a most extraordinary manner ; *that Sir David was urged both by Mr. Home and by yourself* to look under the cloth and under the table, *that he did look under it, and that whilst he was so looking, the table was much moved, and while he was looking, and while the table was moving, he avowed that he saw the movement.*

"Sir David Brewster further writes, that on this same evening the spirits were very active, prolific of raps of various intonations, making tables heavy or light at command, tickling knees, male and female, but always on the side next the Medium. I was repeatedly touched on either knee, and on the lower leg, but I experienced no sensation at all akin to 'tickling,' neither did any of those present, who were similarly touched say that they were—or give any token of being 'tickled.' Moreover I affirm that Sir David Brewster, who sat next to me, declared to me at the time of being touched that he was touched on *both knees.* . . . Nor did he then speak of being '*tickled.*'

"Indeed the phraseology of this part of his letter is matter of the greatest astonishment to me. For it should seem wholly impossible that a man of Sir David Brewster's character, standing, and social position, in the grave and public examination of a question on which a young man's honour and character depend, if no yet higher interests are concerned, should intentionally seek to prejudice the issue in the minds of his readers, by a vulgar jest, puerile to those earnest enquirers who disbelieve the Spiritual origin of these phenomena, inexpressibly revolting to those who believe therein, and which, falling from less respected lips, would by all be termed mere ribaldry.

"I must add one more remark on other passages of Sir David's letter. 'The party present at Mr. Cox's,' he writes, 'sat down to a small table, Mr. Home having previously requested us to examine if there was any machinery about his person, an examination however which we declined to make.' A few lines further on he says, with reference to the phenomena which then occurred, '*I conjecture that they might be produced by machinery attached to the lower extremities of Mr. Home.*' Now I submit, that these two statements should not stand together. It appears to me both morally unjust, and philosophically unsound, in the examination of evidence, first to decline the proferred means of ascertaining the absence of machinery, and then to assume its presence.

"I should not, my dear sir, do all that duty I think requires of me in this case, were I to conclude without stating very solemnly, that after many opportunities of witnessing and investigating the phenomena caused by, or happening to, Mr. Home, I am wholly convinced that be what may their origin, and cause, and nature, they are not produced by any fraud, machinery, juggling, illusion, or trickery on his part.

"I am, my dear Sir,

"Always most faithfully yours,

"T. Adolphus Trollope.

"To John Smith Rhymer, Esq., Ealing."

Here this episode in connection with Sir David Brewster must rest. It is of importance that it should be recorded in this place for several reasons. First—Although the correspondence might with more justice to the young gentleman so harshly attacked and condemned without trial or evidence,

---

* This statement is emphatically denied by Mr. Cox in letters preceding Mr. Trollope's.

have been maintained in private, its publication served to obtain for Spiritualism, hundreds of investigators, few if any of whom could be found to duplicate Sir David Brewster's views of common sense, morality, or justice.   Next—The position occupied by the disputants, commanded a notoriety for the case which it could scarcely have else obtained, and finally, the palpable animus which could have induced a man in Sir David Brewster's position, to descend to misrepresentation, evoked, as it deserved, a sentiment of indignation, which operated most favourably, both for Mr. Home, and the cause he represented.   The young Anglo-American became all the fashion. *Fêted* by potentates and nobles, courted, honoured, and sought for in every direction, it is not too much to allege, as the author can confidently do from many years' knowledge of this famous medium, that he preserved under all circumstances, his integrity and singleness of purpose. He sought no favours, accepted no fees (though he became the recipient of princely gifts and tokens of royal munificence). He was never vain-glorious, conceited, nor presumptuous. At times he was what he himself called "out of power," and though these seasons of incapacity to produce phenomena, sometimes lasted for weeks, the author can positively assert on her own, as well as on the testimony of hosts of the most authentic witnesses, that he was never known to supplement these mediumistic recessions by the smallest attempt at fraud or deception. Thus, though he became the subject of universal attack from those whose interest or predilection determined their antagonistic attitude towards Spiritualism, he also became the centre of attraction to vast multitudes, who owed to him their first demonstrable proofs of the soul's immortality, and restoration to those, whom bereaved mourners had deemed for ever lost to them.

CHAPTER XIX.

SPIRITUALISM IN GREAT BRITAIN (CONTINUED).

MR. D. D. HOME'S MANIFESTATIONS.

IT may appear strange to those who consider how unprecedented in modern experience all the phenomena of Spirit communion are, that their recital excites so little attention and the repetition of spiritualistic narratives so soon palls upon the minds of the recipients ; but the truth is, there exists too little variety amongst these phenomena to render reiteration tolerable.

Then again, Spirit communications are for the most part addressed to individuals, and the innate selfishness of humanity renders personal matter wholly uninteresting except to the parties immediately concerned.

As the intention of this work is to prepare a record for the use of future generations, we feel compelled to avoid the tedium of useless repetition on the one hand, and on the other to send down to posterity a complete set of such representative cases as will display the nature of the spiritual phenomena manifested in the nineteenth century. It is with this view that we select a few of Mr. D. D. Home's remarkable manifestations, as representative cases which it would be difficult to transcend in interest. The following narrative, published in the London *Spiritualist* of March 30th, 1877, was communicated by the charming authoress, Mrs. S. C. Hall, and reads as follows :—

EASTER EVE—IN 1867.

BY MRS. S. C. HALL.

"The near approach of, perhaps, the happiest of our Festivals, sends my memory back to, I think, the most marvellous of all my experiences in Spiritualism : there may be among your readers some who will thank me for preserving and publishing a record of it.

"I did not write concerning it at the time it occurred ; yet I can recall vividly every one of the remarkable incidents : they are as fresh in my mind to-day as they were ten years ago, for they 'happened' on the Easter Eve of the year 1867 : and the Easter Eve of 1877 is now nigh at hand.

"Although my recollection of the scene and circumstances is very vivid, I remembered that my friend Mrs. Henry Senior (the widow of Colonel Senior) had made some notes concerning them. I wrote to her on the subject, and the letter she has written in reply I ask you to print in the number of your publication that you will issue on the Easter Eve of the present year.

"I need do little more than endorse, which I do, every sentence in her letter. I have had more startling experiences in Spiritualism ; but none at once so wonderful and so beautiful, so intensely convincing, so happy in comforting assurance of its holy truth, thoroughly upholding and confirming the faith that has, thank God, been my blessing through the whole of a long life.

"It was not a dark sitting, but the light was subdued, and for a few minutes entirely excluded, when an absolute blaze of light filled the conservatory. We saw shadows (but having forms) pass and repass repeatedly, brought out into distinctness by the brilliancy of the light. When Mr. Home was 'raised' (as he was twice) the gas in the chandelier was lit : although reduced, it was quite strong enough to mark his gradual progress upwards from the chair to the ceiling."

Then follows Mrs. Senior's paper, which is quoted *verbatim*, with a few unimportant excisions :—

"5, Prince of Wales's Terrace, Tuesday.

"Last Saturday (Easter Eve) we had a most wonderful *séance* at Mr. Hall's. I had long been telling him that I was convinced that allowing scoffers and unbelievers to come to our *séances* spoiled them, and that if he would but harden his kind heart for once, and allow us to have a *selfish séance*, I was sure it would be good—and last week he said to me laughingly that I *should* have my wish before I returned to Ireland, that Daniel had promised to come to them on Saturday, and that there should be no one asked but myself and Lady Dunsany—and so it was arranged. Lady Dunsany called for me on her way. We found Mr. and Mrs. Hall alone, but Daniel arrived soon after, and said when he entered the room that he had a very bad headache, which would, he feared, spoil our *séance ;* however, he sat down and chatted a little, and I then asked him to come over to the piano and "croon," as I called it, as I had observed that his doing so always gave us a good *séance.* He played and sang several things, and then Lady Dunsany asked him for a soft Russian air of his wife's. He had not been playing it more than a minute, when a chair, which was at some distance from the piano, *slid* up to it, and placed itself beside him. I was sitting close to the piano on the other side, and saw it move before he did— 'Oh!' he said—'Here is Sacha' (his wife, who had left earth), and he went on playing some time longer, though his hands became perfectly stiff, and it was evident that they were not moved by his own volition. After a time his hands were withdrawn from the piano, and he became entranced, turned round the piano stool, and knelt down, and with hands clasped, poured forth a most beautiful prayer. . . . Mr. Home then came out of his trance, quite refreshed and pleased, and asked us to sit down at the table, which at once began to vibrate and 'tremble,' whilst loud and heavy knocks were heard upon it, upon the floor and the furniture. Presently the accordion was touched, and by the alphabet was spelt out 'We will play the earth-life of one who was not of earth.' Mr. Hall said 'That's nonsense,' but I answered, 'It must be our Lord's life,' and so it proved. First we had sweet, soft, simple music, like a lullaby, for a few minutes, then it became intensely sad for some time, and then we distinctly heard through the music the *regular tramp* of a body of men marching, and we exclaimed, 'The march to Calvary.' Then the tapping sound of a hammer on a nail, the ringing sound of metal upon metal, then a pause, and afterwards came a *crash*, and a burst of wailing, which seemed to fill the room and the house ; it was followed by the *most glorious* triumphal music we any of us had ever heard ; it thrilled to all our hearts, and we were in tears when it was over—it certainly was not of earth. It evidently meant the resurrection of our Lord. We still sat at the table, but nothing more was done for some time ; then the muslin curtains were draped round Mr. Home ; and he was raised from the ground in them. . . . Then Mr. Hall's face and chest shone like silver, and they spelled out, 'He who giveth shall receive light.' The accordion was carried round the circle, played on Mr. Hall's head, then placed on my shoulder next it, and went to Mrs. Hall, on my right hand, and played on her head ; then played in the air round the circle (Mr. Home's hand not being near the instrument) 'The Last Rose of Summer,' and several other airs. Afterwards a great deal of martial music was played by a cousin of Lady Dunsany's, who had been in the Dragoons, and who had 'passed away' in India, and who always comes to her. After this the spirit of a child, whose mother had sent Mrs. Hall flowers that morning, came and gave us each a flower. Mr. Home was then lifted to the ceiling. We heard his nail against it, and he said, 'Oh, I wish I had a pencil to make a mark.' However, he then came down, and Mr. Hall handed him a pencil, in case he should be again raised ; and five minutes afterwards he was again lifted up, and made a mark on the ceiling, which will remain there as a proof of what was done. When Mr. Home returned to the table we were all touched by hands on our brows and on our hands. Sacha gave each of us her peculiar little pinch, and I was touched by both H—— and E——, and Lady Dunsany's cousin flipped all our hands with a flower. After a little time the spirits spelled out, 'We can do no more. Good night. God bless you ;' and we heard the knocks and sounds die away in the distance out of doors, and *we felt* that it was all over. We were all beyond measure grateful for being allowed to witness what we could never forget as long as our lives lasted. That burst of music was still thrilling in all our hearts—nothing composed by mortal could ever touch it. I should have said that just before Mr. Home was lifted up to the ceiling the first time, his face and his chest shone with a silvery light, as Mr. Hall's had done. But, indeed, I have not told many of the minor things that took place. It was an evening of wonders."

The next illustrative *séance* which we deem it necessary to associate with this record is supplied by the late Henry D. Jencken, Esq., barrister—a gentleman too well known in the *élite* of London professional society as well as among the Spiritualistic ranks, to need any additional proof of the authenticity of his narrative.

Mr. Jencken himself was a witness of the facts narrated, and we may here add that Professor William Crookes in his published work entitled "Phenomena of Spiritualism," alludes to the *séance* about to be detailed, affirming that he received the narrative from the lips of three of the witnesses, namely, Lord Lindsay, the Earl of Dunraven, and Captain Wynne.

Mr. Jencken, writing for the February number of *Human Nature*, says:—

"MANIFESTATIONS THROUGH MR. HOME."

"Mr. Home had passed into the trance still so often witnessed ; rising from his seat, he laid hold of an arm-chair, which he held at arm's length, and was then lifted about three feet clear off the ground ; travelling thus suspended in space, he placed the chair next Lord Adare, and made a circuit round those in the room, being lowered and raised as he passed each of us. One of those present measured the elevation, and passed his leg and arm underneath Mr. Home's feet. The elevation lasted from four to five minutes. On resuming his seat, Mr. Home addressed Captain Wynne, communicating news to him of which the departed alone could have been cognisant.

"The spirit form that had been seen reclining on the sofa, now stepped up to Mr. Home and mesmerised him ; a band was then seen luminously visible over his head, about 18 inches in a vertical line from his head. The trance state of Mr. Home now assumed a different character ; gently rising he spoke a few words to those present, and then opening the door proceeded into the corridor ; a voice then said—'He will go out of this window and come in at that window.' The only one who heard the voice was the Master of Lindsay, and a cold shudder seized upon him as he contemplated the possibility of this occurring, a feat which the great height of the third floor windows in Ashley Place rendered more than ordinarily perilous. The others present, however, having closely questioned him as to what he had heard, he at first replied, 'I dare not tell you;' when, to the amazement of all, a voice said, 'You must tell; tell directly.' The Master then said, 'Yes; yes, terrible to say, he will go out at that window and come in at this; do not be frightened, be quiet.' Mr. Home now re-entered the room, and opening the drawing-room window, was pushed out demi-horizontally into space, and carried from one window of the drawing-room to the farthermost window of the adjoining room. This feat being performed at a height of about 60 feet from the ground, naturally caused a shudder in all present. The body of Mr. Home, when it appeared at the window of the adjoining room, was shunted into the room feet foremost—the window being only 18 inches open. As soon as he had recovered his footing he laughed and said, 'I wonder what a policeman would have said had he seen me go round and round like a teetotum!' The scene was, however, too terrible—too strange, to elicit a smile; cold beads of perspiration stood on every brow, while a feeling pervaded all as if some great danger had passed; the nerves of those present had been kept in a state of tension that refused to respond to a joke. A change now passed over Mr. Home, one often observable during the trance states, indicative, no doubt, of some other power operating on his system. Lord Adare had in the meantime stepped up to the open window in the adjoining room to close it—the cold air, as it came pouring in, chilling the room; when, to his surprise, he only found the window 18 to 24 inches open! This puzzled him, for how could Mr. Home have passed outside through a window only 18 to 24 inches open. Mr. Home, however, soon set his doubts at rest; stepping up to Lord Adare, he said, 'No, no; I did not close the window; I passed thus into the air outside.' An invisible power then supported Mr. Home all but horizontally in space, and thrust his body into space through the open window, head foremost, bringing him back again feet foremost into the room, shunted not unlike a shutter into a basement below. The circle round the table having re-formed, a cold current of air passed over those present, like the rushing of winds. This repeated itself several times. The cold blast of air, or electric fluid, or call it what you may, was accompanied by a loud whistle like a gust of wind on the mountain top, or through the leaves of the forest in late autumn; the sound was deep, sonorous, and powerful in the extreme, and a shudder kept passing over those present, who all heard and felt it. This rushing sound lasted quite ten minutes, in broken intervals of one or two minutes. All present were much surprised; and the interest became intensified by the unknown tongues in which Mr. Home now conversed. Passing from one language to another in rapid succession, he spoke for ten minutes in unknown languages.

"A spirit form now became distinctly visible; it stood next to the Master of Lindsay, clad, as seen on former occasions, in a long robe with a girdle, the feet scarcely touching the ground, the outline of the face only clear, and the tones of the voice, though sufficiently distinct to be understood, whispered rather than spoken. Other voices were now heard, and large globes of phosphorescent lights passed slowly through the room."

Mr. H. D. Jencken, in the March number of *Human Nature*, continues his interesting account of the spirit manifestations through the mediumship of Mr. D. D. Home, as personally witnessed and carefully examined by himself and other competent investigators. He narrates an instance of the elongation of Mr. Home's body, and gives the measurements (carefully made at the time) of the elongation of each part of the body. The most unique and striking portion of the phenomenon in this instance was the elongation and shortening of the hand. Mr. Jencken says:—

"As the weight of the testimony depends much upon the accuracy of the tracing taken, I will describe my method in making the outline. I caused Mr. Home to place his hand firmly on a sheet of paper, and then carefully traced an outline of the hand. At the wrist joint I placed a pencil against the 'trapezium,' a small bone at the end of the phalange of the thumb. The hand gradually widened and elongated about an inch, then contracted and shortened about an inch. At each stage I made a tracing of the hand, causing the pencil point to be firmly kept at the wrist. The fact of the elongating and contracting of the hand 1 unmistakably established, and, be the cause what it may, the fact remains; and in giving the result of my measurements, and the method adopted to satisfy myself that I had not been self-deceived, I am, I believe, rendering the first positive measurement of the extension and contraction of a human organism.

"The phenomenon of elongation I am aware has been questioned, and I do not quarrel with those who maintain their doubt, despite all that may be affirmed. In my own experience I have gone through the same phases of doubt, and uttered disbelief of what I was seeing. The first time I witnessed an elongation, although I measured the extension of the wrist, I would not, could not, credit my senses; but having witnessed this fact some ten or twelve times, and that in the presence of fifty witnesses, from first to last, who have been present at these *séances* where those elongations occurred, all doubts have been removed; and that the capacity to extend is not confined to Mr. Home, was shown some months ago at Mr. Hall's, where, at a *séance* held at his house, both Mr. Home and Miss Bertolacci became elongated. The stretching out and contracting of the limbs, hands, fingers, above described, I have only witnessed on this one occasion, and I was much pleased to have a steady Oxonian to aid me in making the measurements above detailed."

Mr. Jencken also relates the following incident of this *séance*:—

"Mr. Home (in trance), now took a violet and a few leaves, and, kneeling down at the hearth, stirred the fire with his hand. He then showed us the flower, and seizing it with the fire-tongs, placed it in the fire. I distinctly saw the leaves burn away, and, on withdrawing the fire-tongs, only the stem was left. Twice he repeated the burning of the flower, then, handing the fire-tongs to Miss Bertolacci, he stepped on one side, and we saw the flower being replaced between the nippers of the fire-tongs. I asked whether they had re-formed the flower, to which he replied, 'No; the flower has never been burnt, only shielded, protected from the fire; the freshness of the flower has, however, been destroyed.' He then handed me the violet and leaves, which Miss Bertolacci took, and I believe has preserved. Mr. Home then showed his hands, which felt harsher and harder than in their normal state."

Mr. Jencken adds that at a recent *séance* with Mr. Home, tongues of fire formed in an irregular circle round Mr. Home's head, flickering in fits and starts, from one to three inches long.

The author would only add in this connection that she has herself witnessed Mr. Home's elongation several times in circles held at the residence of John Luxmoore, Esq., 16, Gloucester Square, Hyde Park, London, and also been present on occasions when Mr. Home laid his head on a blazing coal fire without injury, handled blazing coals and placed the same in the hands of John C. Luxmoore, Esq.,—the host—Professor Plumtree, Madame Maurigy, of 51, Albion Street, Hyde Park, and the author.

We might enlarge this list of wonderful phenomena to the dimensions of a thick volume and still fail to relate all the marvels that Spirits have been enabled to display through the mediumship of Mr. D. D. Home. We must however conclude our notices of his remarkable powers by the following extracts from the work already referred to, namely "Researches in the Phenomena of Spiritualism," by Wm. Crookes, F.R.S.

This eminent scientist was not only for some time an industrious investigator into the phenomena of Spirit communion, but he was bold enough to publish the result of those researches, and to maintain the purely occult origin of the manifestations he witnessed, in lengthy controversies with his fellow scientists, and divers members of the journalistic fraternity.

Professor Crookes was aided and sustained in his brave and unconservative position, by Dr. Higgins, Sergeant Cox, and others of an equally eminent rank in the realms of science.

Professor Crookes' papers were first published in the *Quarterly Journal of Science*, but it is from the volume of his collected articles that the following excerpts are now taken. He says:—

"That certain physical phenomena, such as the movement of material substances and the production of sounds resembling electric discharges, occur, under circumstances in which they cannot be explained by any physical law at present known, is a fact of which

I am as certain as of the most elementary fact in chemistry. My whole scientific education has been one long lesson in exactness of observation, and I wish it to be distinctly
understood that this firm conviction is the result of most careful investigation."

"Among the remarkable phenomena which occur under Mr. Home's influence, the
most striking, as well as the most easily tested with scientific accuracy are, first, the
alteration in the weight of bodies ; and second, the playing tunes on musical instruments
(generally the accordion for convenience of portability) without direct human intervention, under conditions rendering contact or connection with the keys impossible. Not
until I had witnessed these facts some half-dozen times, and scrutinised them with all the
critical acumen I possess, did I become convinced of their objective reality. Still, desiring
to place the matter beyond the shadow of a doubt, I invited Mr. Home on several occasions
to come to my own house, where, in the presence of a few scientific inquirers, these phono-
mena could be submitted to crucial experiments."

Mr. Crookes then proceeds to detail with unnecessary accuracy the pre-
cautions he used to surround his experiments with indubitable proofs that
Mr. Home had no agency in their production.

The substance of the experiments was as follows. In a large room well
lighted with gas, a wire cage was used in which the accordion could freely
expand and contract without the possibility of human contact, with the
single exception that it was held suspended in the cage by one of Home's
hands extended over and resting upon the upper wire of the cage. This
was under the table, but in such a position that the company could witness
all the proceedings ; Professor Crookes's assistant being permitted even
to go under the table and give an accurate report of what was going
on. In this position there was first the regular accordion movements and
sounds with the instrument suspended from Home's hand ; then it was
taken out and put in the hand of the next sitter, still continuing to play ;
and finally, after being returned to the cage it was clearly seen by the
company generally, moving about with no one touching it. The final
paragraph of this description we give in the language of Mr. Crookes
himself :—

"The accordion was now taken without any visible touch from Mr. Home's hand,
which he removed from it entirely, and placed upon the table, where it was taken by the
person next to him, and seen, as were now both his hands, by all present. I and two
others present saw the accordion distinctly floating about inside of the cage with no
visible support. This was repeated a second time after a short interval. Mr. Home
presently re-inserted his hand in the cage and again took hold of the accordion. It then
commenced to play, at first chords and runs, and afterwards a well-known sweet and
plaintive melody, which it executed perfectly in a very beautiful manner. Whilst this
tune was being played, I grasped Mr. Home's arm below the elbow, and gently slid my
hand down it until I touched the top of the accordion. He was not moving a muscle.
His other hand was on the table, visible to all, and his feet were under the feet of those
next to him."

Prof. Crookes occupies quite a considerable amount of his work by
republishing the vigorous lines of defence he was compelled to take up
against his brother scientists, whose virulent opposition was awakened by
the immense importance attached to his (Prof. Crookes') statements, consequently also to the influence which the obnoxious and unquenchable
facts of Spiritualism derived from the allegations of so cautious and capable
an investigator.

On the multitude and variety of his researches he says :—

"I may at once answer one objection which has been made in several quarters, viz. ;
that my results would carry more weight had they been tried a greater number of times,
and with other persons besides Mr. Home. The fact is, I have been working at the subject

for two years, and have found nine or ten different persons who possess psychic power in more or less degree ; but its development in Mr. D. D. Home is so powerful that having satisfied myself by careful experiment that the phenomena observed were genuine, I have, merely as a matter of convenience, carried on my experiments with him, in preference to working with others in whom the power existed in a less striking degree. Most of the experiments I am about to describe, however, have been tried with another person other than Mr. Home and in his absence."

It would be unnecessary to follow out these experiments, with the result of which most Spiritual investigators are familiar; we would only show how thorough they were by the following remarks :—

"My readers will remember that, with the exception of cases especially mentioned, the occurrences have taken place *in my own house, in the light, and with only private friends present* besides the medium.

"I have seen luminous points of light darting about and settling on the heads of different persons; I have had questions answered by the flashing of a bright light a desired number of times in front of my face. I have seen sparks of light rising from the table, and again falling upon the table, striking it with an audible sound. I have had an alphabetical communication given by luminous flashes occurring before me in the air, whilst my hand was moving about amongst them. I have seen a luminous cloud floating upwards to a picture. Under the strictest test conditions, I have more than once had a solid, self-luminous, crystalline body placed in my hand by a hand which did not belong to any person in the room. *In the light* I have seen a luminous cloud hover over a heliotrope on a side table, break a sprig off, and carry the sprig to a lady : and on some occasions I have seen a similar luminous cloud visibly condense to the form of a hand and carry small objects about.

"The forms of hands are frequently *felt* at dark *séances*, or under circumstances where they cannot be seen. More rarely I have *seen* the hands. I will here give no instances in which the phenomenon has occurred in darkness, but will simply select a few of the numerous instances in which I have seen the hands in the light.

"A beautifully formed small hand rose up from an opening in a dining-table and gave me a flower; it appeared, and then disappeared three times at intervals, affording me ample opportunity of satisfying myself that it was as real in appearance as my own. This occurred in the light, in my own room, whilst I was holding the medium's hands and feet.

"On another occasion a small hand and arm like a baby's appeared, playing about a lady who was sitting next to me. It then passed to me, and patted my arms and pulled my coat several times.

"At another time a finger and thumb were seen to pick petals from a flower in Mr. Home's button-hole and lay them in front of several persons who were sitting near him.

"The hands and arms do not always appear to me to be solid and life-like. Sometimes, indeed, they present more the appearance of a nebulous cloud partly condensed into the form of a hand. . . . .

"To the touch, the hand sometimes appears icy cold and dead, at other times warm and life-like, grasping my own with the firm pressure of an old friend.

"I have retained one of these hands in my own, firmly resolved not to let it escape. There was no struggle or effort made to get loose, but it gradually seemed to resolve itself into vapour, and faded in that manner from my grasp.

"On one occasion I witnessed a chair, with a lady sitting on it, rise several inches from the ground. On another occasion, to avoid the suspicion of this being in some way performed by herself, the lady knelt on the chair in such a manner that its four feet were visible to us. It then rose about three inches, remained suspended for about ten seconds, and then slowly descended. At another time two children, on separate occasions, rose from the floor with their chairs, in full daylight, under (to me) most satisfactory conditions ; for I was kneeling and keeping close watch upon the feet of the chair, and observing that no one might touch them.

"The most striking cases of levitation which I have witnessed have been with Mr. Home. On three separate occasions have I seen him raised completely from the floor of the room, once sitting in an easy chair, once kneeling on his chair, and once standing up. On each occasion I had a full opportunity of watching the occurrence as it was taking place.

"As in the former case, Mr. Home was the medium. A phantom form came from a corner of the room, took an accordion in its hand, and then glided about the room, playing the instrument. The form was visible to all many minutes, Mr. Home being seen at the same time. Coming rather close to a lady who was sitting apart from the rest of the company, she gave a slight cry, upon which it vanished."

Such are some of the phenomena obtained by a gentleman who pledges a name and fame standing as high as that of any scientist in the nineteenth century for the truth of all he alleges ; who backs up his own testimony with that of numerous other equally reliable and eminent witnesses, all of whom have everything to lose, and nothing to gain by the assertions they make. It only needs to add, that all the phenomena above alluded to were produced in the light, in private houses, and under circumstances which rendered the interposition of human agency impossible.

If the Spiritualists themselves would but remember that—until Spirit communion is the common experience of the race—the world at large, and investigators seeking for truth in especial, have the right to demand that the records of phenomena shall be placed on equally unquestionable bases, the columns of the Spiritual journals would no longer be desecrated by the unseemly charges of bare-faced fraud from one party and savage recriminations from another. Spiritualism would ascend to the majestic pedestal of immutable truth like a phœnix rising out of the ashes of dead faiths and fleeting superstitions, and ere long it would compel the acknowledgment of humanity that it was the divine science of soul, and the religion of science.*

CHAPTER XX.

SPIRITUALISM IN GREAT BRITAIN (CONTINUED).

THE effect of Mr. Home's presence in England, the wide-spread reports of the marvels occurring through his mediumship, combined with the furious journalistic warfare which these reports elicited, acted like firebrands thrown into the midst of combustible materials, the sparks from which filled the air, and set the entire mental atmosphere ablaze with Spiritual influences.

True it is, that the young medium's marvellous gifts were displayed only amongst that high class of society in which circumstances had contributed to cast his lot, and through whose personal interest he became the guest of many of the nobles and notables of the day.

Still the contagion of the Spiritual outpouring was in the air, and vast numbers of persons to whom Mr. Home's *séances* were but a report, became stimulated to the endeavour to obtain manifestations through private experiments in their own families. The result was—as all experienced Spiritualists would anticipate, that demonstrations of medial power began to arise in vast numbers of family circles, and those who could not enjoy the privilege of investigating through the Transatlantic medium, were soon enabled to prove for themselves the wonderful facts of which rumour had informed them.

---

* For further account of Mr. Home's mediumship and special *séances*, consult his own biography entitled "Incidents of my Life: By D. D. Home," files of the London *Spiritual Magazine*, Owen's "Footfalls on the Boundaries of Another World," and other English Spiritual publications of this century.—(AUTHOR.)

The chances are, that we should very generally find the *modus operandi* of individual investigation exemplified by the experience of Mrs. De Morgan—the wife of the celebrated mathematical professor—who, having been assured by Spirit friends communicating through Mrs. Hayden, that she could have equally good manifestations with those she then witnessed in her own house, at once proceeded to put in practice the instructions given, and form circles, the result of which soon became apparent in the development of remarkable medial powers in Mrs. De Morgan herself, in some members of her household, her friends, and not a few of her servants.

Experiences of this character soon began to multiply. Professor De Morgan, although not avowedly interested to the same extent as his estimable lady, candidly rendered his testimony to the occurrence of the marvellous phenomena which proved Spirit communion. In a short space of time after the advent of Mr. Home in England, the circles known to be held constantly, in various families, might be numbered by the thousand, and those who publicly ranged themselves as advocates of the truth of the communion, included some of the most distinguished and noteworthy persons of the day. Amongst the latter, and especially remarkable as being the earliest of the avowed believers of Spiritualism in England, may be named, Mary and William Howitt and Samuel Carter and Maria Hall; all authors celebrated for their admirable writings, and ladies and gentlemen as much esteemed for their irreproachable private lives as for their eminent literary abilities—Dawson Rogers; a gentleman of high social standing and influential press associations—the Countess, now Duchesse de Pomar, and Countess of Caithness, a lady who takes the highest rank both as an authoress and leader of aristocratic European society; T. P. Barkas, F.R.S.; Lady Otway, Frederick Tennyson, Robert Owen, and his son, Robert Dale Owen; Lord Brougham, Lord Lytton, Archbishop Whateley, the Earl of Dunraven, Lord Adare, the Master of Lindsay, Lady Shelley, Mr. Sergeant Cox; Wm. Wilkinson, Esq., the eminent solicitor, and other members of his family; Sir Edwin Landseer; more than one member of the eminent literary family of the Trollopes; Mrs. Browning, the celebrated poetess; George Thompson, the well known philanthropist; Major Drayson the eminent astronomer; Benjamin Coleman, Esq., and his amiable wife and daughter; John Jones, Esq., of Enmore Park, Norwood; Sir Chas. Isham, Bart., of Lamport Hall, Northampton; the Countess of Paulett; Mrs. McDougall Gregory, widow of the celebrated Dr. Gregory of Edinburgh; Lady Dunsany, Lady Helena Newenham, J. C. Luxmoore, Esq.; Professor A. R. Wallace, the celebrated naturalist; Cromwell Varley, F.R.S.; the renowned electrician; W. F. Barrett, Professor of Physics in the Royal College of Science, Dublin; Lord Rayleigh, F.R.S., Professor of Physics, Cambridge University; the Earl of Crauford and Balcarres, F.R.S., President of the Royal Astronomical Society; Dr. Lockhart Robertson, F.R.S., Editor, *Journal of Science;* Drs. Ashburner and Elliotson, Dr. George Wylde, Dr. Robert Chambers, F.R.S.; Professor Cassel, LL.D.; Captain R. F. Burton, the celebrated traveller; Dr. Fenton Cameron, Henry D. Jencken, barrister; Professor Crookes, the renowned chemist; Mrs. Anna Cora Ritchie, Thos. Shorter, Esq., known under the *nom de plume* of "Brevior;" Dr. Jacob Dixon, the eminent homœopathist; Wm. Tebb, Esq., and his lady; Gerald Massey, the renowned poet; C. C. Massey, the barrister; Hon. J. L. O'Sullivan, Rev. Sir Wm. Topham, A. Gooch, M.P.; Dr. Gully, of Malvern; Chas. Blackburn, Esq., of Parkfield, Didsbury, Manchester;

Jno. Fowler, Esq., of Liverpool, and Jas. Wason, Esq., barrister, of the same place ; Mrs. Honeywood, of Warwick Square, Belgravia ; Dr. Hitchman, LL.D., John Scott, Esq., of Belfast ; John Rymer, Esq., of Ealing ; M. and Madame Maurigy ; W. Cox, Esq., Jermyn Street, St. James', and a long list of other ladies and gentlemen whose names we are not privileged to mention—to say nothing of hundreds of persons in the middle ranks of life, whose advocacy was of equal credit to the cause.

It need hardly be added that since the above-named ladies and gentle- men contributed their influence and honourable names to bear the heat and burden of the early days of spiritual warfare, hundreds of others, scarcely less eminent or noteworthy, have graced the ranks of Spiritualism. Those who have become associated with the moving incidents of the grand historical drama will of course be mentioned hereafter, but a still larger number must necessarily be excluded, though most reluctantly on the author's part, from this over-crowded record.

We recall the few names already cited, chiefly for the purpose of showing the class of individuals against whom the small wits of English journalism amused themselves by directing the shafts of ridicule and contempt, and that simply because they chose to believe what the testimony of their own senses proved to be truth. For this cause and for this only, the above-named parties were virtually branded either as *fools*, incapable of forming correct opinions, or *knaves* wicked enough to join in a world-wide system of imposition upon others. No doubt the *critics* had hardly calculated the sum of the insolence of which they were guilty ; still its substance meant neither more nor less than the assertion that the believers in Spiritualism— be they whom they may—were either all deluded or all deluders, however wise or honest they may have been on every other subject but Spiritualism.

Now it must be borne in mind that neither the gifts nor the messages of Spiritualism were limited to the aristocratic circles of Great Britain.

In a great many cases it was found, that some of the best Mediums were developed amongst the poor patients who sought aid at the Mesmeric Infirmary. The servants in great families also, who were often summoned to attend the circles of their masters and mistresses, at the suggestion of the communicating Spirits, frequently proved to be endowed with remarkable mediumistic powers, and these carried the tidings of the new revelation to persons of their own class, by whom quiet unostentatious methods of enquiry into Spiritualism were proceeding, with far more abundant results than the world at large was at all prepared for.

Still there were circumstances tending to limit the earlier manifestations of Spirit power in Great Britain to private families, and the isolation of individual experiences. In the first place, there were no professional Mediums in England, but such as came from America, for some years.

When European Mediums were either called upon or *compelled*—as was often the case—to abandon all other modes of gaining a livelihood, to devote themselves entirely to the exercise of their Spiritual gifts, it became an inevitable necessity that they should be recompensed for the time and labour involved in their services. It is only just to say, that in America—where every description of labour normal to the individual per- forming it, is recognised as natural and honourable—Mediumistic power was—from the incipiency of the movement—classified with every other faculty, and as such acknowledged to be a legitimate means of earning a livelihood.

In Great Britain the attempt to establish a pharisaical distinction between what is sacred and secular, ever has, and still does, stigmatize *professional* mediumship as "a desecration," &c., &c.   Making all due allowance for the fraudulent spirit so common to human nature, and therefore, so certain to be found in the ranks of Spiritualism as well as amongst all other classes of society, we have yet to see why professional mediumship is not as legitimate an occupation as professional editorship, or professional work done in any other capacity for which the Creator has fitted the creature.

We have yet to learn what gifts are specially *sacred* and what—by converse—are *profane.*   When we have sufficiently *proved* these distinctions, we may be in a position to denounce the Mediums who claim the labourers' hire for their work.   It is but justice to the sticklers for "sacred and profane" gifts in humanity, to add, that they never affix these awkward lines of demarcation to the workers of any other denomination than those of Spiritualism ; the clergy as a body—from the archbishop who receives his twenty-five thousand pounds a year for Spiritual ministrations, to the poor curate upon his stipend of one hundred per annum — being deemed legitimately entitled to receive *whatever they can get,* unrebuked and unquestioned.   Whether we are to consider the clerical calling as "profane" and therefore entitled to recompense, or *"too sacred"* to be called in question at all, we have not yet been able to ascertain, but we do know for an absolute fact, that many an Englishman who does not hesitate to pay his quota of heavy rates to support the Church, has shrunk back in holy horror from paying a sixpenny fee to hear a fine Spiritual lecture, and excused himself on the ground that Mediumship was a " sacred gift," and should not be made the subject of mercenary traffic, &c., &c.   Whether these assertions are designed to insinuate, that the Spirit Medium's gifts are from the Lord, and should not be paid, and those of the Bench of Bishops are from the other party, and may therefore become the subject of traffic, we cannot exactly determine.   The inference is strong that way, and therefore, were it only for the sake of resisting the wholesale insult which this line of argument hurls against the clergy of all denominations, we ought to disregard such distinctions, or at least hold them in abeyance, until the line between the sacred and profane in human endowments is clearly defined. Meantime, the results of these curious opinions were not favourable to the general dissemination of Spiritualism in Great Britain.   For many years the belief was a close communion affair ; the luxurious entertainment of those who could afford to encourage Transatlantic Mediums as their guests, or devote leisure time to the culture of spiritual gifts in small retired family circles.

For a long time, the attempt to disseminate the knowledge thus obtained by aid of professional mediumship was so severely frowned down, that its earliest public exhibitions—as in the case of the Davenport Brothers— became occasions for the display of violence and ruffianism that would have disgraced the darkest of ages.   We may also understand why—with an immense array of titled names and distinguished literary and scientific celebrities as its patrons—Spiritualism remained for many years unrepresented by any public demonstration.

In 1859, Mr. Rollin Squire, the young American gentleman mentioned in our French section, paid a brief visit to Europe, for the purpose of recruiting his health and enjoying a holiday tour.

Both in this country and on the Continent, Mr. Squire exercised his medial powers for the edification of large circles of admirers.   Still, like Mr. Home, Mr. Squire was only known within the charmed limits of aristocracy, or such journalistic commentators as were from time to time invited as witnesses of the marvels enacted in his presence. Mr. P. B. Randolph, an eccentric trance speaker, and Mrs. A. E. Newton, a vision seeress and clairvoyant, were also received amongst the *haut ton* of European Spiritualism, and each contributed their quota as honoured American visitors, in disseminating spiritual light amongst the more favoured part of the community. In 1864 the far-famed Davenport Brothers visited England for the first time. They were the only Mediums except the trance speakers, who had yet appeared in Europe through whom manifestations of spirit power could be given in public audiences.

Professional Mediumship as above suggested, was at that time regarded with so much unreasoning distrust, that the announcement that what had hitherto been regarded as the "most sacred of gifts," was now to be made the subject of paying exhibitions, caused a thrill of horror to pervade even the minds of Spiritualists themselves. It was in deference then to this orthodox view of spiritual power and gifts, that the Davenports and their *Entrepreneur*, were induced at first to tender their inaugural manifestations in private circles, or gatherings convened according to custom, at the houses of the privileged few.

As we feel justified in asserting that no subsequent phases of mediumship exhibited on public platforms, have ever equalled in TEST conditions and clearness, the manifestations produced through the Davenport Brothers in the early days of their public career, we deem it a necessary part of the present record, to give a brief account of the phenomena which ordinarily transpired in their presence, and this we prefer to do, by reiterating a published statement attested by a large number of respectable witnesses, rather than offer the author's own unsustained views of these young men's Mediumship.

Dr. Nichols, author of a sketch of the Davenport Brothers, during the very early portion of their career, says : "On the night of October 11th, 1864, a very distinguished company assembled at the residence of Mr. Dion Boucicault to witness the manifestations which are given in the presence of the Brothers Davenport." An account of the proceedings which transpired, Dr. Nichols alleges to have been drawn up and published by Mr. Boucicault himself. The following is a *verbatim* copy of the report in question :—

" To the Editor of the ' Daily News.'

"Sir,—A *séance* by the Brothers Davenport and Mr. W. Fay, took place in my house yesterday in the presence of Lord Bury, Sir Charles Nicholson, Sir John Gardiner, Sir C. Lennox Wyke, Rev. E. H. Newenham, Rev. W. Ellis, Captain E. A. Inglefield, Mr. Chas. Reade, Messrs. Jas. Matthews, Algernon Borthwick, T. Willes, H. E. Ormerod, J. W. Kaye, J. A. Bostock, H. J. Rideout, Robt. Bell, J. N. Mangles, H. M. Dunphy, W. Tyler Smith, M.D., E. Tyler Smith, T. L. Coward, John Brown, M.D., Robert Chambers, LL.D., and Dion Boucicault.

"The room in which the meeting was held is a large drawing-room, from which all the furniture had been previously removed excepting the carpet, a chandelier, a table and sofa, and twenty-six cane-bottomed chairs.

"At two o'clock six of the above party arrived, and the room was subjected to careful scrutiny.

"It was suggested that a cabinet to be used by the Brothers Davenport, but then erected in an adjacent room, should be removed into the front room, and placed in a spot selected by ourselves.

"This was done by our party, but in the process we displaced a portion of this piece of furniture, thus enabling us to examine its material and structure before we mended it. At three o'clock, our party was fully assembled and continued the scrutiny. We sent to a neighbouring music seller for six guitars and two tambourines, so that the implements to be used should not be those with which the operators were familiar. At half-past three the brothers Davenport and Mr. Fay arrive.d They found we had altered their arrangements by changing the room which they had previously selected for their manifestations.

"The *séance* then began by an examination of the dress and persons of the Davenports, and it was certified that no apparatus or other contrivance was concealed on or about their persons. They entered the cabinet, and sat facing each other. Captain Inglefield then with a new rope, provided by ourselves, tied Mr. W. Davenport hand and foot, with his hands behind his back, and then bound him firmly to the seat where he sat. Lord Bury in like manner secured Mr. Ira Davenport. The knots on these ligatures were then fastened with sealing wax and a seal affixed. A guitar, violin, tambourine, two bells, and a brass trumpet were placed on the floor of the cabinet.

"The doors were then closed, and a sufficient light was permitted in the room to enable us to see what followed.

"I shall omit any detailed account of the Babel of sounds which arose in the cabinet, and the violence with which the doors were repeatedly burst open and the instruments expelled, the hands appearing as usual at a lozenge-shaped orifice in the centre door of the cabinet. The following incidents seem to us particularly worthy of note.

"While Lord Bury was stooping inside the cabinet, the door being open, the two operators seen to be seated and bound, a *detached* hand was clearly observed to descend upon him, and he started back remarking that he had been struck.

"Again, in the full light of the gas chandelier, and during an interval in the *séance*, the doors of the cabinet being open, and while the ligatures of the brothers were being examined, a very white thin female hand and wrist quivered for several seconds in the air above.

"This appearance drew a general exclamation from all the party. Sir Charles Wyke now entered the cabinet and sat between the two young men, his hands being right and left on each, and secured to them. The doors were then closed and the Babel of sounds recommenced. Several hands appeared at the orifice, amongst them the hand of a child. After a time, Sir Charles returned amongst us and stated that while he held the two brothers, several hands touched his face, and pulled his hair ; the instruments at his feet crept up, played round his body, and over his head, one of them lodging eventually on his shoulders. During the foregoing incidents the hands which appeared were touched and grasped by Captain Inglefield, and he stated that to the touch they were apparently human hands, though they passed away from his grasp.

"I omit mentioning other phenomena, an account of which has been rendered elsewhere.

"The next part of the *séance* was performed in the dark. One of the Messrs. Davenport and Mr. Fay seated themselves amongst us. . . . Two ropes were thrown at their feet, and in two minutes and a half they were tied hand and foot, their hands behind their backs, bound tightly to their chairs, and their chairs bound to an adjacent table. While this process was going on, the guitar rose from the table and swung or floated round the room and over the heads of the party, slightly touching some. Now a phosphoric light shot from side to side over our heads. The hands and shoulders of several were simultaneously touched or struck by hands, the guitar meanwhile sailing round the room, now near the ceiling, now scuffling on the head and shoulders of some luckless wight. The bells whisked here and there, and a light murmuring was maintained on the violin.

"The two tambourines were rolled hither and thither on the floor, now shaking violently, now visiting the knees and hands of our circle, all these foregoing incidents being simultaneous. Mr. Rideout, holding a tambourine, requested it might be plucked from him, when it was almost instantaneously taken. At the same time Lord Bury made a similar request, and a forcible attempt was made to pluck a tambourine from his grasp, which he resisted.

"Mr. Fay then asked that his coat should be removed.

"We heard a violent twitch and here occurred a most remarkable fact. A light was struck before the coat had quite left Mr. Fay's person, and it was seen quitting him, and plucked off him upwards.

"It flew up to the chandelier, where it hung for a moment and then fell to the ground. Mr. Fay was seen meanwhile bound hand and foot as before. One of our party now divested himself of his coat, and it was placed on the table. The light was extinguished and this coat was rushed on to Mr. Fay's back with equal rapidity.

"During the above occurrences in the dark, we placed a sheet of paper under the feet of the two operators, and drew with a pencil an outline around them, to the end that if they moved it might be detected.

"They of their own accord offered to have their hands filled with flour, or any similar substance to prove they made no use of them, but this precaution was deemed unnecessary ;

we required them however to count from one to twelve repeatedly that their voices constantly heard might certify to us that they were in the places where they were tied. Each of our own party held his neighbour so firmly that no one could move without two adjacent neighbours being aware of it. At the termination of this *séance* a general conversation took place on the subject of what we had witnessed.

"Lord Bury suggested that the general opinion seemed to be that we assure the Brothers Davenport and Mr. Fay that after a very stringent trial and strict scrutiny of their proceedings, the gentlemen present could arrive at no other conclusion than that there was no trace of trickery in any form, and certainly there were neither confederates nor machinery, and that all those who had witnessed the results would freely state in the society in which they moved that so far as their investigations enabled them to form an opinion, the phenomena which had taken place in their presence were not the product of legerdemain. This suggestion was promptly acceded to by all present.

"Before leaving this question, in which my name has accidentally become mixed up, I may be permitted to observe that I have no belief in what is called 'Spiritualism,' and nothing I have seen inclines me to believe in it—indeed the puerility of some of the demonstrations would sufficiently alienate such a theory, but I do believe that we have not quite explored the realms of natural philosophy—that this enterprise of thought has of late years been confined to useful inventions, and we are content at least to think that the laws of nature are finite, ascertained, and limited to the scope of our knowledge. A very great number of worthy persons, seeing such phenomena as I have detailed, ascribe them to supernatural agency; others wander round the subject in doubt, but as it seriously engages the feeling and earnest thought of so large a number in Europe and America, is it a subject which scientific men are justified in treating with the neglect of contempt?

.   •   ,   •   •   •   ,   •

"I am, &c.,

"Dion Boucicault.

"Regent Street, October 12, 1864."

It may be asked with some point, why we republish accounts of phenomena so well known and which have long since been put into the shade—in the opinion of many Spiritualists—by the marvels of what they term "form materializations?" On the other hand, there has been a kind of fashion in the assertion, both within and without the ranks of Spiritualism, that the Davenport Brothers are "impostors," and many assume, without any known grounds for the assumption, that they have been *proved* to be impostors. To all classes of objectors we would carefully commend a perusal of the *séance* reported above. Let it be remembered that it is written by one who only admits that his name is "*accidentally*" mixed up in the affair, and who guards that name with unnecessary caution from the charge of *being a Spiritualist*.

All those who have witnessed the Davenports' *séances* know, that their phenomena were performed with lightning speed; that no singing was called for—"loud, louder, louder still"—during the dreary waiting time when Spirits are "materializing," and all who read the report of these press men, scientists, and sceptics, will observe, how often they insist upon their own caution in examining, and of the utter impossibility of their detecting fraud, or the personal agency of the Mediums in the phenomena.

Now, uninteresting as the facts themselves may be, the above report shows a set of conditions under which human agency or contrivance was simply IMPOSSIBLE. Our aim in dwelling upon this *séance* is to show, that in the case of the Davenports, as in those so often described as occurring with Mr. Home, stringent tests do not hinder the manifestations, neither does the presence of sceptics destroy them.

Here are conditions under which conjurers may be defied and scepticism baffled; and though imposture is impossible, true Mediumship could not fail to come out of such trials triumphant and unimpeachable. But these conditions are "too degrading for sensitive Mediums to submit to," urge their apologists, "and you who demand it of them, are no true Spiritualists; you are *Spirit grabbers*, Mediums' enemies, the worst foes of Spiritualism," &c., &c., &c.   To this class of talkers and writers, we have no answer to make, neither desiring nor intending to hold intercourse with them; but to the confiding victims whose heart strings are wrung, and whose pockets are so often robbed to sustain impostors, we would say, See what Spirits could do, and did do, through the mediumship of the Davenports, and have no hesitancy in refusing to accord faith to any professions of Spiritual agency that are not equally well guarded round, against possibility of human interference and deception.

That the poor Davenports were often inhumanly, and even brutally treated, we not only admit, but are about to demonstrate; but the tests applied by the party whose record we have given, neither degraded nor insulted the Mediums; on the contrary, they submitted to them cheerfully, and often, to the author's personal knowledge, suggested still more stringent tests, with which their manifestations could readily be given.

The truth is, the Davenports have seldom been fairly dealt with.   The people that could not explain their manifestations, have contented them-selves, like Mr. Boucicault, by denying that they could be "Spiritual," because they were too *puerile*, whilst multitudes of Spiritualists who will gaze with rapture upon the tinsel ornaments sewed on to cheap finery by *Mediums*, whilst their masked dummies are contemplated with awe, stretched out on sofas, will turn with disgust from the obvious and unmis-takeable proofs of Spirit power, furnished through the Davenports, because they come from "such very low Spirits!"   Had we an opportunity of questioning Mr. Boucicault concerning his opinion as to what becomes of the great mass of mankind that sit nightly to watch his dramas, perhaps we might be in a position to show that the taste of the majority inclines to puerility only, and that anything that was not puerile, would not represent the vanished millions that have passed through the gates of death to the life beyond, where it is exceedingly doubtful, if puerile Spirits become wise in the twinkling of an eye, or low men and women suddenly become exalted angels.   Meantime the question is not one of *quality* but kind. Were the manifestations recorded above, made by the Davenports, if not, by whom and what?

These are the real questions at issue, and those manifestations can no longer be called "puerile," which defy the whole realm of science to explain, nor those Spirits be tabooed as "too low" for pious company, which prove the fact of man's spiritual existence, better than all the sermons that were ever preached from the mere standpoint of belief without knowledge.

Following immediately upon the *séance* recorded above, with the Daven-ports, were others of a more or less wonderful nature.

These exhibitions were at first confined to private circles held in the houses of the nobility, or of scientific persons; at length however, the Mediums enlarged their borders, and appeared at the Queen's Concert Room, Hanover Square, attracting select and distinguished audiences, by whom they were still esteemed as entirely free from all shadow of fraud or suspicion.   For some time the gentlemen of the press, especially those who were favoured with invitations to attend the more exclusive circles, were fair and candid in their statements concerning what they had witnessed. No sooner did it appear however that the Mediums seemed in a fair way to remunerate themselves for time and service by successful public exhibitions, than the press suddenly became alive to the "impiety," "American audacity," &c., &c., of the whole affair.

Dr. Nichols in his biography of the Davenport Brothers quotes the press utterances of this character at large, and to judge by their general tone, the Davenports had become unmistakably popular, and were very generally *fêted* and patronised by the highest rank of society, whilst their success in "making money" by their public exhibitions, and baffling all attempts of the scientific or learned to "find them out," very *naturally*, and very *justly*, merited the united storm of journalistic indignation from all parts of the country, and the united "anathema maranatha" of every pious professor of Spiritual doctrines, who could not prove what they professed, quite as well as the Davenports. So the storm raged, and so the enemies of the cause contributed to feed the flame by the virulence of the persecution directed against it. The culminating point of these proceedings however was reached, in a demonstration of *popular sentiment* displayed towards the Davenports on the occasion of their visit to the north of England. Although the character of this incident is such an one as no English writer would care much to descant upon, we feel obliged, in the interests of truth, to give the narrative in all its ugly details; still we prefer to let others tell the tale. We shall therefore place it before the reader in the language of the parties most nearly concerned, and as the following letter from the Brothers Davenport contains published facts which for many years have remained uncontradicted, we cannot do better than reprint it in their own words.

The following quotation, explanatory of the letter, is written by the Rev. J. B. Ferguson, A.M., LL.D., a gentleman from one of the Southern States of America, who having become well acquained with the Davenports, and placing implicit faith in their honesty, and the thoroughly Spiritual nature of their endowments, had consented to accompany them to England, as a travelling companion, and was well advised of all the facts which were published indeed under his own supervision.

Writing to the author Mr. Ferguson says:—"The Brothers Davenport have been subjected to a series of extraordinary outrages in some of the provincial towns of England, which show that the spirit of opposition manifested by a portion of the public press is likely to take more violent form when it falls into a lower stratum of society. The facts connected with the riots at Liverpool, Huddersfield, and Leeds are very clearly stated in the following address of the Brothers Davenport to the British public, which, as a portion of the history of the movement, deserves a place in these records:—"

"THE BROTHERS DAVENPORT TO THE BRITISH PUBLIC.

"We appeal to the free press and the enlightened and fair-dealing people of the British Empire for a candid consideration of the following statement, and for the even-handed justice usually given in this country to all persons, rich or poor, citizens or strangers. We ask, also, as a matter of justice, that journals which have published accounts of the recent riots at Liverpool, Huddersfield, and Leeds, of which we were the victims, should also give the facts contained in this statement.

"We beg, furthermore, most respectfully to commend to the consideration of the Right Honourable Sir George Grey and the magistracy and police authorities of the United Kingdom, the fact that within two weeks, in three of the most important provincial towns in England, without any fault of our own, transgressing no law of the realm, and offering no violence or injury to any person, we have been made to suffer in property, and have been menaced with extreme personal injury, with apparent danger to our lives, as will appear by the following statement of facts:—

"After having given over two hundred public and private *séances*, or exhibitions of physical phenomena, such as have been described in all the leading journals of Europe and America, and in our published biography, at the Queen's Concert Rooms, London, and the mansions of the nobility and gentry of England, we visited Liverpool on the 13th of February, and, as is our custom, gave a private *séance*, to which the members of the press and others were invited, who reported the satisfactory character of the exhibition. February 14th we gave two public *séances* at St. George's Hall with like results ; a private *séance* at a gentleman's mansion and a public morning performance on Tuesday were alike satisfactory.

"On Tuesday evening we were proceeding with another exhibition, when two persons, a Mr. Hulley and a Mr. Cummins, acting as a committee from the audience, in attempting to tie our wrists, caused so much pain that we were compelled to protest against the torture they were inflicting. We were willing to be tied with entire security, as we have been many hundreds of times by riggers, sailors, engineers, and other skilled persons, or to give any reasonable test in proof that we have no active part in the phenomena witnessed in our presence ; we had no fear of a 'Tomfool knot, or of any mode of fastening that did not inflict unbearable torture. We declined to be bound by a committee whose unfairness and even brutality were soon manifest. Hulley and Cummins refused to retire and give place to another committee ; the audience was made to believe that it was the form of a particular knot, and not the cruelty of its application, to which we objected, and we were compelled by an unappeasable tumult to return the money taken for tickets, and postpone further proceedings.

"On the following evening printed regulations were given to every person entering the hall, and read from the platform, in which we distinctly claimed the right of rejecting any person on a committee whom we should find acting with unfairness. This would be our right were we criminals on trial for felony. Before commencing, we invited all persons who were not satisfied with these regulations to retire from the hall, and receive the money they had paid for entrance.

"Messrs. Hulley and Cummins, backed by a crowd of their friends, came again upon the platform, and, from their previous unfairness, were promptly rejected by us as a committee. They insisted upon tying us, and appealed to the audience to support them in their demand. They refused to leave the platform when requested, took possession of our cabinet, and in various ways excited violent manifestations in the audience.

" We were then assured by a gentleman of Liverpool that unless we submitted to the demands of these men there would be a furious riot. He promised that they should not be permitted to injure us, and we finally yielded to his assurances. But they had no sooner placed the cords upon our wrists than they inflicted a degree of pain which could not be endured. We protested against this violence, but in vain, and, refusing to submit to it longer, had the cords cut from our wrists, and left the platform, which was instantly invaded by the mob ; our cabinet was broken in pieces, and Hulley and Cummins, the heroes of this assault of some hundreds of brave Englishmen upon four unarmed, unoffending, and unprotected foreigners were borne from the hall upon the shoulders of their friends, apparently proud of their triumph.

" Our cabinet destroyed and our business interrupted, with heavy pecuniary damage in Liverpool, we returned to London, had a new cabinet constructed, and on the following Monday returned to Halifax, where we gave our usual public and private exhibitions without interruption.

"Our next engagement was at Huddersfield, February 21st. On our arrival we were informed that Hulley and Cummins, the heroes of the Liverpool mob, had been telegraphed to, and were coming with a strong deputation from that town, to break up our exhibition. The infuriated mob was the common talk of the town. We appealed to the police, and we are happy to say that, in this instance, a sufficient force was promptly sent to the hall for our protection. The crowd that assembled gave many indications of being prepared for violence. When our representative had stated the regulations adopted, and that we proposed simply the presentation of certain facts, without any theory, and asked for the appointment of a committee, two gentlemen, instructed, it was said, by Hulley and Cummins, came upon the platform and commenced to tie our wrists together behind us, which they did with needless severity. We bore the pain, however, until carrying the ropes through the hole in the seat, they drew the backs of our hands down upon it with such violence as to threaten dislocation, placing their knees upon the seat, and in one instance upon the hands of one of us to give them greater purchase. This torture, deliberately, and to all appearance maliciously inflicted, we of course could not bear, and at our demand the cords were instantly severed. We exposed our livid wrists, in which every strand of the cord was visibly imprinted, to the audience, who, to the credit of their humanity, cried out 'Shame !' But the mob organized to break up our exhibition had no such feeling, and made a simultaneous rush for the platform, where, however, an efficient police force saved our property from destruction and us from a violence which, under the stimulating addresses of the heroes of the Liverpool outrage, expended itself in hootings and howlings.

"We had engagements for two nights at Hull, but on our arrival we were informed by the gentleman who had engaged us, the chairman of the hall committee, and the police superintendent, that there were such indications of a violent mob, that we could not be permitted to give our exhibition, and we received from the gentleman chiefly interested the following note :—

"'Music Hall, Jarret Street, Hull.
"'22nd February, 1865.

"'Sir,—As I believe there is reason to apprehend a disturbance at the hall this evening, if the *séance* of the Davenport Brothers takes place, I have come to the conclusion that it would be advisable to postpone the *séance*. I am sorry to do this, particularly as yourself and the Messrs. Davenport have arrived in Hull, and are ready to fulfil your engagement ; but I am driven to do so by the *organized attack* which I am given to understand is in preparation. I am also urged to do so by the proprietors of the hall, who are alarmed lest their property should be damaged by any disturbance.
"'I remain, yours faithfully,

"'ROBERT BOWSER.
"'Rev. Dr. Ferguson, Royal Station Hotel, Hull.'

"Failing to find at Hull that protection in our legal rights which we had supposed was extended to every man on English ground, we went to meet our next engagement at Leeds, where the scenes of Liverpool and Huddersfield were re-enacted with increased violence. We were met by an organized mob, and were refused the protection of the police when it was demanded. When the ringleaders or agents of the mob, taking possession of the stage, had subjected us to the same violence that had been planned and practised upon us at Liverpool and Huddersfield—the mob again destroying our property, smashing the cabinet and breaking up or purloining our musical instruments, and we were protected from personal violence, amid the smashing of door panels and the howling of an enraged populace, by the tardy arrival of a detachment of police and the brave and firm conduct of one of its members—our agent, contrary to all justice, was compelled to order the return of the admission money paid by those who had come for the very purpose of making the riot from which we suffered. On the same day we had given a public *séance*, attended by the members of the press and some of the most respectable citizens of Leeds, in which the famous 'Tom-fool knot' was used, and in which, so far as we were able to judge, the phenomena exhibited gave entire satisfaction.

"It remains but to state two or three facts which may throw further light on these proceedings.

"In Liverpool, as reported in the *Mercury*, Mr. Hulley, when accused of acting unfairly to, and being an enemy of the Davenports, said, 'I avow it. I am a bitter foe to the Davenports.' After such an avowal, what right had he to act on a committee whose duty was strict impartiality ?

"We wish to be just to the police. At Huddersfield, though they could not give us order, we were protected from actual violence. At Leeds such protection was withheld until too late to save our property.

"At Liverpool the *Mercury* says :—

"'The appearance of Inspectors Valentine and Southwell, with a force of thirty men, did not stop the process of demolition. The police, indeed, *did not attempt to interfere so long as only the property of the Davenports was threatened.*'

"The *Leeds Mercury*, reporting the violent proceedings against us at Huddersfield, says :—

"'Mr. Walker, not considering that his hands could pull the rope tight enough, *used his knee to assist him,* and the brother he was operating on again protested. . . . . Several persons had at that time gone to the cabinet, and Davenport showed his wrist to some of them. *It had a livid mark fringed with red, about the breadth of a finger, and in the hollow of this mark there were the marks of the individual strands of the rope.*'

"Yet some have been found to insist on inflicting this brutal torture upon us, with howling mobs to back them, as if we were malefactors or wild beasts. It may be doubted if such an amount of violence, wrong, and outrage has been inflicted on any unoffending men in England since Clarkson was mobbed by the slave-traders of Liverpool, and Priestly by the mad bigots of Birmingham. . . .

"(Signed)

"IRA ERASTUS DAVENPORT.
"WILLIAM HENRY DAVENPORT.
"WILLIAM M. FAY."

CHAPTER XXI.

SPIRITUALISM IN GREAT BRITAIN (CONTINUED).

ANOTHER of the abnormal personages who made a deep mark upon tne faith of European society, was Miss Nichol, better known as Mrs. Guppy, the wife of a gentleman of wealth and good social position, who previous to his union with Miss Nichol, had become remarkable in the Spiritualistic ranks as the author of a singular book entitled "Mary Jane." The speciality of this publication, which was issued in two handsome volumes, was to this effect.

Previous to the decease of his first wife, Mr. Guppy's attention had been drawn towards a succession of extraordinary disturbances occurring in his own house, and which continued for many months, in the form of rappings, movements of furniture, direct writings, and at last, when advised by Spiritualistic friends to try and obtain communications with the unseen tormentors through the ordinary methods of the Spirit circle the manifestations changed to intelligent question and answer, rendered through rappings, table tilting, and planchette writings. Being of a somewhat materialistic turn of mind, and greatly interested in the study of the natural sciences, Mr. Guppy—whilst compelled to admit the supra-mundane character of the new development in his household—attributed it to *a species of aromal force, given off unconsciously, from certain human organisms, and combining itself into a sort of magical impersonal personality*, to which he gave the anomalous designation of "Mary Jane." As the said "Mary Jane" manifested a remarkable amount of intelligence, often transcending that of any member of the household, and betrayed moreover, tokens of a strong will of her own, Mr. Guppy conceived such an amount of respect for his "Ariel," that he proceeded to write her history, and completely filled the two volumes above alluded to, with accounts of her strange freaks, varied accomplishments, and demonstrations of preternatural power.

After the death ot his first wife, Mr. Guppy being introduced to Miss Nichol, found in that lady's Mediumship, a very striking counterpart of his invisible friend Mary Jane's performances. The interest thus excited, not only ended in Mr. Guppy's complete conversion to Spiritualism, but also in the transformation of Miss Nichol into the wife of the wealthy scientist, in which position, as a *non-professional Medium*, Mrs. Guppy was enabled to exert a widespread influence both in England and many of the Continental cities.

As Mrs. Guppy's Mediumship is of that representative character which it is the aim of this work to depict, we avail ourselves of the accounts given of Mr. Guppy's *séances*, published by several authoritative witnesses.

The first whose testimony we cite, is the late eminent jurist, Serjeant Cox, who, in a paper read before the Psychological Society of Great Britain, relates in very minute detail, how he one day called at Mrs. Guppy's residence at Highbury, and solicited the favour of her company at a Spiritual circle, to be held that evening at his own residence. Serjeant

Cox candidly states, that he desired to take Mrs. Guppy unaware of his invitation, and the lady in her own simple and amiable way, immediately complied with the request preferred.

It was winter time, and the ground was covered with snow. Mrs. Guppy having arranged her dress, entered the hired cab which Serjeant Cox had brought, and drove with him some four miles to his residence. From the time of her arrival at his house, till the period of the *séance*, about five hours later, Serjeant Cox or the ladies of his family never for one moment lost sight of Mrs. Guppy, and yet within three minutes of the time that the circle had assembled, in a room which had been thoroughly searched, the one door locked, and the key deposited in Serjeant Cox's pocket, when the light was extinguished, heavy thuds were heard on the table, the lights were called for by signal, and the table was found to be covered with heaps of pure white snow. When this unwelcome freight of matter had been removed, the party re-formed, and the gas extinguished, more deposits were heard falling, fresh signals were made for lights, and the table was found literally piled up with lovely hothouse flowers, arranged with exquisite taste into divers fanciful groups.

The author on one occasion, in a locked room, too thoroughly searched to admit of the concealment of a single article however small, was presented, at her own request, with a live pigeon, which fluttered down upon her lap, almost as soon as asked for. The bird being released, and flowers asked for, when the signal was given for lights, an immense pyramid of flowers was found tastefully built up around a pot of tulips. The lights— at the request of the Spirits—being again put out, the flowers, including immense branches of ferns, were so completely hidden or removed from the room, that though the one door was locked, and the key in the pocket of one of the company, the strictest search failed to reveal a single leaf. All that was left was the pot of tulips, on which was found a paper with very small writing, presenting the tulips as a gift to the author, "from the Spirits."

One of the most curious narratives in connection with this lady's Mediumship, is given in the following account, which was published as the statement of a *séance*, in which a gentleman present was suddenly, mysteriously, and unconsciously transferred from the locked circle room of Mr. Guppy's house, to the locked and closed premises of a friend of his, two miles distant. Quite twenty reliable witnesses at the two ends of the line, signed their names to an attestation, one party declaring the gentleman was in their midst at nine o'clock p.m. in a locked room, the key of the only door being in the pocket of one of the company, and the other party witnessing that the same gentleman suddenly made his appearance, at nine o'clock also, in a yard, locked, shut up, and enclosed on every side against the possibility of entrance, except by the locked and barred gate ; also, that on that night, *when the rain was pouring*, and the streets were covered with mud, this transfer of a human being, through two miles of space, was made, without leaving one trace of dampness or mud upon his clothing.

The names of the twenty witnesses are those of well-known and respectable persons, but as the gentleman himself would not allow his name to be published in connection with the circumstance, we simply allude to it, without ranging it in the category of the narratives given in this volume ; indeed we only reprint thus much of the details because the account which was sent to several London papers for publication, was prefaced by a concise summary of a similar event occurring in the experience of Mrs. Guppy, of which the most exaggerated accounts have been put in circulation.

The following brief statement has been pronounced to be so reliable and accurate by all parties concerned, that we deem it in order to republish it. It must be understood, that it was printed in connection with the narrative of the gentleman before alluded to, in the *New York Sun*, from which we give the following extract:—

"Before entering upon particulars, it is desirable to advert to a somewhat similar circumstance that took place on June 3rd, 1871, upon which occasion Mrs. Guppy, the famous medium, was conveyed instantaneously from her breakfast parlour at Highbury (where she was engaged making up her housekeeping accounts) to a locked room at 61, Lamb's Conduit Street, where she was suddenly found in a state of trance or unconsciousness, upon a table around which ten persons were sitting for the investigation of alleged spiritual phenomena, in the presence of Messrs. Herne and Williams, the widely known professional mediums. A minute and circumstantial report of this event appeared in the current spiritual journals, as well as in several newspapers, attesting, not only her unexpected arrival, but also the fact, amongst many others, that she held in her hand her housekeeping book and pen with the ink still liquid—such report being signed by all present at the *séance* in question—viz., N. Hagger, 46, Moorgate Street; Caroline Edmiston, Beckenham; C. E. Edwards, Kilburn Square, Kilburn; Henry Morris, Mount Trafford Eccles, near Manchester; Elizabeth Guppy, 1, Morland Villas, Highbury Hill Park, N.; Ernest Edwards, Kilburn Square, Kilburn; Henry Clifford Smith, 38, Ennis Road, Stroud Green; H. B. Husk, 26, Sandwich Street, W.C.; Charles E. Williams, 61, Lamb's Conduit Street; W.C.; F. Herne, 61, Lamb's Conduit Street, W.C.; W. H. Harrison, Wilmin Villa, Chaucer Road, S.E. Three members of this party (as a deputation), to fully test the circumstance and to prevent collusion, escorted Mrs. Guppy home, and took the testimony of Mr. Guppy and Miss Neyland to the fact of Mrs. Guppy's presence in her home at Highbury, immediately preceding her appearance at Lamb's Conduit Street."

In this case it must be borne in mind that Mr. Guppy—a gentleman of unquestionable probity—his housekeeper, and Mrs. Guppy's maid, testified to her presence in her house at Highbury about half-past eight in the evening, and at or about the same time, ten persons sitting in a third floor room, locked and bolted, in Lamb's Conduit Street, a distance of at least four miles, holding a dark circle, with the window closed, the one door locked, and the key in the pocket of one of the sitters, hearing a sudden noise on the table—struck a light, and found Mrs. Guppy in a state of partial consciousness, arrayed in a loose morning gown, housekeeping book in hand, sitting in their midst, on the table.

Let it be noted also, that the whole of the witnesses were credible, respectable persons, and though their testimony was received with the fool's argument of ridicule, and bald denial, it was of a reliable character, and from persons whose witness thus given, would have been received in any court of judicature as undeniable.

The next and last account we can give of Mrs. Guppy's Mediumship is one published by Miss Houghton in her "Record of Spirit Séances," and confirms numbers of other and similar statements made by Professors Wallace, Varley, Serjeant Cox, the late King Victor Emanuel of Italy, General Garibaldi, Prince George of Solms, Mr. R. D. Owen, and numerous other notables for whom Mrs. Guppy often sat, and who have freely testified to manifestations occurring in their presence of exactly the same character as the following extract from Miss Houghton's book:—

"In October, 1868, a *séance* was held, at which eighteen persons were present, Miss Nichol being the chief medium. Each of the sitters wished for fruit, the wish being in every instance granted. The following were brought and dropped on the table around which the company sat: A banana, two oranges, a bunch of white grapes, a bunch of black grapes, a cluster of filberts, three walnuts, a dozen damsons, a slice of candied pine apple, three figs, two apples, some almonds, dates, pears, a pomegranate, two greengages, a pile of currants, a lemon, a bunch of raisins, which, as well as the figs and dates, were quite plump, as if they had never been packed, but brought direct from the drying ground. While the wishing was in progress a lady said, ' Why does not some one wish for vegetables, such as a potato or an onion?' and even while she was speaking a potato and an onion fell into her lap."

In recalling the phenomenal personages who between the years 1860 and 1880 have contributed most liberally to the diffusion of Spiritual light and knowledge, it would be ungenerous to omit a notice of Mr. David Duguid, of Glasgow, a young man occupying the humble position of an industrious mechanic, and one whose limited means of education entirely precluded the expectation of an exhibition of his powers in the direction of the fine arts. The following account however, furnished to the London *Spiritual Magazine* by Mr. Benjamin Coleman, one of the most persevering as well as disinterested observers of Spiritual phenomena, will give a fair illustration of the modes by which Spirit influence can evolve latent faculties and cultivate unknown germs of talent, even from the most unpromising sources.

In the *Spiritual Magazine* of June, 1866, Mr. Coleman writes :—

"There are several other mediums in Glasgow, one among them, Mr. David Duguid, a working cabinet-maker, is likely to be distinguished as a drawing medium. One very remarkable and interesting fact connected with this young man it is my purpose to relate, which I do upon the authority of Mr. H. Nisbet and Mr. James Nicholson, with whom I had the pleasure of becoming acquainted whilst in Glasgow.

"After David had been recognised as a medium for the ordinary manifestations, he developed as a drawing medium, but made little progress at first without the aid of a young lady who formed one of the circle. When she placed her hand on the back of his, it would move with great facility, and at this stage his *left hand only* was used.

"At the third sitting David became entranced with his eyes shut before commencing to draw. At each succeeding *séance* his powers increased as the trance condition became more intense, and his eyes more firmly closed.

"The objects usually drawn at first were human heads and flowers; but, when a certain proficiency was obtained, flowers, fruits, and a rough landscape were done in colours, the pencils and brushes being now taken in his right hand.

"At the fifth sitting, a remarkable painting in water-colours was commenced and finished, representing the entrance to an arcade, the archway being surmounted by the figure of Justice, standing upon a globe, around which a serpent is coiled, with the figures on either side of Hope and Charity. These figures are very masterly in conception. The interior of the arcade is panelled with niches, in which figures and vases of flowers are placed. The floor is carpeted, and at the extreme end there is a rotunda, in the centre of which a cross is placed. The picture is a transparency, and, when held up to the light the cross dissolves into a throne, upon which a figure is seated with a halo of glory surrounding the head, supported by twelve figures, six on each side. *Those present were anxious to know the name of the artist, but he declined for the present to satisfy them, giving as a reason that he would ultimately give them the means of establishing his identity.* Subsequently, they were told that he was an artist of celebrity, who had lived in the seventeenth century; that he was born in 1635, and died in 1681; and that he was contemporary with Steen, the celebrated Dutch painter; that he had not been accustomed to paint figures, but that his delight had been to represent Nature, and that he would attempt at their next sitting a sketch of one of his paintings—his masterpiece.

"Accordingly, on the evening of the 18th of April the promised sketch was pencilled out, and on the 21st it was finished in water-colours, in the short period of four hours, and in the left hand corner the initials "J. R." were placed. This painting is considered a very able production.

"Up to this time, none of the party had the least idea of the name of the spirit-artist, and their curiosity was unsatisfied until Mr. Logan brought an artist friend to see the picture, who was much struck with it, and said he was sure he had seen the painting somewhere, though he could not at the moment name the painter.

"A day or two after, Mr. Logan's friend informed him that he had made the desired discovery, and showed Mr. Logan a volume of Cassell's *Art Treasures' Exhibition*, where, at page 301, there is an engraving, nearly *fac simile* of the spirit drawing, from a painting of 'The Waterfalls,' by Jacob Ruysdael, acknowledged to be his *chef d'œuvre.*

"This circumstance was communicated to the persons forming the circle ; but they determined to keep the medium in ignorance of the fact, being satisfied that in his normal condition he knew nothing of it.

"At the next sitting, on the 28th April, David became deeply entranced, and after the usual short conversation between him and the spirit-artist, the latter spoke through the medium, and informed the company that he was aware of the discovery they had made 'that his name was Ruysdael.' They then placed before the medium Cassell's volume, which also contains a portrait of the painter, and invited the spirit's inspection of it. The spirit remarked that the engraving of the picture was a good copy, and the likeness tolerable when at the age of thirty. They then pointed the spirit's attention to the absence of figures in the new drawing which were in the original. The spirit replied, 'That the figures in his paintings were not by himself, but were put in by an artist friend !' which, upon reference to a biography of Ruysdael, they found to be correct.

"It remains to be stated that Mr. David Duguid, the medium, has no knowledge whatever of drawing, and that he is, as I have already said, a plain working man ; that the drawing was executed in the presence of several persons, including those I have named, in four hours, whilst the medium's eyes were fast closed ; and, further to satisfy the scepticism of some of those present, there was a bandage put over them during part of the time. The medium declares that he had no knowledge of the existence of Ruysdael's picture, nor that such an artist had ever lived, and there is no reason to doubt his asseverations."

For the satisfaction of those who deem that the impelling motive with humanity in general, and Spirit Mediums in particular, is "the greed of gain," and the desire "to make capital" out of the world's interest in Spiritual phenomena, we must here state, that David Duguid, although pursuing steadily the cultivation of his mediumship for many years—up to the time indeed of this present writing—has never done so professionally, but still lives by his mechanical labours, following out his simple unosten tatious career, producing in the brief leisure hours he can afford to give to his mediumship, hundreds of paintings, drawings, and sketches, some of rare merit and others more indifferently executed, but all without the slightest attempt to convert his extraordinary gift to the same means of compensation, which would be freely accorded to any other form of artistic production.

We shall conclude this brief notice of our excellent and self-sacrificing Medium's career, with the following short excerpt, the nature of which speaks for itself. It is taken from *The North British Daily Mail* (Glasgow) of March, 1870, and reads thus :—

"So much has been said and done lately regarding 'the exposure of Spiritualism,' that a few notes may be of interest as to what the writer witnessed the other night at a private *séance* given by Mr. David Duguid. This gentleman was comparatively unknown until publicly challenged by Mr. Bishop during his recent 'exposure of Spiritualism.' Mr. Duguid has never courted publicity, but at the same time he has always been very willing to give every information regarding his manifestations. The *séance* took place in his parlour, and was attended by ten gentlemen, five of whom were rank heretics regarding all Spiritualistic phenomena. Immediately on Mr. Duguid taking his seat at a small table he went into a trance condition, his eyes closing and a smile playing on his countenance. A piece of cardboard, about six inches by nine inches, which had been previously examined by the company, was then handed to him. After breathing on it Mr. Duguid made a rough pencil sketch, and then picking up his palette and brushes commenced to paint a landscape with his eyes firmly sealed. To make assurance doubly sure, a handkerchief was firmly bound across his eyes, but he did not appear to be the least inconvenienced by this arrangement, and painted away quite briskly, first rubbing in the sky, and then the faint outline of the distant mountains ; and finally boldly dashing in the foreground with a few vigorous strokes. At the suggestion of a gentleman present the light was put out, but this made no difference, the action of the brushes being quite audible in the darkness. After the expiry of half an hour the sketch was complete, and was a most remarkable picture to be produced under such peculiar conditions. What in

Spiritualistic circles is called a 'direct drawing' was then attempted. A common card, coated with iodine, was placed on the table before Mr. Duguid, whose hands and feet were firmly secured with silk handkerchiefs. The gas was turned off, and the company, joining hands, sang the 100th Psalm. After the lapse of about five minutes a rap was heard on the table, and on the gas being lit Mr. Duguid was found sitting as firmly bound as before, and on turning up the card on the table, a nice little miniature landscape was observed, the colours being quite wet and newly painted. Without attempting to give an opinion or explain how such manifestations could be accomplished, we simply narrate the circumstances of the *séance* as they occurred."

Besides the remarkably-endowed Mediums above mentioned, a large number of ladies and gentlemen moving in various distinguished circles of Great Britain have manifested extraordinary spiritual gifts and exercised them freely, in a non-professional way, for the benefit of their friends and acquaintances. Medium power indeed has been exhibited in every class of society throughout the United Kingdom, and for some years it would have been impossible to visit any town or hamlet, without discovering way-marks of Spiritual power in the form of healings, trance speaking, Spirit drawing, writing, seership, or physical force manifestations.

Besides the large number of private Mediums, of whose gifts we are not privileged to speak, except in these general terms, there are a great many excellent and disinterested labourers in the Spiritual vineyard, who *give* their services to the public in the capacity of clairvoyants, and trance speakers. Very few of these persons will receive compensation for their services, and many of them—especially in the North of England—voluntarily travel from place to place each Sabbath day, incurring a vast amount of fatigue and freely bestowing time and service, for the purpose of disseminating the glad tidings of Spiritualism, to all who will come to hear them. Throughout the large and thickly-populated districts of Yorkshire, Lancashire, Durham, and Northumberland, scores of these self-sacrificing missionaries may be found. Many of them are miners, pit men, weavers and factory hands, who, notwithstanding the unceasing toils of the week, cheerfully devote themselves to the duties of the Spiritual rostrum on the Sunday; and though they are simply "children of the people," and wholly untrained to such work, their rude natural eloquence, heightened by the afflatus of the spirit intelligences that speak through their lips, produces a much deeper influence upon audiences of their own class, than the metaphysical arguments of more polished speakers could do. The very fact too, that wholly uneducated men and women can give correct diagnoses of disease, make cures that the medical faculty could never succeed in, and pour forth moving strains of exalted eloquence, far in advance of their normal capacity, clearly proves the control of some outside power, and brings conviction to many minds, that could not be reached by all the subtle logic of well-trained orators.

We are not pleading in this category either for the expediency of non-professional Mediumship, or advising the exercise of inspirational powers upon the public rostrum, which are liable to be marred in transmission through illiterate channels, but in reporting the status of Spiritualism as it really exists, we should omit one of the most important factors in Spiritual progress amongst the rank and file of society, if we failed to render justice to the self-devoted labourers who throughout England, but especially in the North, have for years rendered invaluable services as healers and speakers, with few to thank, and none to compensate them, save the consciousness of the good they have performed, and the approbation of the angels whose servants they are. If any readers are curious to learn who these self-sacrificing individuals are, let them turn to the plan of speakers for the Yorkshire districts as advertised in the *Medium and Daybreak*, the reports from the Lancashire, Durham, and Northumberland towns and mining districts, together with a few reports from the South and West, and they will there find a list of humble names recorded, whose place will surely be found, in the day when the MASTER OF LIFE "numbers up his jewels."

Before quitting the subject of non-professional Mediumship in England, we must call attention to the inestimable services rendered in higher and more influential grades of society than those above named—in fact, amongst the most distinguished and aristocratic circles of the metropolis—by Mrs. Everitt, a lady of independent position now residing at Hendon, formerly of Islington, London. Mrs. Everitt's Mediumship has been distinguished by the variety and intellectual character, no less than the force of the manifestations given in her presence. Besides loud rappings and the movement of heavy bodies which have been brought through closed doors and carried hither and thither in broad light, often *without human contact*, Mrs. Everitt is a remarkable Medium for the production of the direct Spirit voice, and writings executed in the most minute form of caligraphy, in an almost incredibly short period of time. The illustration (given on another page) of these spirit writings, purported to come from Dr. Burns, a clergyman of London, and one eminent alike for his noble character, his eloquence as a preacher, and the fearless candour with which he avowed his belief in Spirit communion. Dr. Burns granted the use of his Church to Dr. Newton for the purpose of practising therein his marvellous gift of healing. He attended several of Mrs. Everitt's circles ; publicly expressed his entire belief in their supra-mundane character, and after passing into spirit life, returned to those circles, to add his testimony as a spirit, to that which he had borne on earth as a mortal. The writing, of which a facsimile is given, was produced *in nine seconds* upon a piece of marked paper—in the presence of some ten witnesses—honoured guests of Mr. and Mrs. Everitt.

Mr. Everitt has in his possession hundreds of similar writings—most of them produced under the most crucial test conditions. The writing here exemplified was produced by the Spirit of one well known to the parties present, and is of a thoroughly characteristic style.

Sometimes the house in which the *séances* were in session has been shaken as in an earthquake. On other occasions the circle room has been filled with delicious perfumes or strong currents of air.

The intelligence rendered by the direct writings, no less than the Spirit voices conversing with the company, is for the most part of a religious or moral character. The writings have not unfrequently been given in Greek, Latin, and Oriental languages, all of which are totally unknown to Mrs. Everitt. As an example of the preternatural mode in which these writings are produced, the following incident may be narrated. At a *séance* held in a semi-darkened drawing-room, with closed doors, and a company of some twenty persons assembled, a very large and splendidly illustrated book with paper covers, suddenly fluttered down from the ceiling and dropped in view of all present on the table in their midst.

The book had been kept for many previous months in a locked drawer, in a room above that wherein it now appeared, and no human being at that time, *could* have had access to the place from which it was taken.

This book was passed round amongst the company, of whom the author was one, and the illustrations being very fine, it was examined with so much

My dear very dear friends it gives me exceeding pleasure and great happiness to meet you here this evening You are advocates of truth so am I and always have been I earnestly sought for this one great truth and was willing to pay toil for the truth must be bought and is never gained except at a sacrifice I have now proved that great truth and here I am able to come again with those beloved friends who still live on the earth sphere do not think you friends who have slipped over are free from you we are no we feel by an means to you believe you here now the condition we are in a clever enter with as the only real bond of union that in spiritual union that is possible for man to hold consumer with the deported is the one great truth I have refused to meet I have found it I wish show it when you have turned it like me only enough to prove what you believe to be true it met not only higher great self denial to possess it but goal courage to profess it The kingdom of heaven is a slowly kingdom that spiritual kingdom which country and you try as the clear on the light of heaven whose silent movement breaking upon the world dispersing the darkness of the night it comes with such goodness that it does not disturb the sleeping If the infant be light expressly spiritual light must have this darkness loudness and gentleness to come forward a hither to this great truth

Your husband and fellow laborer

L Brown

attention by all parties present, that not a leaf could have escaped observation. Whilst the visitors were commenting on the astonishing though by no means unprecedented manner in which this manifestation had occurred, the Spirits spelled out by rappings the request that the lights should be put out. This was promptly done, but in less than twenty seconds another well-known signal was given for the restoration of the lights. Deeming that some preliminary had been forgotten which the Spirits wished attended to, the chandelier was hurriedly relighted, when it was found that the margins of two leaves, at the place where the book was lying open, were covered with very fine pencilled writing. On further examination, it appeared that over twenty of the leaves were similarly marked, thus making in all, nearly three hundred words inscribed upon paper, that, sixteen seconds previously, had been proved to be entirely blank.

It must be added, that although Mr. and Mrs. Everitt's position in the social scale placed them on an equality with all their guests, this excellent lady has ever cheerfully submitted to the most *exigéant* demand for tests, and furnished opportunities for thorough and searching investigation as gracefully, as if she had been a professional medium, or had not been in her own estimable character beyond all possibility of doubt or suspicion. For many years she devoted her varied gifts to the service of her friends, and such guests as could obtain an introduction to her delightful *séances.* Here the noble, the scientific, and the learned, no less than the plain, untitled citizen, were freely welcomed, and ever hospitably entertained by the master and mistress of the mansion, and the author is in a position to affirm, that *thousands* of persons in this generation, owe their assurances of immortality, and their happiest hours of pure communion with blessed ascended ones, to the inimitable gifts of Mrs. Everitt, and the genial hospitality of her noble husband.

Mrs. Everitt was also a seeress, and could readily receive impressions by mental telegraphy, from her friends.

The author has often exchanged messages with this lady, when separated by miles of distance, such messages being invariably found subsequently to be correct. In Mr. Everitt, the cause of Spiritualism has found an equally indefatigable and able champion, Mr. Everitt's eloquent expositions of Spiritualism upon every available opportunity having attracted large audiences, and respectful consideration, whenever presented.

If we speak somewhat in the past tense of Mr. and Mrs. Everitt, it is not because their devotion to the cause of Spiritualism has waned, or the lady's Spiritual gifts have failed, but in the retirement of the family from the busy metropolis to the seclusion of a suburban residence, the opportunities for the exercise of Mediumship to all comers, have necessarily become very infrequent, and it is now only in the family circle and its immediate visitors, that Mrs. Everitt's charming phases of mediumship can be witnessed.

We shall now direct the reader's attention to another wonderful display of Sibylline power manifested in the family of Mr. Bertolacci, a gentleman too well known and esteemed by his wide circle of friends, to incur the slightest shadow of suspicion, either in respect to the disinterestedness of his motives, or the truth of his statements. As Mr. Bertolacci was very free in placing the Mediumistic power of his family at the service of numerous credible witnesses, his testimony is susceptible of full verification in every particular.

After eleven years of astounding and continuous demonstrations of Spirit power, Mr. Bertolacci — at the instance of his friends and numerous interested witnesses,—consented to embody his experiences in a small volume, which—in deference to his devoted adherence to the tenets of the Christian religion, or, it may be assumed, as a line of demarcation between himself and less orthodox believers in Spirit communion—he entitled as follows :—*Christian Spiritualism : Wherein is shewn the Extension of the Human Faculties by the Application of Modern Spiritual Phenomena, according to the Doctrine of Christ.* By William Robert Bertolacci.— Published by Emily Faithfull.

The following extracts are taken from a fine analytical review of Mr. Bertolacci's work by Mr. Thomas Shorter, the learned author of "The Two Worlds," editor of the London *Spiritual Magazine*, &c., &c. Mr. Shorter introduces his subject in these words :—

"The experiences of M. Bertolacci extend over a period of eleven years, and this little volume must be regarded as only a synopsis or sample rather than a complete and elaborate history of them. Previously thereto, M. Bertolacci was, he informs us, a 'complete disbeliever in all miracles,' and he adopted the popular talk of 'laws of nature,' 'priestcraft,' and 'weak-minded credulity,' as all-sufficient to explain them. Under the influence of these derided manifestations this unhappy attribute and tone of mind has become changed to one of earnest and devout Christian assurance, as this book sufficiently evinces. But to come to the facts. M. Bertolacci says :—

"'We have produced most of the manifestations witnessed in other circles, such as table-turnings, and tiltings, raps and many sorts of sounds in different parts of the house. Tables and other objects have been raised from the ground without contact ; and have, when in the air, resisted the efforts of a strong man to force them down again. Tables have been made to adhere so fixedly to the ground as to resist every endeavour to raise them ; and in more than one instance, when five or six persons have combined their whole strength, the wooden top, fixed on with strong screws, has been wrenched completely off, while the light framework and legs have remained adhering to the ground ; whereas these, immediately after, have risen quietly up into the air without being touched on being told to do so. Clocks have passed the hour without striking it on being told not to do so.

"'In one circumstance, we obtained direct writing by placing a clean sheet of paper in a drawer overnight, the drawer and room being locked and secured, so that no one could obtain access to them. The next morning, was found written on the paper, as had been foretold through the planchette, "*Christ soit avec vous*," "Christ be with you.'"

"The raps on the table being too slow a process for communicating information, the use of the planchette had been indicated.

"By means of the planchette the author has thus obtained some 1,200 or 1,400 pages of manuscript in English and French, including a work of 500 or 600 pages, explanatory of phenomena of which these writings form a part.

"The *séances* have not been confined to physical manifestations, such as have been already named, nor has the attendance at them been limited to M. Bertolacci and his family ; intimate friends were at first admitted, and these introduced others, and the attendance so increased that after a short time it became requisite to appoint reception days, and on these occasions to hold both morning and evening meetings. These witnesses are, therefore, additional evidence to the facts certified by M. Bertolacci.

"The proceedings of the *séances* were regulated by the planchette writing ; and we learn that—

"'If among those present any one was ailing, or in a state of ill-health, they were generally singled out, and desired to come to the table. When there, they would often be told what their sufferings were, how long they had been ill, &c., although no previous mention had been made of the subject, and while under the surprise which these unexpected communications generally created, they would be told that if they had faith in Christ they should be cured, which was, in several instances, realized immediately.

"'At other times, the *séance* would begin by first one person and then another being selected among the company, and each in their turn being conversed with by means of the planchette-writing. Then, to the astonishment of many present, persons appearing amongst us for the first time would be called by their Christian names, and others by their familiar nicknames, telling them their peculiarities of disposition, their favourite pursuits, and their thoughts at the very moment. It has constantly occurred that at the very time this was going on, the table on which the planchette was writing would be seen to rise into the air, all its four legs being a foot or more from the ground.' . . .

MRS EVERETT.

"Contagious maladies, and even the action of poison, have been arrested, and organic disease successfully treated. The following is an instance :—

"'At one of our receptions, a Madame G——a, of Pontoise, was, by appointment, introduced by mutual friends. The assembly was very numerous—some twenty persons being present. Madame G——a had, for eleven months previous, lost the use of her legs from a paralysis which extended from her waist downwards, resulting from a premature confinement. It was with difficulty she could move about on crutches upon very even ground, and she had to be carried from the carriage which had conveyed her from the railway station to our reception room on the first floor, in the arms of her friends.

"'The *séance* was a very animated one. Many wonderful things occurred ; the planchette had written at once under the hands of persons who had never witnessed anything of the sort before, &c., &c. Madame G——a was then selected, and during fifteen or twenty minutes, she had it all to herself, much in the same way as it occurred with Mrs. K——d previously to her being cured. Many tears were shed by Madame G——a, who was deeply affected by the words of kind and gentle sympathy and of encouraging hope addressed to her by the sublimely inspired phrases written under the planchette. While this was going on, the rest of the company were conversing quietly among themselves in undertones. Then, all present being desired to give their whole attention, we were exhorted to join our hearts in an act of inward and fervent communion, and implore God to show His mercy upon our suffering sister. During the total silence which ensued, a short and impressive prayer was rapidly written under the planchette, which was read aloud, then the Spirit through the planchette, addressing Madame G——a, wrote, "*Do you believe in Christ's invariable goodness and power ?*" to which she answered, "*Yes, truly I do.*" While she was answering, the planchette was writing, "*Then stand upright !*" As though recollecting her weakness, for a moment she seemed to look round for assistance, and at the same instant the words, "*Alone in Jesus Christ's name !*" were written with such rapidity, that they seemed as if they had been struck off upon the paper ; and they had not time to be read, when Madame G——a sprang on her feet, and she was no longer a paralytic. She was then told to walk up and down the room, which feat she accomplished with unhesitating firmness and perfect ease, and was after that sent downstairs to walk, accompanied, but unassisted, by my wife, for five minutes round the garden, where she was all the time in full view of the company assembled on the balcony and clustered round the windows ; and having come up again, she expressed her gratitude towards God for the mercy she had received, amidst the congratulations of all parties, who by that time had begun to be sufficiently recovered from their first surprise to reflect upon and appreciate the miracle which had been performed. We resumed our places. A thanksgiving to God was written through the planchette, and an hour afterwards, Madame G——a's carriage having been previously discarded, she returned with the rest of the company, going on foot to the railway station, about a mile from our house, and was perfectly cured of her paralysis.'*

"Surgical cases were treated in like manner and with like results. M. Bertolacci says :—

"'When any of my girls cut themselves or met with any other accident, such as bruises, sprains, &c., not only is all pain immediately taken away, but indeed the healing is almost as rapid. One day, one of them, in cutting a loaf of bread, gave herself a deep gash across the left hand, an inch long. The blood was flowing very copiously and had quite wetted a towel, which she had wrapped round it, through and through many folds, by the time she came to me, though she lost no time, however, in so doing. The towel was taken off, and I held the lips of the wound together, while those present joined us, during eight or ten seconds, in communion, the name of Jesus Christ having been invoked. The blood ceased to flow, and the wound was closed. Not more than four hours afterwards, some friends having come to pass the evening with us, she played several long pieces on the pianoforte, and had totally forgotten that she had cut herself in the day. Nevertheless, the wound was sufficiently severe to leave a scar still very plainly to be seen, although it is now somewhere about seven years since the accident occurred. On another occasion since that, one of her sisters cut the top of her thumb from one side to the other, down to the very bone, and was cured in the same manner, as completely and as instantaneously.

"'I have mentioned these two cases in particular to give my reader a notion of the efficacy of the cures ; but, indeed, it is almost of daily occurrence with us, either for one thing or the other—a cut, a bruise, and the blistering of an arm from the effects of a poisonous plant, having, the very day on which I write this narration, been cured, each in the space of eight seconds. A few days back, it was a hand and wrist which had been

---

* Compare this case with the analagous and equally remarkable one of Miss Fancourt, as given in Brevior's "Two Worlds,' pp. 230-235.

pretty smartly scalded with boiling water. Toothaches and caries are as effectually stopped, even to the destroying of the nerve, in order to obviate any recurrence of the pain from extraneous causes. On one occasion, when the request was made that the nerve should be destroyed, the most complete insensibility immediately succeeded; but we were told, that as the tooth was only slightly attacked, if it were stopped within a few days, in order to keep the air and moisture from it, it would be preserved; but that, if that were not done, in ten days it would begin to fall to pieces. It was *not* done, and on the tenth day, a large portion of the tooth fell off, and, in a very few days more, nothing but the bare root was left, which, however, was very easily extracted without occasioning the least pain.'

"There can be no mistake about cases like these, the facts are recent, and are published to the world; the witnesses are living, and well known as persons of credit and integrity. The faculty and the press may ignore or deny the facts; from their antecedents it may be expected that they will do so; but this, though it should affect their own credit, will not affect the facts, which are neither made nor destroyed by the opinions which may be formed about them.

"We omit, from want of space, the magnetic and clairvoyant phenomena related, but the spiritual education of his family, as M. Bertolacci relates it, is something so unique that notwithstanding our already copious extracts we quote it *in extenso.* After a chapter on 'Initiation,' he proceeds :—

"'With this foundation to work upon, and confiding in the revelations and spiritual guidance by which we had already attained the degree of spiritual strength shewn in the preceding narration, I boldly withdrew my two younger daughters from the school they daily attended; and in spite of the opposition and common-place arguments of other parties, began their new mode of education in the manner indicated by our invisible spiritual conductor, which was pursued much in the following order :—

"'Lessons were learnt by heart by reading to my students in their magnetic sleep, ordering them to retain in their memory when they awoke, all they had heard. Lessons were next learnt by heart by the pupils reading, themselves, once over, in their magnetic sleep, one or more pages of a book. When this began to become familiar, and the organs of memory showed that they were in a fit state of rapid obedience, the action of the organs of outward perception upon the memory was submitted to the strong developing power of the soul's direct influence, and lessons were learnt by the simple inspection of (or staring at) the open page of a book,—the students being in their normal waking state. In the beginning, the inspection, or staring, was made to last a certain number of seconds, and that number being gradually reduced, after a short space of time, the duration of a single second or a mere glimpse at the page was sufficient for the pupils to retain in their memory the whole contents of it.

"'In this manner and in the following, the daily lessons of my children, equal at times to a week's corresponding school tasks, were learnt in the space of a few seconds; lessons that take hours to interrogate them upon, with any degree of detail. Lessons are also learnt by a simple act of pious concentration from books closed or totally out of sight. In this case, we have usually named the page where the beginning of the lesson is to be found, for we have, as yet, had recourse to the process less as a matter of immediate utility than as a practice of the powers of distant clairvoyance. It will be easily conceived that by a slight extension of this faculty, or rather by the special direction being given to it, it may be applied to obtain references from, and even the perfect knowledge of, works one does not oneself possess, but which are known to exist in certain libraries and other places, rendered either by their distance, our own want of time or otherwise, inaccessible to us.

"'DICTATION.

"'Dictations were given by the teacher reading from a book in the ordinary manner; but without naming the stops or any of the other signs, these being seen by the students through their pre-acquired clairvoyant capacities, the phrases becoming visible to them as soon as they are dictated. The mental dictations.—In this case the pupils are made acquainted—*by the knowledge of their "inner man," and the perfected obedience of the organs of their "outer man,"*—with the contents of the page held open in a position visible alone to the eyes of the teacher—and as the latter desires to communicate a phrase to the pupils, they hear a voice dictating it aloud to them in the air, although no person is speaking at the time.

"'HISTORY.

"'The direct clairvoyance gives the student a correct sight, with regard to the historical persons and facts treated of in the lessons learnt by the inspection of books, either open, closed, or at a distance—as explained in the foregoing.

"'NATURAL HISTORY AND PHILOSOPHY.

"'THE SIGHT OF THE PLANTS, FLOWERS, MINERALS, ANIMALS, &c., described or mentioned in their books, as also such other useful details as may have been omitted by the author, or belong to a more minute study of the subject, is enjoyed in the same manner.

"'GEOGRAPHY AND ASTRONOMY.

"'GEOGRAPHICAL AND ASTRONOMICAL STUDIES FROM CHARTS OR GLOBES.—When a locality is named by the teacher, or is to be designated for any purpose in the course of study, the forefinger of the pupil is, *by inspiration*, instantaneously drawn to the exact spot of the map or globe where it is to be found. This action takes place before the reason of the students can have given them the slightest notion of the relative position or bearing of the place, the head following the movement of the hand, instead of directing it. THE STUDENTS ARE ALSO, BY THE FACILITY THEY ACQUIRE FOR RECEIVING INSPIRATIONS, SO PERFECTLY IDENTIFIED WITH EVERYTHING BELONGING TO THE PLACES SPOKEN OF IN THEIR STUDY OF GEOGRAPHY, THAT THEY FEEL AS THOUGH THEY WERE ON THE SPOT. So correct are the impressions made by the ubiquitous power of their souls on all the organs of the body in their temporarily perfected condition, that they appear to themselves to be, not where the lessons are going on, but in the very places therein referred to ; seeing, hearing, and feeling all that they are required or desirous to see, hear, or feel.'

"M. Bertolacci has written in a tone of moderation and a religious spirit ; and he disclaims all idea 'that there is any peculiarity in his nature or that of his children, by which they are exceptionally qualified for the attainment of the gifts they have received.'"*

Whilst no persons who have ever become acquainted with Mr. Bertolacci, or conversed with his witnesses—of whom hundreds are still living—are capable of questioning his veracity or impugning his statements, we know we are drawing heavily on the faith of those readers who are not personally cognizant of the overwhelming mass of testimony which surrounds the case and its narration.

Perhaps in future ages, the substance of what we are now so reticent in offering to the acceptance of modern readers may be deemed trivial or insignificant, in comparison with the soul growth to which humanity may have then attained—meantime, where does our duty lie ? Why, even in turning to the motto of this volume, and accepting practically as well as theoretically the charge to proclaim "THE TRUTH AGAINST THE WORLD."

CHAPTER XXII.

SPIRITUALISM IN GREAT BRITAIN (CONTINUED).

BESIDES the merely phenomenal phases of Spiritualism illustrated by the narratives given in the last few chapters, THE MESSAGE which relates to the conditions of life hereafter, and the religious element which grows out of Spiritual communion, has not been lacking in its full share of representation, in England, although there was a strong desire manifested on the part of some of those who stood in the position of "Leaders" in the ranks of English Spiritualism, to keep all questions of a religious and controversial nature in the background.

The author's experience has ever been in this, as in all other departments of human thought and interests, when connected with Spiritualism, that Spirits themselves are at the helm of the new movement, and with or without the sympathy of mortals, they will raise up instruments, and create

---

* This review may be found in full in the London *Spiritual Magazine* for October, 1865.

opportunities for the impartation of whatever ideas they may determine to communicate. Thus it was, that whilst certain believers in Spirit communion, who were still steadfast in their adhesion to the Christian Church, and its belongings, were constantly deprecating the attempt to incorporate religious ideas with Spiritualism, and protesting—often in no measured terms—against the "infidelities" of the American trance speakers, the Spirits on the other side of the Atlantic were opening up opportunities, and presenting impelling motives to those very speakers, to visit the mother country, and widen the borders of Spiritualism from its conservative position in private families, to the more diffusive arena of the public rostrum.

It has been quite a common practice amongst many European Spiritualists, to endeavour to narrow down the diffusion of Spiritualism to the private circle, or the perusal of such "well digested" literature, as was specially prepared to warn *preaching Spirits* off the sacred preserves of orthodoxy.

All would not do however. The stream whose sources are not on earth, has made its own channels, and swept away all barriers that intervened to check the course laid out for its flow, by higher wisdom than that of humanity.

It was under this special guidance, and in virtue of her commission from a well-tried band of Spiritual guides that the author—a Medium for many phases of Spirit communion, but chiefly recognised as a speaker under Spiritual influence, was impelled after many years' pilgrimage in the New World to return, with her venerable mother, to settle once more in her native city of London. Mrs. Hardinge* reached England in the fall of the year 1865, a period that may truly be called, the blossoming time of Spiritualism in Great Britain. Her intention was to retire from her long and toilsome career as a public speaker into the quiet of home and literary occupations, but her arrival had been already anticipated by generous notices in the London *Spiritual Magazine*, and immediately on landing, she found herself surrounded by hosts of warm sympathizers, who although strangers—in the ordinary sense of social relations—were still one in heart with the new comer, in the desire to promote the interests of a much loved cause. It was in this spirit that Mrs. Hardinge, soon after her arrival in London, found herself compelled to abandon her projected seclusion, and once more to enter upon the vortex of effort to promulgate the truths of Spiritualism, by means of rostrum addresses.

Early in the winter succeeding Mrs. Hardinge's arrival, a series of "winter soirées" were inaugurated, chiefly at the instance of Mr. Benjamin Coleman, Mr. William Wilkinson, Mr. Thomas Shorter, and other leaders of the Spiritual cause, interested in the promulgation of its philosophy.

The scene of these gatherings was the Beethoven Rooms, Harley Street, Cavendish Square, where a splendid suite of *salons*, capable of seating several hundred persons was engaged, and where the guests were admitted in evening costume, by subscription tickets, or introductions permitted by the Committee.

The company included many persons of the highest rank or eminence in literature and science, and at these gatherings Mrs. Hardinge gave weekly addresses in her capacity as an inspirational speaker during a period of many months.

The subjects of the lectures were most generally selected by the audience, and questions on all manner of abstruse, scientific, and metaphysical points, were answered at the close of the addresses.

---

* Now Mrs. Hardinge Britten.

The proceedings were received with tokens of the highest interest, and at the close of each series announced, Mrs. Hardinge was induced to renew her lectures, at the earnest solicitation of the friends of the movement.

How gladly the chief promoters of these meetings welcomed the opportunity of extending phenomenal Spiritualism into the realms of philosophy and mental science, may be gathered from the glowing accounts that were published from time to time in the London *Spiritual Magazine,* especially the numbers for 1865-6. However gratifying these eulogiums might have been to the speaker, they can find no place here, and are only alluded to in order to mark the deep interest which inspirational addresses awaken, even in the minds of those least disposed to sympathize with the speaker's views, and to show how the cause progressed from phenomenal to intellectual phases of the movement.

During her long and arduous career as a speaker in America, Mrs. Hardinge, having taken special interest in tendering the consoling doctrines of Spiritualism to the masses, was unwilling to narrow down her ministry to the exclusive and aristocratic listeners of the Harley Street soirées. She therefore proposed to her friends, that public meetings of a more general character should be inaugurated, the first to consist of three lectures on "America," to be given in St. James's Hall, the next to enter at once and publicly on the subject of Spiritualism in a course of Sunday evening addresses of the same character as those given at the winter soirées, to which all classes of the public should be admitted. To both these propositions Mrs. Hardinge's Spiritualistic friends lent their willing and generous aid.

The secular lectures were at once undertaken, and called forth even from the London *Times* wonderfully complimentary notices of the lady lecturer and her pretensions ; in fact, as these addresses were totally unconnected with the obnoxious, and all too popular Spiritual *bête noir* of the age, they were received with the most laudatory notices from the press in general ; so enthusiastic indeed was the tone of commendation adopted by the leading journals of the metropolis, that Mr. Benjamin Coleman, a *Machiavelli* of strategy, as well as an indomitable general of strategical forces, collected these reports from the various papers, and published them in pamphlet form for general distribution.

As the very next appearance of Mrs. Emma Hardinge's name in the public journals was an announcement of her Sunday evening *Spiritual* lectures, Mr. Coleman was generally thought to have stolen a march on the secular press, which might have induced them to regret that they had contributed so large a share of advertising to " the Spiritualists' new Pythia," as one of the repentant journals now designated the lady, who but a short time ago had been the subject of unqualified laudation.

Not any longer from the columns of the secular press, but in the London *Spiritual Magazine* came the announcement of the next move on the Spiritual chessboard, which was to the effect that the Sunday evening lectures were attracting such immense and enthusiastic audiences, that they would be continued for an indefinite period, or at least, as long as the speaker could remain in the country to give them.

About this time a valuable impulse was communicated to the Spiritual movement by the publication of a new paper called *The Medium and Day-break*—started by Mr. James Burns, now so well known in connection with this and other periodicals, as well as being the founder of the Spiritual Institution, Southampton Row, Bloomsbury. The assistance which an editor of ability and a devoted Spiritualist like Mr. Burns was able to render, in publishing and distributing Mrs. Hardinge's lectures, can scarcely be estimated.   The secular journals had obviously entered into a conspiracy of silence in regard to meetings which were attracting immense and over-flowing audiences every Sunday.

In this juncture Mr. Burns—of whom we shall have more to say here-after—devoted himself heart and soul to the work of publishing the addresses, which were issued, some in the columns of *The Medium*, others in tract and pamphlet form, whilst the Harley Street lectures were collected into small volumes, and distributed broadcast by hundreds, and on special subjects by thousands.   By the indomitable energy of Mr. Burns, the press found themselves defeated by their own weapons, and from the time when this spirited publisher commenced in earnest his work of literary propagandism, the movement acquired a diffusive popularity which made a deep mark upon public opinion both in the metropolis and in the provinces.

Hitherto, circumstances had not favoured the dissemination of Spiritual teachings through the platform.

English Spiritualists had been honoured with a visit from the celebrated American inspirational speaker and poet, the Rev. T. L. Harris, known in the Spiritual ranks as "The Medium," through whom was communicated the charming poems entitled, "A Lyric of the Morning Land," and "An Epic of the Starry Heavens."

Unfortunately, Mr. Harris's visit failed to promote any interchange of kindly sentiment between the American and English Spiritualists, the former having incurred Mr. Harris's wrath for refusing to install him into the position of a settled ministry.   The results of this disappointment he ex-pressed in his English addresses, wherein his former associates and fellow labourers were so roundly abused, that it was evident to his grieved listeners that the ex-reverend gentleman was afflicted with a very *unspiritual* form of Spiritualism; hence his ministrations served rather to retard than advance the cause in England.   Mr. B. P. Randolph, another American Spiritual lecturer, had also essayed the platform, but failed to reconcile his hearers to his marked eccentricities.   A far more satisfactory expositor of the Spiritual doctrines had been found in the Rev. J. M. Peebles, formerly an American clergyman, but then a speaker on Spiritualism, whose eloquence created a deep impression on audiences gathered to hear him, on both sides of the Atlantic.   At the time of Mr. Peebles' first visit, however, there was no available organization to give effect to his public efforts, hence, however valuable, they were not appreciated as they should have been.   On several subsequent occasions Mr. Peebles' platform addresses were listened to with deep interest, and his visits to England welcomed with tokens of high appreciation.   Time and circumstances combined to favour the effect of Mrs. Hardinge's advent in London, hence the results of her inaugural meetings were most influential in opening up opportunities for platform work in other directions.

Although Mrs. Hardinge could never reconcile herself to a permanent residence in England, and for the last fifteen years has only revisited the country for limited periods of time, the kind greetings and cordial farewells—often accompanied by substantial tokens of interest—which these flying visits called forth, served to create pleasant "revivalisms," which heightened the effect and popularity of her labours.

One of the most talented of the lecturers that succeeded Mrs. Hardinge during her absence in the United States was Mrs. Cora Tappan, a lady whose high reputation as an able and eloquent expositor of the Spiritual philosophy, stands unrivalled on both sides of the Atlantic.

Mrs. Tappan's lectures were not only pronounced to be miracles of eloquence by the *élite* of the London Spiritualists, but by her efficient missionary labours in the provinces, she succeeded in awakening a widespread interest in Spiritualism throughout the country.

We have already alluded to the remarkable test facts of Spirit presence, afforded by the visit of Mr. Charles Foster, an American medium renowned for exhibiting names of deceased persons, and test facts of Spirit presence, by writings in raised letters, on the arm.   Besides this remarkable personage, England was visited by Messrs. Redman, J. B. Conklin, and Colchester, all powerful physical test mediums.

The fact that they were professional mediums and demanded liberal fees for their services, was of course a subject of reproach, which the opposition could not afford to pass by unheeded.   Not that the English people are grudging in their dealings, whether in trade, commerce, or art ; but, as we have already noted, the orthodox method of regarding Spiritual gifts as "Divine endowments," which must not be desecrated by association with "filthy lucre," threw an absurd and superstitious glamour over the subject, which exempted it from the ordinary methods of justice and common sense. When this unreasonable spirit was met on its own ground, and mediums, visiting the country from foreign lands, refused to take compensation for their services, rich presents were often pressed upon them in greater prodigality than their services could have commanded as payment, but when set fees were required, the whole community was aroused to the iniquity of making *God-like gifts* the subject of traffic, &c., &c.

We shall devote the remainder of this chapter to a brief notice of another Transatlantic visitor whose reputation for the beneficent use he made of his marvellous powers of healing by touch, had long preceded him ; we speak of Dr. J. R. Newton of Rhode Island, U.S., who arrived in this country for a second visit during the month of May, 1870.

Stimulated by the reports of his many wonderful cures, the leading Spiritualists of London met together at the "Beethoven Rooms," Harley Street, on Thursday, May 12th, to tender to Dr. Newton a cordial welcome in the form of a public reception.

The meeting was not only a representative one, the Spiritualists of eminence from the provinces as well as from the metropolis flocking in from all parts of the country, but those who attended were prompt to bear testimony to the excellent services of their distinguished guest, by relating several incidents in connection with his powers as a healer, the recital of which must serve in this place, as a sample of the good work performed by Dr. Newton during his brief residence in England.

In the course of their several addresses, Messrs. Coleman, Tebb, Shorter, the Rev. J. M. Peebles—who happened to be in England at the time— and Mr. S. C. Hall, gave pointed and interesting delineations of the real status of English Spiritualism at the period in question, and the unpremeditated testimony borne by these gentlemen at a time when their utterances were not given for effect on the outside world, may be received as of more value than any elaborately prepared statements.

Mr. Benjamin Coleman, the chief promoter of the meeting, was unanimously called upon to preside, and the exercises of the evening proceeded as follows.   The Chairman, after stating that the object of the meeting was to give Dr. Newton a hearty welcome, closed a pertinent speech on the value of the healing power with the following remarks :—

"In America Dr. Newton stands pre-eminent for his healing powers, as proved by recorded facts spread over the last fourteen years, and many of the cures effected by him were of a very wonderful description. When in New York and Boston, I heard of Dr. Newton's powers in this respect. One gentleman told me of a case where Dr. Newton had restored sight to a blind man, who had been unable to see for seven or eight years previously, and who was cured by Dr. Newton in a few minutes. Dr. Newton only arrived in Liverpool last Saturday, May 7th, and he was asked to go on the following day and see Mr. Ashley, of that town, who had been afflicted with a very serious illness for some time, and Mr. Wason, who is present, has given me the following statement of what took place :—

"'Mr. Ashley resides at 5, Catherine Street, Liverpool. On the 27th December last he was at Oxford and broke a blood-vessel in the lungs. A leading medical man, Mr. Freeborn, was called in, who prepared Mrs. Ashley for the worst, and told her that there was no hope ; that her husband would go off in a rapid consumption, and none could say how soon ; he advised that he should not be removed to Liverpool, as his strength was not equal to the journey. Mrs. Ashley prayed fervently for Divine aid, that she might be comforted and directed according to her trial, feeling assured that her husband would shortly depart—and turning to her Bible, opened it at a venture, and found her finger, she knows not how, on the text in St. John, where Jesus, speaking of Lazarus, says, "This sickness is not unto death, but for the glory of God." From that moment she felt assured that her husband would not die, and she told Dr. Freeborn her strong impressions. Some little time after this Mr. Ashley was removed to Liverpool on a bed fitted up in a railway carriage. For about five months he was confined to his room, no one expecting his recovery except his wife. Once Mr. Gardiner carried him like a child down stairs, and had great difficulty in getting him back, and fears were entertained that he would not recover the shock. Last Saturday, May 7th, Dr. Simmons prepared Mrs. Ashley for the worst, and intimated that the great change might take place at any moment. Last Sunday, the 8th of May, Dr. Newton and myself went in a cab to Mr. Ashley's ; the Doctor went upstairs to Mr. Ashley's sick-room, requesting that none should follow but Mrs. Ashley. In about five or six minutes, Dr. Newton brought Mr. Ashley down stairs, and took him into the open air and said he was cured ; he told him that he could walk a mile and a half, which he urged him to do, and to eat a beefsteak and drink a pint of ale for dinner—although his doctor had fed him on slops for the last five months. Mr. Ashley came to the evening service and stood alone a considerable time, whilst Dr. Newton told the audience of the case, which Mr. Ashley confirmed in all respects. Mr. and Mrs. Ashley gave me this account yesterday (Monday), at their house, after Mr. Ashley had been out, and eaten a mutton chop with pudding and ale, and after a long walk. . . . Previous to Dr. Newton's seeing him, *he had not been out of his bed for five months.*'"

Mr. Coleman then went on to say :—

"I cannot in this short address give one-hundredth part of the cases on record, some of which have taken place very recently. Mr. Watson, who has come over from America with Dr. Newton, told me that he had lost the sight of one eye, in consequence of a piece of steel getting into it by accident ; inflammation set in, and he lost the sight of the other eye. Two years ago his wife was impressed to induce her husband to go with her to Montreal from New York, to visit Dr. Newton. They arrived in Montreal as Dr. Newton was on the point of leaving it, and directly Dr. Newton saw the patient, whose eyes were covered with a bandage, he told him that he would do good to one of them, thereby showing a knowledge that both of them were not in the same state. He then removed the bandage, and said, 'You can see, can't you ?' and although he had only been in the room seven minutes, he found that he could read small print. Mr. Watson is present, and can testify to the truth of these facts.

"In London Dr. Newton will doubtless encounter plenty of opposition ; if he does not succeed the medical profession will call him a sharper, and if he does succeed they will call him a lunatic ; they are sure to say that he is mad, because he has announced his intention not to charge a fee to anybody during his stay in England.

"I do not believe that Dr. Newton will cure everybody, nor indeed half of those who call upon him, but there is no doubt that he can effect very wonderful cures, and that he has a great work to do in this country."

After the reading of a cordial, and scholarly address, from the pen of Mr. Thos. Shorter, that gentleman was called upon to speak, which he did in substance as follows :—

"I had the good fortune to make the personal acquaintance and friendship of Dr. Newton on the occasion of a brief visit he paid to this country in the autumn of 1864. I was then deeply impressed, as I think all who know him must be impressed, with his great simplicity and gentleness of character—his ingenuousness of disposition, singleness of purpose, and entire disinterestedness. I allude to this, not for the purpose of compliment, but because I believe that these qualities of character—this large-heartedness and quick active sympathy has had much to do with the marked success as a healer which Dr. Newton has achieved. On the occasion of that visit, as but little previous notice of it had been given, and it was at the time of year when most of our friends were absent from town, there were but few to meet him and hold out to him the hand of welcome. However, a genuine man with a high sense of duty, and who delights in the execution of a noble mission, is not easily discouraged, and I am glad to find that the untoward circumstances to which I have referred, have not deterred Dr. Newton from repeating his visit under happier auspices, and I hope it will be found with more satisfactory results. During the interval that has elapsed since his first visit the position of Spiritualism in England has changed very much for the better ; public opinion on the subject has grown and ripened ; publications and books devoted to its exposition and advocacy have multiplied ; the platform, too, as well as the press, has been called into requisition— lectures have been delivered, conferences held, Sunday services established, various forms of associative effort instituted, and societies and individuals have been stimulated to its investigation ; and thus conviction has spread, and a better understanding of the subject has been reached ; and to-night, instead of the few friends who welcomed Dr. Newton on his first visit, I am glad to see so goodly an assemblage. I trust that the work which Dr. Newton has begun so well in Liverpool will be continued in London, and that he will be as successful in curing disease in England as he has been in America. Many no doubt will think him mad, but looking at the results of this so-called insanity, I can only hope that it may soon become contagious. . . . . Some four or five years since, when Dr. Newton was in Philadelphia, he was brought before a magistrate on some trumpery charge at the instigation of the doctors. Those whom he had cured, naturally indignant at the treatment of their benefactor, came forward unsolicited to the number it is said of about fifteen hundred, thronging the court and all its avenues, eager to tender their unsought-for evidence of the reality of their cure— these included the cures of blindness, deafness, lameness, paralysis, and other chronic maladies, seemingly incurable. Of course the charge was summarily dismissed. I will refer to one other case nearer home. The Rev. Frederick Rowland Young, pastor of the Free Christian Church, Swindon, was not only a minister of the Gospel, but a believer in the gracious word of the Master, 'The works that I do shall ye do also,' and when evidence was brought before him of the cures wrought by Dr. Newton in America, so strong was his faith, that he crossed the Atlantic to be cured by him. His faith was rewarded by an immediate cure. Not only did he return cured of the neuralgia with which he had been afflicted for many years, and which physicians had been unable to remove, but he himself received through Dr. Newton the gift of healing, which he has freely exercised in his own town and neighbourhood, as well as for the benefit of persons living at a greater distance. Last summer, while at Swindon for a few days, I heard much of these cures, and one case came under my notice of a poor woman who had lost her eyesight for many years who had been cured by Mr. Young by the simple laying on of hands and prayer ; and she was then going about her ordinary household occupations. Whether Dr. Newton will be as successful here as in America I cannot say. When I consider the educated prejudice and indurated scepticism with which he will have to contend, I confess my expectations are greatly moderated. All the more credit to Dr. Newton, who, knowing all this, and in the face of these repellent influences, has ventured again to come amongst us. The least we can do is to acknowledge his great kindness in doing so, and by our sympathy and co-operation to aid him all we can in the great and good work in which he is engaged—the relief of suffering humanity, irrespective of all considerations of sect, party, country, class, or creed."

"Mr. William Tebb said : 'I do not rise to make a speech : there are those here, some of whom have already addressed you, who are accustomed to speak in public assemblies, and I am not. I cannot, however, refrain from expressing my concurrence with the sentiments contained in the address just read, and my satisfaction in seeing so many assembled here this evening to do honour to so distinguished a philanthropist as Dr. Newton. It is related of Faraday, that when he made a new discovery he would show

12

it and explain it to his friends, evincing a delight which they could not always appreciate, and the question was frequently put to him, "What is the use of it?" To which the Professor would reply, "Wait, and we'll find some use for it." Now, this question is frequently put with regard to Spiritualism, and I confess that if it was confined, as many seem to suppose, to the phenomena of raps, table-tipping, and the like, one might be puzzled to answer the question satisfactorily. But when it is shown there is a continuous influx from the spiritual world, which is manifested in all the variety of forms witnessed in the Apostolic age, in healing the sick, as illustrated by our guest Dr. Newton ; in inspirational speaking, so powerfully instanced in this hall by Mrs. Hardinge ; in the power to cast out evil spirits ; and when the facts of modern Spiritualism demonstrate the truth of all the most cherished beliefs of humanity, showing the ever-watchful interest which those who have gone before take in those that remain, and giving us clearer and better views of the future as well as of the present life, I think we may affirm that the good is unquestionable. I do not, however, intend to pursue this subject, but permit me before taking my seat to assure Dr. Newton that the kindly feelings he has expressed in his letters to Spiritualists in this country are reciprocated by Spiritualists here towards himself and his fellow-workers. We in England owe a deep debt of gratitude to the earlier advocates of the movement in America, to public men like Governor Tallmadge, of Wisconsin, and Judge Edmonds, of New York ; to clergymen like the late Rev. John Pierpont, of Boston, the successor of the celebrated Dr. Channing, and Adin Ballou ; to men eminent in the scientific world, like the late Professor Mapes, and Dr. Hare, of Philadelphia ; to men like Dr. Willis, and A. E. Newton, who for their faith as Spiritualists have been expelled from college and from church, and many others—with noble women not a few, who have borne the loss of worldly position, the ridicule, vituperation, and all that general hostility which ever seems to follow those who identify themselves with the advent of unpopular truths.'

"Mr. J. M. Peebles said : 'I feel some embarrassment in making any remarks, as this is a meeting of noble-hearted Englishmen to welcome a distinguished friend of my own from America. I am exceedingly happy to be in your midst, and especially to be upon this platform alongside a friend and brother whom I have known, loved, and respected for many years. . . . . Truly it is often asked, "What good does Spiritualism do?" It gives demonstration of a future existence, for even now clear-headed men often ask the question, "If a man die, shall he live again?" Once, as a minister, I attended a funeral of an only child. My text was "Suffer little children to come unto Me, and forbid them not, for of such is the kingdom of heaven." The whole of my sermon was about "faith," but as the mother baptized the coffin with her tears, she turned and said to me, "Tell me what you *know* about the immortal world ; my aching heart asks for more than faith—for knowledge." She added, "Tell me what you know of that world ; shall I know my child? Will my child know me?"—and *I was dumb.* But now, since I have talked with the angels, and have heard their lute-like voices, I no longer talk only about "faith," for now "We know that we have a house eternal in the heavens." Spiritualism teaches us and proves that there is an immortal life beyond the tomb. Spiritualism is spreading to the ends of the earth. I found its phenomena in Smyrna, in Constantinople, in Athens, and upon the Pacific coast ; in fact, wherever thinking men are found, there is this living truth proclaimed. I know much of Dr. Newton, for hundreds have clasped my hand who have been healed by him. To pick out solitary instances from among the large number is like trying to select some specially bright star from the thousands in the midnight heavens. In Buffalo, several years ago, I was present at the house of Dr. Newton, when a gentleman was brought in upon his bed, who for years had had paralysis ; Dr. Newton looked at him, simply laid his hands upon him, and said, "Disease, I bid you depart ! Arise ! you are well ;" and the man left the bed and crossed the room, then stood before Dr. Newton weeping with joy. "Stop," said Dr. Newton, "it is not I ; it is the spirit power of which I am but the humble instrument." On another occasion a lady could not get near him, and Dr. Newton was impressed to say, "It does not matter, she is well," and she was cured. He has cured the lame, the dumb, and the blind. . . . . As Mrs. Hardinge stands at the head of American inspirational speakers, so Dr. Newton stands at the head of all the healing mediums connected with the movement. Before him disease departs, and when it does not depart at once, it sometimes departs very shortly afterwards, because of its cause being removed—a stream will flow for a little time after its sources of supply have been cut off. I have great faith in Dr. Newton's cures, far more faith than has been expressed by some of those who have spoken before me, because I have seen more of Dr. Newton's work than they have. I know that Dr. Newton will nobly do his work, and that he will be blessed by God and His holy angels : I trust that all present will extend to him love and warmth of soul. Personally, the more time I spend in England, the better I comprehend and love Englishmen, and I wish to bespeak for Dr. Newton cordial welcomes and greetings while he remains in this country.'

"Dr. J. R. Newton then rose amid loud and continued applause. He spoke under spirit influence, with slowness and frequent pauses, and said: 'I feel overwhelmed by your cordial welcome. I stand before you as a plain man, and feel like a little child. I am a practical Christian, and am ready at any time to make a sacrifice of myself for the sake of Christianity. It is a wonder to me that few men ever try to live daily as Jesus lived. When I became Christian in life, spiritual gifts were showered upon me, and this was as wonderful to myself as to those whom I address. I believe in spirit communion, and I even know the names of some of the spirits who control me in the exercise of my gifts. . . . . As to the power of healing, it is merely an illustration of the power of love. When any sick person comes before me, I lay my hands on that person and feel that I love him, and if the patient is not antagonistic, he is almost sure to be healed ; tell them I love them, and when this opens their hearts to me, the disease must depart. I make no profession to be a public speaker. I am entirely under the control of the spirits. . . . . I cannot say that I have come to England at any sacrifice, because it was the will of my Father that I should come. I have not come to London to make money, and I shall receive rich and poor alike. The welcome I have received prevents me from speaking as freely as I wish to do. I have much to say, but I feel overwhelmed at the reception you have given me. I am heart and soul with you. . . . . . It is not a matter of belief with me that spirits control me—it is knowledge. Pythagoras, Socrates, and Plato walk the earth to-day, and so do all the great and good men who have gone before us. I shall meet you again next Sunday, and wish you all well, with many thanks and blessings for your kind attention.'

"Mr. S. C. Hall said : Before the meeting closes, I should like to say a few words of congratulation to Dr. Newton. I believe that I express the sentiments of all Spiritualists when I say that it is their desire to give a cordial greeting to all Americans ; and that it is a great duty to bring Americans and Englishmen closer together, that they may understand each other better than they have done. I should not have risen at all except to call attention to one point. I want to tell Dr. Newton that Spiritualism is making great progress in this country among great men and great thinkers, and men who will become great authorities. I rejoice to tell him that a Society the other day called witnesses before them, and made clear and close inquiry ; that that Society is about to send forth a report which will do much good among outsiders. . . . I believe that the report of the Dialectical Society will go far towards the removal of the chief obstacles in the path of Spiritualism, and make it easier to help on our divine belief. We shall then be, I trust, the humble instruments in God's hands of destroying the Materialism of the present age, for this I consider to be the great purpose of Spiritualism. . . . I have myself full knowledge of the truth of Spiritualism, and I hope that many who are not Spiritualists will take my testimony as worth something when I express that certainty of belief. The more Spiritualism has been inquired into, the more its truth has been exhibited ; I thank God for having given us opportunities of proving that which we now believe and know. Dr. Newton has reached London at a good time, with less difficulties than of old to encounter, and with less probability of being considered mad or dishonest.'

"Thanks having been voted to the Chairman, the business part of the meeting then came to a close, and it assumed the character of a *conversazione*." . . .

. . . .

"DR. NEWTON AT THE CAVENDISH ROOMS.

"On Sunday evening at the close of the service, and after a very excellent discourse by Mr. Peebles, Dr. Newton invited all who were afflicted with disease or pain to come forward. Many did so ; and declared themselves either cured or greatly benefited by the Doctor's treatment. These included headache, deafness, stammering, neuralgia, heart disease, &c. His success in one case was very marked ; that of the son of Mr. F. Cowper, 388, Edgware Road, who had been unable to walk without crutches for eight years past. After Dr. Newton's treatment, the lad was able to walk home—a distance of about two miles. On Monday he attended at the Cambridge Hall, and had his spine straightened, which has made him measure about four inches taller. He now walks with a stick, and improves daily. On Sunday, May 22nd, a similar scene was witnessed, and on both occasions the hall was densely crowded."

"DR. NEWTON AT THE CAMBRIDGE HALL.

"The *Medium* says : 'Dr. Newton commenced a regular course of treatment of the poor on Monday morning, May 16th, in the Cambridge Hall, Newman Street, Oxford Street. He attends between the hours of nine and twelve, and will accept no money for his services. A large number came to be healed, and they have steadily increased each day. Many remarkable cures have been made. It would be of little use to fill our columns with an account of the remarkable instances of benefit which could be culled from the Doctor's treatment on one morning only. Dr. Newton commenced on Wednesday morning by removing a curvature from the spine of a young lady, the daughter of Lady Helena Newenham. A lad who had not spoken, except in a whisper, for three years, was enabled to speak, so as to be heard distinctly over the hall. Mr. Hubbard, of Rathbone Place, was cured of asthma of long standing. Mr. Watts, Rathbone Place, was cured of lameness from wounds. Mr. Charles Clutterbuck, 74 years of age, had been totally blind for six years; after treatment, he could see faces and tell the colour of Mr. Watson's beard. Mrs. Anna Crisp, 23, King Street, had been paralyzed for three years; cured by one treatment. She had been affected on one side throughout. Robert Andrews, 151, Metropolitan Meat Market, was blind of one eye, and had pains in the head and hand; after treatment he pronounced himself "all right." James Armstrong, 44, Brindley Street, Harrow Road, was afflicted with paralyzed legs for nearly two years. He could walk with difficulty on a pair of crutches, but he went away with his crutches over his shoulder. Many who were not perfectly cured were much relieved. Some were pronounced absolutely incurable. "It would be as easy to make new eyes as to cure you," said the Doctor to several who were entirely past recovery. Others were benefited, and some were told to come again; others that their diseases were mitigated, and would pass away in a few weeks.'"

" DR. NEWTON AND MR. ASHLEY.

" Since the foregoing was in type, we have received the following communication :—

"' *To the Editor of the Spiritual Magazine.*

"' May 23rd, 1870.

"' Sir,—I have received a letter this morning from Mr. Wm. Ashley, of Liverpool, whose case I alluded to at Harley Street, and which was the first case upon which Dr. Newton tried his healing power after his arrival in England. Mr. Ashley now writes :

" May 22nd.

" You will be pleased to hear that I am gaining strength daily. I generally walk out one or two hours when the weather permits, either alone or with my wife. I enjoy my food as much as ever I did, and have no doubt but in a short time I shall be in robust health—thanks to dear Dr. Newton."

"' You can make whatever use you please of this communication.

"' You will see that the press is in full blast against the Doctor; the *Telegraph* of this day being most violent; the *Echo* of Saturday publishing a letter from a patient who was not healed; the *Advertiser* denouncing him as a humbug.

" The only fair account was given in the *Daily News* of Saturday; but the writer did not half state the facts he witnessed. I was there, and many cases were marvellous— unmistakable !

" Yours truly,

" Benj. Coleman."

" DR. NEWTON AND THE PRESS.

" The *Liverpool Mercury* has a long article on Dr. Newton's proceedings in Liverpool. On Sunday, May 8th, he attended two meetings and operated on from thirty to forty persons, and all, it is admitted, with one exception, professed themselves benefited. A portion of the London press has begun to *Telegraph* false reports and *Echo* dirty insinuations. ''Tis easy as lying,' said Shakespeare, and newspaper scribes well know how easy that is.

" The *Daily News* in a long article gives a tolerably fair account of some of the proceedings during what the writer calls Dr. Newton's morning performance, and this tolerable fairness was so much a surprise to Dr. Newton, amidst the furious blasts of others of the press, that he had the innocence to thank the *Daily News* and even to 'bless' the editor. This was too much for the editor, and he has hastened to repudiate the blessing, and to withdraw all his fairness, saying, with great truth, that such a thing was never in his mind. A great deal more of this is of course in store for Dr. Newton, and he has made up his account to meet it. Perhaps the source of the Doctor's power to heal may itself render him not the most philosophic or prudent person in speaking, and he may not be a good exponent of the philosophy of the subject. In this way additional difficulties may be thrown in his own way, and in that of the public, to prevent their understanding the *rationale* of this power, even to the small extent to which it can be understood. . . . . But apart from this, we should be glad to know why a benevolent gentleman cannot assert this power in his own person, and endeavour to exercise it at his own cost, without drawing down on himself the blind ferocity of the press and the public. We do not know why he should be called a blasphemer and an impostor, and have the whole pack of the press, like so many hounds, yelping at his heels. In America, where we have watched his course for many years, he has relieved and cured thousands, and is a poorer man to-day than he was five years ago, though his powers of healing are said to be greater. Already he has been the means of curing many in England during this short visit; and we should have thought the wise plan would have been to watch the result and tabulate his work, and see what it comes to before becoming abusive. It suits the temper of the press, and its ignorance of such matters, to begin by abuse; and so we must be content to let them go on in their own way. Anything above mere physics always produces this unholy rage. We wish that some healer could be found who could cure this public madness."

Our Spiritualistic readers have, no doubt, like the author herself, too often heard the parrot cry of *Cui bono* to marvel why—even with all the excisions of extraneous matter we have made—we should have published the above account *in extenso* from the pages of the London *Spiritual Magazine* of December, 1870.

To non-spiritualistic readers who may perchance glance over these pages we would say, "Read, mark, learn, and inwardly digest" the above account, before you again ask the ten thousand times answered question, "What is the use of Spiritualism?"

CHAPTER XXIII.

SPIRITUALISM IN GREAT BRITAIN (CONTINUED).

OF SPIRITUAL ASSOCIATIONS,

IN 1865 an association was formed under the name and style of "The Association of Progressive Spiritualists of Great Britain," and the following is a brief summary of its aims as reported in the London *Spiritual Magazine* for December, 1865 :—

"The 'Association of Progressive Spiritualists of Great Britain,' which recently held its first convention at Darlington, has issued—'A circular respectfully addressed to the friends of Spiritualism and the public generally;' in which, accepting as their definition of Spiritualism the motto of the *Spiritual Magazine*, they state that :—

"'The principal objects we have in view, are, as an association, to meet once a year, or oftener, if it be deemed advisable, for the purpose of social communion, interchange of sentiment; to record our united experiences, and the progress which Spiritualism is making in and around us; to devise means for diffusing among our fellow men and women the principles of this Divine philosophy, by the distribution of the best tracts and books we have upon the subject, and the delivery throughout the kingdom of lectures by persons of approved character and ability.'

"A second convention is announced for the last week in July, 1866, at Newcastle-on-Tyne. The secretary of the Association is Dr. McLeod, of Newcastle."

Of the Convention announced as above, the reports were scarcely as favourable as could have been desired. A general lack of unity seemed to pervade the assembly and the papers presented were not calculated to edify those outside the ranks of Spiritualism, however interesting they might have been to the writers. The following remarks conclude a report of this gathering furnished by the London *Spiritual Magazine* : —

"Amid much that is crude and undigested in the papers and speeches here reported, there are some well worthy a better companionship, especially one by Mr. Etchells, on The Atmosphere of Intelligence, Pleasure, and Pain ; or a Chapter from the Harmony of Matter, as unfolded in the Circles of Spiritualists who meet at Brothers Chapman, Varley, and Etchells', Huddersfield.' This paper has evidently been prepared with great care ; the facts it relates, especially those concerning the phenomena of 'the Double,' are of great interest ; and the circles named by Mr. Etchells can hardly be better employed in the interest of Spiritualism than in the further prosecution of these investigations."

For a few succeding years, conventions were held either in London or the provinces, but these gatherings were seldom participated in by the majority of the English Spiritualists, nor were they conducive to any very important results.

Conventions appear to be more in harmony with the genius of American than English Spiritualism, and we have but few evidences that their action in England has promoted the progress of the cause or the spirit of unity amongst its supporters.

The invariable struggle between the extremes of Radicalism and Conservatism which so often disturbs the harmony of associative bodies, is a prevailing condition, of which the Spiritualists have had to learn, by painful experience.

One of their most severe lessons in this direction was read to them in the determined opposition manifested by "The Royal Society of Great Britain," against the admission of "Spiritualism" as a theme of discussion worthy the attention of that august body. Several of the Fellows were earnest believers in Spiritualism, and thinking they perceived in its phenomena, subjects quite as worthy the attention of eminent scientists as the genesis of a worm or the precise number of markings on a fossil trilobite, they made strenuous efforts to introduce papers on the subject of the marvellous demonstrations of unknown force which the phenomena of Spiritualism display. It was in the amazing assumptions of contempt and indifference with which these propositions were repelled, that the Spiritualists were led to believe that Societies in general are banded together for the defence of the old against the innovations of the new, and those who presume to try and enlighten the said Societies upon the subject of new ideas, must be taught, that anything a very learned, especially a Royal Society, does not already know, cannot exist, or if it presume to maintain an existence without the pale of such an authoritative body, cannot be worth knowing.

It was doubtless under the influence of this high-toned monopoly of all knowledge worth the having, that Professor Tyndall, Mr. Palgrave, and other members of the Royal Society of Great Britain, maintained a long and acrimonious correspondence with Mr. William Wilkinson, Professors Wallace and Cromwell Varley, Sir J. E. Tennant, and others, on the question of bringing the phenomena claimed to be "Spiritual," before the members of the Royal Society, and although the Mediumship of Mr. D. D. Home was courteously tendered as an illustration of the assertions made by the Spiritualists, the scornful rejection of this offer seemed necessary to convince the zealous propagandists, how useless it is to try and convince those, who neither desire nor intend to be convinced of any facts they do not originate, or any truths they do not themselves already know.

Although the action of Societies as a general rule appears to be ephemeral in connection with Spiritualism, its use being simply available for temporary purposes of propagandism, there have been a vast number of attempts at organization in the ranks of Spiritualism. One of the most permanent and influential associations that has ever been formed in Great Britain has been known under the name of "The British National Association of Spiritualists." It may not be generally understood that this organization owes its first foundation in the metropolis to the steadfast though quiet and unobtrusive efforts of Mr. Dawson Rogers, of Rose Villa, Finchley. This gentleman—one of the veteran Spiritualists of London— has for many years laboured unceasingly to promote the interests of Spiritualism, and both by purse and person has maintained every good work which has tended to advance "the cause." Besides devoting himself with tireless energy to the foundation and conduct of the "British National Association of Spiritualists," the movement owes to Mr. Dawson Rogers the foundation of the admirable periodical entitled *Light*. With the exception of the London *Spiritual Magazine, Light* is unquestionably the highest toned, and most scholarly periodical that has ever issued from the Spiritual Press, and Mr. Dawson Rogers's good services to the cause of Spiritualism have been for many long years pursued so faithfully, so effectively, yet with such a total absence of personal display, that we feel but too happy in offering this humble tribute to one, whose way marks in the path of progress have been far more prominent, than his honoured name. To return to Mr. Rogers's first great public effort in promoting the foundation of the British National Association of Spiritualists. In a brief sketch of this important movement published a few years since in the London *Spiritualist*, the editor says :—

"Some time in 1873 it was resloved to form a national organisation of Spiritualists in Great Britain. This was done at a meeting at Liverpool, to which everybody had been invited by means of advertisements and special letters to well-known men. Thus was the standard raised of "Friendly union among Spiritualists." Fierce attempts were made to kill the organisation, more especially by the press, but the workers fought their way, and succeeded in planting a central establishment in London, and in doing some public work in addition, more especially the founding of fortnightly meetings to consider public questions relating to Spiritualism."

Soon after its first inauguration, the Society issued a well-prepared tract, in which was published the list of distinguished persons who became its members and associates. Although it would be impossible to give *in extenso* a list which includes more than a hundred names and addresses, it may not be out of place to make the following selection from amongst the most noteworthy personages of the association :—

"BRITISH NATIONAL ASSOCIATION OF SPIRITUALISTS (ESTABLISHED 1873.)

PRESIDENT.

Alexander Calder, Esq., 1, Hereford Square, West Brompton, S.W.

VICE-PRESIDENTS.

Blackburn, Charles, Parkfield, Didsbury, Manchester.
Coleman, Benjamin, 1, Bernard Villas, Upper Norwood.
Fitz-Gerald, Mrs., 19, Cambridge Street, Hyde Park, W.
Fitz-Gerald, Desmond G., M.S.Tel.E., 6, Loughborough Road North, Brixton, S.W.
Gregory, Mrs. Makdougall, 21, Green Street, Grosvenor Square, W.
Honywood, Mrs., 52, Warwick Square, S.W.

ALLIED SOCIETIES.

The Liverpool Psychological Society. Secretary, S. Pride, Esq., 8, Grampian Road, Edge Lane, Liverpool.

L'Union Spirite et Magnetique. Secretary, M. Charles Fritz, 121, Rue de Louvain, Brussels.

The Brixton Psychological Society. Hon. Sec., H. E. Frances, Esq., 22, Cowley Road, Brixton, S.W.

The Spiriter-Forscher Society, Buda-Pesth. Secretary, M. Anton Prochaszka, Josefstadt Erzherzog Alexander-gasse, 23, Buda-Pesth, Hungary.

Dalston Association of Enquirers into Spiritualism. Hon. Secretary, T. Blyton, Esq., 74, Navarino Road, Dalston, E.

Cardiff Spiritual Society, Hon. Sec., Mr. A. J. Smart, 3, Guildford Street, Cardiff.

Sociedad Espiritista Espanola, Cervantes 34, 28, Madrid. President, El Visconde de Torres-Solanot.

Sociedad Espirita Central de la Republica Mexicana. President, Senor Refugio T. Gonzalez, 7, Calle de Amedo, Mexico.

Sociedad Espirita di Bogota, Colombia, South America. President, Senor Manuel Jose Angarita.

For several years this Association has maintained its meetings, established a library, held soirées, investigating circles, and social gathings, with an amount of fidelity specially commendable in a movement so fluctuating as Spiritualism. Many internal changes have of course taken place, especially in its officers and directors. Many of its once prominent members have been removed by transition to a higher life; others have been impelled to withdraw from personal motives, and still many eminent persons not enumerated in the first list, have become affiliated with the organization. So much influence for good however has been exerted by the persistent energy of its leaders, that we feel pleasure in adding a notice of the last change that has been effected in its arrangements. The excerpt we are about to subjoin was only published in May, 1882, and is taken from *Light*.

The annexed report is the last announcement of the British National Association of Spiritualists under that name, the society being henceforth destined to be known as " The Central Association of Spiritualists."

The article is headed :—

" BRITISH NATIONAL ASSOCIATION OF SPIRITUALISTS.

" ANNUAL MEETING.—The annual general meeting of this Association was held on Tuesday evening last, at 38, Great Russell Street, Mr. E. Dawson Rogers, vice-president, in the chair. The principal business of the meeting was to receive the annual report of the Council and statement of accounts, and to consider a recommendation involving a change in the name and constitution of the Association. The report was unanimously adopted, as was also a proposition in favour of the adoption of the name 'The Central Association of Spiritualists,' by which designation, therefore, the Association will hence-forth be known. The change, we think, is a wise one; but after eight years' familiarity with the title of the ' B.N.A.S.,' we give it up with some regret."

Then follows an elaborate report of the Council, by which it appears that the society is still in a flourishing condition. The following items, however, may possess some interest to the reader, because they allude to the depart-ture of more than one honoured friend of the Spiritual cause, and give further particulars of the status of the association under its new designation in 1882. The report concludes thus :—

"The following is a concise summary of the history of the Association since the last annual meeting :—

"Changes in the Membership.—Number of new members elected, 52 ; number of resignations 16. Deaths during the year—M. Léon Favre, Prof. Friedrich Zöllner, Rev. Sir Wm. Dunbar, H. D. Jencken, M.R.I., Alex. Thorn, Mrs. Hook, A. E. Hunter, B.A. (Cantab). Present number of honorary and subscribing members, 294.

"Allied Societies.—The Gateshead Society for the Investigation of Spiritualism, the South African Spiritual Evidence Society, and the Paris Psychological Society have allied themselves to the Association during the year, making a total number of sixteen in friendly union.

"Work of the Association.—A series of Discussion and Social Meetings has been kept up through the season. Many of these have been highly interesting and successful.

"Mr. T. P. Barkas, F.G.S., was appointed as a representative of the Association at the discussion on Spiritualism at the Church Congress held in October of last year. This discussion, and the extent to which the report of it was circulated, has done much to raise the position which the whole subject of Spiritualism occupies in the public mind.

"On the 5th and 6th of January last, conferences of an excedingly interesting character were held in the rooms of the Association, on the invitation of Professor Barrett, of Dublin. These conferences have resulted in the formation of a 'Society for Psychical Research,' which, while working to some extent on similar lines to those of the B.N.A.S., does not commit itself to a belief in Spiritualism, but aims at approaching the inquiry solely from a scientific standpoint. The Council feels that there is abundant room for such a society without in any way affecting the necessity for a Central Association avowedly for the investigation and propagation of Spiritualism."

The new organization alluded to in the last report sufficiently indicates its aims by its nomenclature—namely, " The Society for Psychical Research."

The announcements put forth by this Society point to the lines of de marcation which separate it from any thoroughly pronounced Spiritual organizations ; in fact, the addresses of its President and Members on the occasion of its first general meeting, which took place in July, 1882, clearly show, that though Spiritualists may and do take part in its researches, a belief in Spirit communion is by no means the leading principle upon which the association is based. To illustrate this position still more forcibly, we append a note which the Society print in connection with their prospectus. It reads as follows :

" To prevent misconception, it is here expressly stated that Membership of this Society does not imply the acceptance of any particular explanation of the phenomena investinated, nor any belief as to the operation, in the physical world, of forces other than those recognised by Physical Science."

After publishing the list of eminent literary and scientific ladies and gentlemen who compose the officers and members of this association, the prospectus gives the following, which may present a satisfactory synopsis of the subjects of proposed research.

"(1) Committee on Thought-reading ; Hon. Sec., Professor W. F. Barrett, 18, Belgrave Square, Monkstown, Dublin.

"(2) Committee on Mesmerism : Hon. Sec., Dr. Wyld, 12, Great Cumberland Place, London, W.

"(3) Committee on Reichenbach's Experiments ; Hon. Sec., Walter H. Coffin, Esq., Junior Athenæum Club, London, W.

"(4) Committee on Apparitions, Haunted Houses, &c. ; Hon. Sec., Hensleigh Wedgwood, Esq., 31, Queen Anne Street, London, W.

"(5) Committee on Physical Phenomena ; Hon. Sec., Dr. C. Lockhart Robertson, Hamam Chambers, 76, Jermyn Street, S.W.

"(6) Literary Committee, Hon. Secs., Edmund Gurney, Esq., 26, Montpelier Square, S.W. ; Frederic W. H. Myers, Esq., Leckhampton, Cambridge."

Besides these well selected subjects for consideration, and the marked ability of the gentlemen who have consented to aid in their investigation, the success of the undertaking is guaranteed by the high standing and literary attainments of the parties under whose direction the work is announced to proceed. Any committee of investigators into psychic phenomena which includes the names of the subjoined officers and Council can scarcely fail to command the respect of the community at large and the sympathy of every earnest investigator into the subjects under consideration :—

PRESIDENT.

Henry Sidgwick, Esq., Trinity College, Cambridge.

VICE-PRESIDENTS.

Arthur J. Balfour, Esq., M.P., 4, Carlton Gardens, S.W.
W. F. Barrett, Esq., F.R.S.E., 18, Belgrave Square, Monkstown, **Dublin.**
John R. Holland, Esq., M.P., 57, Lancaster Gate, London, W.
Richard H. Hutton, Esq., Englefield Green, Staines.
Rev. W. Stainton-Moses, M.A., 21, Birchington Road, London, N.W.
Hon. Roden Noel, 57, Anerley Park, London, S.E.
Professor Balfour Stewart, F.R.S., Owens College, Manchester.
Hensleigh Wedgwood, Esq., 31, Queen Anne Street, London, W.

COUNCIL.

W. F. Barrett, 18, Belgrave Square, Monkstown, Dublin.
Edward T. Bennett, 8, The Green, Richmond, near London.
Mrs. Boole, 103, Seymour Place, Bryanston Square, London, W.
Walter R. Browne, 38, Belgrave Road, London, S.W.
Alexander Calder, 1, Hereford Square, South Kensington, **London, S.W.**
Walter H. Coffin, Junior Athenæum Club, London, W.
Desmond G. FitzGerald, 6, Akerman Road, Brixton, S.W.
Edmund Gurney, 26, Montpelier Square, London, S.W.
Charles C. Massey, 1, Albert Mansions, Victoria Street, London, S.W.
Frederic W. H. Myers, Leckhampton, Cambridge.
Francis W. Percival, 28, Savile Row, London, W.
Frank Podmore, 16, Southampton Street, Fitzroy Square, London. S.W.
C. Lockhart Robertson, M.D., Hamam Chambers, 76, Jermyn Street, S.W.
E. Dawson Rogers, Rose Villa, Church End, Finchley, N.
Rev. W. Stainton-Moses, 21, Birchington Road, London, N.W.
Morell Theobald, 62, Granville Park, Blackheath, S.E.
Hensleigh Wedgwood, 31, Queen Anne Street, London, W.
G. Wyld, M.D., 19, Great Cumberland Place, London, W.

Many other associations besides those already named have been formed with kindred aims. Some have maintained a more or less permanent existence—but whether they still survive or have passed out of being, all have achieved some use as temporary levers in the spiritual progress of the race.

CHAPTER XXIV.

SPIRITUALISM IN GREAT BRITAIN (CONTINUED).

SPIRITUALISM AND THE LONDON DIALECTICAL SOCIETY.

IT now becomes necessary to give a brief account of a movement which has exerted a marked influence over the progress of Spiritualism in Great Britain, namely, the investigations and published report of " The London Dialectical Society," the action of which in connection with Spiritualism arose thus. In January of the year 1869, an association composed of ladies and gentlemen distinguished for their literary and scientific attainments, entitled " The Dialectical Society," determined to investigate the subject of modern Spiritualism.

The minute of the proceedings which inaugurated this investigation reads in their published report as follows :—

"At a meeting of the London Dialectical Society, held 6th of January, 1869, Mr. J. H. Levy in the chair, it was resolved,—' That the Council be requested to appoint a Committee to investigate the phenomena alleged to be Spiritual manifestations, and to report thereon.' "

In consequence of this resolution, the members issued a circular couched in courteous terms, inviting the leading Spiritualists of England to assist them by personal or written testimony in the investigations they proposed to pursue.

One of the first respondents to the call issued by the Council was the author of this work, who happened at that time to be in England, and who, in company with J. C. Luxmoore, Esq., of Gloucester Square, Mr. and Mrs. Everitt, and a few other Spiritualistic friends, waited on the Society at a meeting appointed for that purpose on the evening of March 16th, 1869. After offering such testimony as she felt to be apposite to the place and time, Mrs. Hardinge gave a long address upon the main features of the Spiritualistic movement, the characteristics of Mediumship, the Spirit circle, and the difficulties which beset the path of the investigator, all of which will be found duly recorded in the printed report of the Society. The address closed with a strong recommendation to the Society to conduct their investigations, not in general sessions of the whole body, but to form themselves into groups or sub-committees, of from four to eight, or at most ten persons; selecting the members of these groups on the principle of mutual goodwill, or such cordial relations with each other, as would be most likely to produce harmony of feeling, and psychological equilibrium.

In answer to various queries propounded by members of the Committee at this stage of the proceedings, Mrs. Hardinge described in detail the best and most approved methods of forming circles, founding her advice not on her own opinions, but on the well proved experiences of the Spiritualists with whom she had been associated for many years.

During the entire course of this address, which was occasionally interrupted by appropriate questions, listened to with deep attention, and responded to by a cordial vote of thanks, the Spirits, or invisible audience present, availed themselves of the Mediumship of Mrs. Everitt, who was one of the party, to emphasize the entire speech with loud clear raps which resounded in unmistakable cadence to every sentence, on the uncovered library table, at which the Committee were seated.

Both Mrs. Everitt and the speaker were too far from the table to give rise to the supposition that they had any agency in producing the sounds, yet these manifested an intelligence which was so unmistakable that it must have appeared astounding to the sceptics present. On some occasions, the invisibles emphasized the utterances with the customary signals for " yes " and " no," joining in most vociferously with the applause, and taking part throughout the proceedings with a force, spontaneity, and independence, which was as amusing to the Spiritualists as it was startling and unexpected to the rest of the party.

After the official work of the evening was ended, the company amused themselves for some time by questioning the invisible rapper, and though the meeting did not in any way assume the form of a *séance,* or commit itself by making any report of this informal action of their invisible attendants, the curious proceedings obviously made a deep impression upon some of those present, whilst it called forth from others that involuntary spirit of denial, which would rather discredit the testimony even of the senses than recede from the standard of obstinate and preconceived opinions.

It is more than probable that out of the large number of circulars which were sent to other well-known Spiritualists besides Mrs. Hardinge, not one failed to produce a response of more or less interest to the investigators.

Amongst those respondents whose names will be found in the Society's published report, and who attended in person, to give oral evidence of their faith, are the following persons :—Mrs. Emma Hardinge, Mr. H. D. Jencken, M.R.I.; Mrs. Honeywood, Mr. T. M. Simkiss, Mr. E. Laman Blanchard, Mr. J. Murray Spear, Mr. Benjamin Coleman, Mr. George Childs, artist; Mr. J. Enmore Jones, Miss Alice Jones, Miss Douglass, Lord Borthwick, Mr. James Burns, Mr. Thomas Sherratt, Professor Cromwell F. Varley, Miss Houghton, Mr. Thomas Shorter, Mr. Manuel Eyre, Mr. Lowenthal, Mr. Hockley, Mr. D. D. Home, Mrs. Cox, Signor Damiani, Lord Lindsay, Mr. Chevalier, Mr. Percival, Miss Anna Blackwell, &c., &c.

Letters in response to the Society's circular were received from—Mr. George H. Lewes, Mr. Wm. Wilkinson, solicitor ; Dr. Garth Wilkinson, M.D. ; Dr. Davey, Dr. J. Dixon, Mr. Wm. Howitt, Lord Lytton, Mr. Newton Crosland, Mr. Robert Chambers, Dr. Lockhart Robertson, Dr. Charles Kidd, Mr. Edwin Arnold, Mr. J. Hawkins Simpson, Mr. A. Glendinning, Mr. T. A. Trollope, M. Léon Favre, Mrs. L. Lewis, The Countess (now Duchesse) de Pomar, M. Camille Flammarion, &c., &c., &c.

Papers also, though of an antagonistic character, were received and published from Profs. Huxley and Tyndall, Dr. Carpenter, Mr. Bradlaugh, and others.

It would be impossible without giving the substance of a volume of some 400 pages published by the Dialectical Society as their ultimate report, to convey to the reader the least idea of the candour and zeal with which this investigation was pursued, nor the vast sum of testimony which resulted from it ; in short, without any such intention on the part of its authors, the Dialectical Society's report forms one of the best collections of test facts and irrefragible testimony in favour of the Spiritual hypothesis, that has yet issued from the nineteenth-century press.

It seems that the General Committee, acting on the suggestions before named, organized themselves into six groups or sub-committees, at which Mr. Home and other well-known Mediums lent valuable assistance, whilst on many occasions, phenomena of a very convincing character were evolved, no recognised Medium being present. The reports of the Sub-Committees in fact, when read and candidly considered in detail, *are fully sufficient to establish the fact of an unknown super-sensuous and intelligent power communicating with mortals both by physical and intellectual modes, and that without any additional testimony from any other sources."*

"The Dialectical Society's Report on Spiritualism," was first published by the Society, and subsequently reprinted (by permission) with additional matter, by Mr. Jas. Burns, 15, Southampton Row, Holborn, London, where the curious reader can obtain it. Meantime, the following excerpts from the introductory portion of the work will be perused with interest.

The General Council of the Sub-Committee, addressing the Society at large, report as follows :—

"Your Committee have held fifteen meetings at which they received evidence from thirty-three persons who described phenomena which they stated had occurred within their own personal experience.

' Your Committee have received written statements relating to the phenomena from thirty-one persons.

"Your Committee invited the attendance, and requested the co-operation and advice of scientific men who had publicly expressed opinions favourable or adverse to the genuineness of the phenomena.

"Your Committee also specially invited the attendance of persons who had publicly ascribed the phenomena to imposture or delusion.

"Your Committee however, while successful in procuring the evidence of believers in the phenomena and their supernatural origin, almost wholly failed to obtain evidence from those who attributed them to fraud or delusion.

"As it appeared to your Committee to be of the greatest importance that they should investigate the phenomena in question by personal experiment and test, they resolved themselves into sub-committees as the best means of doing so.

"Six sub-committees were accordingly formed.

"All of these have sent in reports from which it appears that a large majority of the members of your Committee have become actual witnesses to several phases of the phenomena, without the aid or presence of any professional medium, although the greater part of them commenced their investigations in an avowedly sceptical spirit.

"These reports hereto subjoined, substantially corroborate each other, and would appear to establish the following propositions :—

"1. That sounds of a very varied character, apparently proceeding from articles of furniture, the floor and walls of the room—the vibrations of which are often distinctly perceptible to the touch—occur, without being produced by muscular action or mechanical contrivance.

"2. That movements of heavy bodies take place without mechanical contrivance of any kind or adequate exertion of muscular force by the persons present, and frequently without contact or connection with any person.

"3. That these sounds and movements often occur at the times, and in the manner asked for by persons present, and by means of a simple code of signals, answer questions and spell out coherent communications.

"4. That the answers and communications thus obtained are for the most part of a commonplace character ; but facts are sometimes correctly given which are known to one of the persons present.

"5. That the circumstances under which the phenomena occur are variable—the most prominent fact being, that the presence of certain persons seems necessary to their occurrence, and that of others, generally adverse—but this difference does not appear to depend upon any belief or disbelief concerning the phenomena.

"6. That nevertheless the occurrence of the phenomena is not induced by the presence or absence of such persons respectively."

Thus far the sub-committees' personal experiences alone are touched upon. The report next proceeds to deal with the testimony of the various witnesses who, orally or by written statements—received as indisputable, in view of the character and standing of the deponents—gave in a vast mass of testimony from which the following numbered extracts are selected :—

"1. Thirteen witnesses state that they have seen heavy bodies—in some instances men—rise in the air, and remain there for some time without visible support.

"2. Fourteen witnesses testify to having seen hands or figures not appertaining to any human being, but life-like in appearance and mobility, which they have sometimes touched or even grasped and which they were therefore convinced were not the result of illusion or imposture. . . .

"4. Thirteen witnesses declare they have heard musical pieces well played upon instruments not manipulated by any ascertainable agency.

"5. Five witnesses state that they have seen red-hot coals applied to the hands or heads of several persons present without producing pain or scorching, and three witnesses state that they have had the same experiment made upon themselves with the like immunity.

"6. Eight witnesses declare that they have received precise information through rappings, writings, and in other ways, the accuracy of which was unknown at the time to themselves or any persons present, and which on subsequent enquiry was found to be correct."

.   .   .   .   .

"9. Six witnesses declare they have received information of future events, and that in some cases the hour and minute of their occurrence have been accurately foretold, even days and weeks before."

In addition to the above, evidence was given of gratuitously false statements alleged to come from spirits ; of spirit drawings produced under conditions which rendered " human agency impossible," also of " trance speaking, healing, automatic writing, the introduction of flowers and fruit into closed rooms ; of voices in the air, visions in crystals and glasses, and the elongation of the human body.

After a careful and almost exhaustive review of the whole subject, notices of the literature, and the various hypotheses put forth by way of attempted explanation, the preliminary report of the General Committee concludes with the following remarks :—

"In presenting their report, your Committee, taking into consideration the high character and great intelligence of many of the witnesses to the more extraordinary facts, the extent to which their testimony is supported by the reports of the sub-committees, and the absence of any proof of imposture or delusion as regards a large portion of the phenomena ; and further, having regard to the exceptional character of the phenomena, and the large number of persons of every grade of society and over the whole civilised world who are more or less influenced by a belief in their supernatural origin, and to the fact that no philosophical explanation of them has yet been arrived at, deem it incumbent upon them to state their conviction that the subject is worthy of more serious attention and careful investigation than it has hitherto received."

With a recommendation that the entire report together with the detailed reports of the Sub-Committees should be printed, here concludes one of the most remarkable, candid, and noteworthy summaries of a series of investigations into the phenomena of modern Spiritualism that the records of that movement can display.

The very popularity of "the cause," the many honourable and distinguished patrons which it had attracted to its ranks, and the possibility of making easy profits by simulating its phenomena, have doubtless been the superinducing motives which have caused such a vast flood of imposture, fraud and pretension to disgrace its honoured name, *since* the Dialectical Society issued their report. Still that volume remains, and the high character of those who constituted the witnesses, their entire disinterestedness and freedom from bias or motive to pervert the truth, and the care, caution, and indefatigable energy with which the research was pursued, will out-weigh with the capable thinker the adverse witness of determined prejudice, or even the soil of ten thousand impure and fraudulent hands laid upon the fair form revealed by the investigations of this brave band of truth seekers. It is only to be regretted that the report of the Dialectical Society has not attained to a far wider circulation than it has hitherto enjoyed—still more that other associations composed of individuals as authoritative in name and place, as capable of judging rightly, and as faithful in seeking for and sifting evidence, have not followed so laudable an example, and by thus formulating and publishing abroad all that was found valuable and important in the movement, they would have tended to repress the atrocious licence, absurd fanaticism, and audacious frauds, that have been foisted upon the name and fame of modern Spiritualism.

CHAPTER XXV.

SPIRITUALISM IN GREAT BRITAIN (CONTINUED.)

IT must not be supposed that the course of Spiritualism in Great Britain moved on to the achievement of its many conquests over materialism and unbelief, without battles to fight, and obstacles to overcome. Besides the persistent opposition directed against this movement from the enemies who may be classified as the would-be monopolists of all knowledge, in religion, science, and literature, many and injurious have been "the foes of its own household," with which Spiritualism has had to contend.

Whether excessive vanity or mercenary motives have been the causes which induced certain individuals, professing to be Mediums for Spiritual phenomena, to supplement the lack of natural endowments by artifice, it matters not now to enquire; but it is an assured fact, that few well-informed Spiritualists would venture to deny, that many manifestations have been exhibited, both by private and professional Media, more or less garbled by fraud, and interpolated by human contrivance.

As our work is understood to record what Spiritualism is, *not what it is not*, we do not feel called upon to dilate farther on the performances of tricksters than to note the fact of their interference, and the injurious effect they have had upon the progress of the Spiritual cause.

It must suffice to say, that Spiritualism, like every other movement in human life worth counterfeiting, has had to endure its share of hindrance and disgrace from the camp followers who are ever found in the wake of the armies of progression.

We know it is constantly alleged by detected impostors, that the frauds they can no longer conceal, were undertaken, "under the influence of *evil spirits*," generally those, who were attracted to the circle by some *evil-minded sceptic.* As to themselves—poor innocents!—they were *wholly unconscious*, and should be regarded merely as *victims*, not as offenders.

To account for the prepared paraphernalia with which their frauds were perpetrated, they generally fall back upon the theory of *conspiracies to ruin them*, amongst the very sitters whom they have attempted to cheat, &c., &c. To *explanations* of this character, alike insulting to common sense, and common honesty, no answer can be made. Unfortunately however, the heartless impostors who have no scruple in robbing their victims, and imposing on the holiest emotions of the heart, generally find hosts of apologists, who not only seek to excuse their turpitude by the miserable platitudes suggested above, but follow up the detection, with torrents of abuse against those who will not tamely submit to be imposed upon.

"Hard words break no bones," says the Spanish proverb. That may be true, nevertheless they are exceedingly hurtful to the feelings, and hence it is, that many an audacious cheat has been permitted to perpetrate his foul work unrebuked, for fear of the clamorous attacks with which the exposer is sure to be met by ill-judged partisanship, or fanatical credulity.

True Mediums, whether professional or otherwise, deserve the most kind consideration and courteous treatment ; but that is a poor rule which does not apply both ways, and therefore the same consideration and courtesy is due to the investigator, especially when it is remembered that such investigations are generally made under the impulse of the most sacred affections, and therefore deserve to be treated with reverence and respect.

Still the effect of detected imposture has been most injurious to the progress of Spiritualism, and though its publicity may have served the purpose of stimulating the investigator to more caution in his researches, it has turned back many an one from seeking divine truth, in a path bristling with the way marks of deceit and lies.

Other causes too, conspired to produce reactionary tides in public opinion, unfavourable to Spiritualism.

Mr. Sothern, a popular actor, who under the alias of "Stuart," had once been the conductor of the well-known "miracle-circle" of New York, thought proper to amuse his English associates by contriving all sorts of caricature performances calculated to bring ridicule and discredit upon Spiritualism.

Mr. Benjamin Coleman in his zeal for the cause he espoused, in exposing Mr. Sothern's performances, unfortunately republished certain statements copied from the New York papers, which gave the pretext for a prosecution on the ground of libel. A trial ensued. The well-known aphorism that "truth is a libel" obtained with unmistakable force in this case, and Mr. Coleman and his publisher, the editor of the paper called *The Spiritual Times*, were mulcted in heavy damages.

It is worth while in this connection to give a curious episode which may not be unimportant in weighing the statements of those, who—because they find fraud in one direction—pass a wholesale verdict of condemnation against the reliability of all phenomena.

A report has often gained currency, that there was *somewhere*, though rumour never condescended to be explicit on the actual whereabouts, a mechanic who had been employed to manufacture apparatus by which a machine, concealed about the person, could produce the phenomena known as "Spirit rapping."

More than one of the antagonists to Spiritualism have made allusion to this floating rumour, treating it as a well proven fact, and alleging that it fully explained the entire formulæ of the (assumed Spiritual) rappings.

Now these allegations have always been made with an amount of indefiniteness which has deprived them of credit, whether with the advocates

13

or opponents of Spiritualism.   For the benefit of both classes, we shall now proceed to give the floating rumour a clear and legitimate parentage.

During the investigations of the Dialectical Society, there was a general flutter of opinion on the part of the antagonists to Spiritualism lest those who were heretofore sceptics, might prove too much and not improbably become themselves converted.

In this direful contingency *some one (whom this record does not care to immortalize)* procured the attendance before the Dialectical Society's Council, of one Mr. William Faulkner, of Endell Street, London, who gave evidence in respect to certain magnets which he claimed to have manufactured, by means of which " artificial raps could be produced," whilst the magnets were concealed about the person of " the Medium."

Being closely plied with questions by the Spiritualists present, this gentleman was unable to show *that he had ever supplied these magnets to a single Medium known to any one in the Spiritual ranks* save a Mr. Addison, the accomplice of Mr. Sothern, and the *gentleman* at whose residence all the tricks were performed, which Mr. Coleman exposed.

It must be remembered that Messrs. Sothern and Addison made it their business to bring Spiritualism into ridicule and contempt by first pretending to produce phenomena and then showing that it was only the result of trickery and deception.   It was in aid of this notable work that Mr. Faulkner's magnets were manufactured, and in this way that Mr. Faulkner's testimony was expected to bring discredit on the entire mass of Spiritual phenomena ; in a word, those who contrived to cite this person, before the Dialectical Society's Council, evidently meant to show that because Mr. Addison's house was fitted up with artificial magnets designed to deceive the unwary and bring Spiritualism into ridicule, so all " Spirit rappings," whether occurring in the palaces of emperors and princes, or the homes of clowns and harlequins, must be produced by magnets manufactured by Mr. Faulkner, of Endell Street, London !

Comment upon this very flimsy attempt to destroy a world-wide truth with a harlequin's bat and ball is unnecessary ; in short, a subject so justly relegated to oblivion would not be recalled at this time, were it not desirable to observe, to what desperate and puerile methods of warfare, the opponents of this great cause have been driven.

Shortly after the Coleman prosecution, another of a still more complex and damaging character arose, in connection with Mr. D. D. Home, and an old lady by the name of Lyon.

Although the details of this case may be fresh in the memory of readers of the present generation it is necessary, for the benefit of posterity, to give the following brief abstract of its salient points.

It seems that Mrs. Lyon, an eccentric old lady, took a sudden and violent fancy to Mr. D. D. Home, and being a widow with a large fortune at her own disposal, she induced the young Medium to become her adopted son and heir.   Settlements were made, and Mr. Home's name was changed to Lyon, by a formal parliamentary act.

For a time all seemed to promise well for the future happiness of the contracting parties.   At length however, the lady grew exacting, the adopted son restive ; she wearied of her fancy, he of his gilded chains. Disputes arose ; then estrangement, and the *finale* was, a demand on the part of the lady, for release from all her promises, and an immediate restitution of the gifts she had bestowed on the creature of her whim.

Unfortunately for Mr. Home, the last-named demand implied an impossibility with which he could not comply. Failing to obtain her exorbitant demands, the whilom *tender mother* had the son arrested, and then commenced a vigorous prosecution against him for the restitution of all the gifts she had bestowed, on the plea, that Mr. Home had worked upon her feelings, and induced her to consent to the act of adoption by *pretended* Spiritual manifestations.

A long trial ensued, in the published reports of which, not one tittle of evidence could be adduced in support of the lady's allegation ; on the contrary, her witnesses discredited and contradicted each other, and her own testimony was so silly and unsupported, that the judge was frequently obliged to advise her to be silent, as "her statements were too contradictory to be accepted." On the other hand it was shown by an immense number of the most respectable witnesses, that Mr. Home yielded to this lady's offers slowly and reluctantly, and that he even sent his friend and legal adviser Mr. William Wilkinson to call on her; to place before her the magnitude of her undertaking, and beseech her to take time and good counsel, before consummating her hasty proposal.

During the entire progress of this protracted trial, the balance of evidence was all on the side of the unfortunate Medium, and judging purely by the testimony adduced, not a doubt existed in the public mind, that Mr. Home would be honourable acquitted, and the prosecution anything but honourably quashed.

But great are the uncertainties of the law ! Mr. Home was found guilty *of exerting undue influence over the mind of an innocent aged lady*, and ordered to give back all that he could restore, and so the matter was supposed to end. End there however it did not. So long as the details of the case were fresh in the public mind, Mr. Home was regarded as the victim of a very unjust verdict, whilst Mrs. Lyon was regarded as very much more of a wolf in sheep's clothing, than as the representative of her kingly name. When the real facts at issue slipped out of the versatile memory of "the dear public" however, and ancient prejudice was permitted to re-assume her sway, the Spiritualists were constantly reproached with the acts of "that wicked Mr. Home," and the wrongs of that amiable and *truthful* old lady, Mrs. Lyon. Nay, the author in her wide wanderings over the world has frequently been reminded "how that dreadful Mr. Home had been *imprisoned for life,* for plundering and imposing upon his benefactress, and how that dreadful delusion of Spiritualism was all exploded in consequence." It was of no avail to urge that Mr. Home was at that very time the honoured guest of the Emperor of Russia, and Spiritualism exerting more power and influence over the masses than ever. The slanderers "knew all about it," for did not every one "say so," and was it not enough that it was testified of by the authoritative tongue of common report ?

At a still later date, other trials and other convictions occurred, and in more than one instance frauds and adventurers received their deserts, and suffered penalties which Spiritualists were as ready to pronounce well merited as were their opponents. Still the result of any judicial trials in which Spiritualism was concerned, invariably ended *unfavourably for the cause*, whatever the merits of the case might be.

It is not to be wondered at then, that antagonistic individuals availed themselves of this mockery of justice in connection with an unpopular movement, and scrupled not to call in the aid of the law to punish the believers whose faith they could not change.

Whatever the present generation may allege, posterity will surely **realize** that it was the prevalence of an unjust and bigoted public sentiment, and the certainty that the law would uphold that sentiment, which stimulated the vexatious prosecution that was quite recently instituted against the celebrated American Medium, Mr. Henry Slade, who, during a brief visit to this country *en route* to fulfil an engagement in Russia, was becoming all too popular with the visitors whom his limited time permitted **him** to receive.

It was no doubt in view of this "perversion of public feeling" and "in the highest interests of morality and religion" that two self-styled scientific gentlemen called on the American Medium, and after endeavouring in every possible way to entrap him into some suspicious act, they openly accused him of fraud, caused his arrest and entered upon a vigorous and relentless prosecution against him.

Again the details of the trial were utterly barren of proof that **the** charge was true. Except that the prosecution could not account for the phenomena produced, and therefore trumped up an imaginary and totally impractical hypothesis as *to how it might or must have been done*, there was not a shadow of evidence to prove fraud on the part of the Medium.

For the defence, a large number of distinguished and respectable persons tendered their witness in favour of Slade's honesty, and the unmistakable character of the supra-mundane phenomena occurring in his presence. Only four of these favourable witnesses were allowed to testify, one of them being the celebrated author and naturalist, Professor A. R. Wallace. Notwithstanding the fact that the magistrate before whom the case was tried, was obliged to acknowledge that the evidence in Slade's favour "was overwhelming," after a most "Dogberry" like summing up, he sentenced Mr. Slade "under the fourth section of the Vagrant Act," to three months' imprisonment with hard labour, "*for using subtile crafts and devices by palmistry or otherwise to deceive*," &c., &c. This notable conviction was soon after "quashed" on appeal to the Middlesex Sessions, for a formal error in the conviction.

But the enemy was not to be deprived of his "pound of flesh." "In the interests of science"—as the prosecutors alleged—they commenced a fresh attack, and although the victim of this pitiful warfare—broken down in health and spirits by the cruel persecution directed against him— insisted upon meeting whatever further proceedings might be taken, his medical attendant declared that "any further attempt to face the storm would kill him outright," and his numerous friends and supporters absolutely forced him to proceed on his way to the Continent, to meet the engagement for which he had come to Europe.

It is but justice to add, that when Mr. Slade's health became sufficiently restored, he wrote to one of his scientific accusers, offering to return to England at his own expense, to give him six *séances* at any place he might choose, under any reasonable conditions he might dictate, entirely free of charge and for the purpose of proving the absence of fraud on his part. This letter, long, clear, and manly as it was, the scientific and gentleman- like accuser doubtless deemed it "in the interests of science" utterly to disregard, even by a single word of reply. The unprejudiced reader may satisfy himself concerning the entire candour and honesty of this letter by perusing it on page 36 of Professor Zöllner's work, "Transcendental Physics."

It might be worth while to compare the facts thus briefly summarized, from already published accounts, with "the lying tongue of rumour," from which source the author has frequently heard, that "Slade had been caught in the act of tricking a party of celebrated professors ; tried, condemned, imprisoned, and that hence, the monstrous delusion of Spiritualism was all exposed and for ever exploded !"

For the rest of Mr. Slade's Continental experiences the reader is referred to the section on "Spiritualism in Germany," and the report of his *séances* with the Leipzig professors.

It only remains to notice one more result of the prosecution, or more strictly speaking, the *persecution*, to which Mr. Slade was subject, and this was, the circulation of a memorial to the British Home Secretary, a few extracts from which will close this chapter.

The Spiritualists of Great Britain probably never expected any other official result from their memorial than a silent smile of contempt from the party whose duty it would be to consign it to the Governmental waste basket—nevertheless they felt that its distribution would serve the purpose of registering the Spiritualists' version of their case, and give the too-trusting public to understand that the Bow Street magistrate's unfavourable verdict, had not yet become the funeral sermon of Spiritualism, also that this irrepressible cause still maintained a vigorous state of being, in which new conversions were effected with each succeeding day and hour.

The *Religio Philosophical Journal*, an old established and excellent Spiritual periodical published at Chicago, U.S., reprinted the above-named memorial, the main points of which, together with the editor's comments, we give in the following extract :—

"The British National Association of Spiritualists has prepared, and is circulating a memorial to the Home Secretary of the British Government, asking that the construction heretofore put upon an Act for the Suppression of Vagrancy, whereby it is made a means of maintaining criminal prosecution against Mediums, may be corrected. The fourth section of the act classes as vagrants, 'Every person pretending or professing to tell fortunes, or using any subtle craft, means or device by palmistry or otherwise, to deceive or impose upon any of his majesty's subjects.' It was under this clause that Henry Slade was prosecuted, and concerning his prosecution the memorial says :

"'As an instance in point your memorialists would refer to the case of Henry Slade, an American Medium, charged at Bow Street Police Court in the year 1876, under the fourth section of the said Act. For the defence the magistrate allowed to be called as witnesses four gentlemen, one of them of great scientific eminence, who were experts in the investigation of Spiritualism, and who had especially tested the Mediumship of the defendant on many occasions. These gentlemen gave evidence of facts wholly inconsistent with the supposition that the defendant was an impostor—evidence which the magistrate himself declared from the bench to be "overwhelming." In attendance were other witnesses prepared to give similar testimony. Yet the magistrate refused to allow them to be called : and, in giving judgment against the defendant, he avowedly put the evidence, which he had described as above, altogether out of consideration, expressly declaring that he based his decision "according to the known course of nature." The law, it is true, does not expressly sanction any presumption against the existence of agencies in nature other than and surpassing those generally known—and these it is, and not "miraculous" or "supernatural" powers that Spiritualists allege—but the persons who administer the law are unavoidably bounded by this common knowledge in dealing with evidence and the probabilities arising therefrom. It results then, that the magistrate who adjudicates "according to the known course of nature" in respect to phenomena which do not conform to such "known course" as interpreted by him, finds it practically unnecessary to hear evidence beyond the mere proof of the alleged occurrence of the phenomena in question in the presence of a certain individual, when no other person also present can be taken to have produced them. The case is therefore prejudged ; and the examination of witnesses to prove that any alleged act of imposture was not really of that character is a superfluous mockery and pretence. It is upon this fact that no tribunal, without going into an exhaustive and impracticable inquiry upon an unfamiliar subject, can do other than take its own knowledge and experience as the standard of probability, that your memorialists chiefly rest their statement of the unavoidable injustice and prejudicial character of these prosecutions.'"

CHAPTER XXVI.

SPIRITUALISM IN GREAT BRITAIN (CONTINUED).

CONCERNING THE LITERATURE OF ENGLISH SPIRITUALISM.

THE first periodical issued in England in connection with the subject of Spiritualism was *The Yorkshire Spiritual Telegraph.* When seeking for authentic information on this pioneer work, the author was referred to the following article which appeared in the year 1882 in the columns of *Light*; and its perusal will perhaps give a better idea than could otherwise be obtained of the regard with which the promoter of this periodical is still remembered :—

" KEIGHLEY.

"An event, unique in character, has recently transpired in this cosy little Yorkshire town, which will long be remembered with pleasure by all concerned, marking as it did the thirtieth anniversary of the introduction of Spiritualism into this country. The celebration, for such in character was the event alluded to, was conceived and executed by the committee and friends of the Keighley 'Spiritual Brotherhood,' Mr. John Pickles, the chairman, working energetically to that end, and being ably assisted by Mr. J. Smith, the hon. secretary. Indeed, so earnestly did all work that a most successful issue was achieved. The proceedings consisted of a public tea and meeting on Saturday, July 8th. The objects the committee had in view were the presentation of the portraits of the three pioneer workers in the movement, viz., Messrs. John Wright, Abraham Shackleton, and David Weatherhead ; the two first-named persons, and the family of the last-named gentleman, who has passed hence, being the recipients of the gifts. In 1853 Mr. David Richmond, from the Shakers, of America, brought the particulars of Spirit phenomena with him to this country, and, paying a visit to Keighley, called upon Mr. David Weather-head to present the matter to the attention of that gentleman. As a result of the interview, a public meeting was held, at which table manifestations were obtained, through mediums discovered in the audience, by Mr. Richmond, who delivered an explanatory address. Mr. Weatherhead became convinced of the truth of Spirit intercourse, and at once entered heartily into the matter, sparing neither time, pains, nor purse in his zeal. He established the first printing press in the movement, printed the first English Spiritual periodical, the *Yorkshire Spiritual Telegraph,* and caused the circulation of innumerable tracts, pamphlets, &c., throughout the kingdom, and subsequently erected, at his own expense, the comfortable and commodious building used by the society at the present time. He contentedly bore all the expenses involved, and during his residence in the flesh was a true pillar of the cause. Messrs. Wright and Shackleton were the two trance mediums developed in the early days ; they have literally grown grey in the work. Their labours have been free of price, and as speakers, healers, and clairvoyants they have rendered valuable service to the cause. To do honour to these workers, and to express the high esteem in which they were held, the recent presentation was arranged. On Saturday the proceedings were opened by a tea, at which a very large company sat down. At seven o'clock the public meeting was opened by the chairman, Mr. J. Clapham, who said : 'Ladies and gentlemen, we are met here to-night to show our gratitude to the late Mr. Weatherhead, and also to Mr. Shackleton and Mr. Wright, for their past services. Keighley was the place where Spiritualism was first promulgated in this country, being introduced to us by Mr. David Richmond, of Darlington, who, with the assistance of Mr

Weatherhead, was enabled to deliver three lectures upon the subject in the Working Men's Hall, in June, 1853. The issues were, that Mr. Weatherhead took steps which resulted in the formation of the society which exists at the present time ; and soon afterwards the mediums named were developed, and they are still serving us to-day. These gentlemen, with Mr. Weatherhead, were the mainstays of the cause, and Mr. Weatherhead, during his life here, spared neither time nor means in spreading abroad this grand truth. It was he who established the first printing press, and distributed tracts, pamphlets, and other literature broadcast, the materials for which were largely obtained through mediumship. He it was who bore the entire expense of the erection of the Lyceum Buildings, and in many other ways testified his earnestness and devotion to the cause. The outcome of his labours has been that to-day we have here a society in a flourishing condition, having one hundred and fifty members on the roll, some five or six active mediums constantly ministering to us, and a Sunday School composed of upwards of a hundred members. As, therefore, a slight mark of esteem and appreciation to these our pioneer workers, we are to-night to present to them the portraits before us, and all will join with me in saying they are most heartily deserved.' The portraits, in oils, which are excellent specimens of the painter's art, were then presented. That to Mr. Wright was presented by Mr. John Scott, of Belfast ; that to Mr. Shackleton by Mr. D. Richmond, of Darlington ; and that of Mr. Weatherhead to his family, by Mr. J. J. Morse, of London ; and suitable acknowledgments were made in each case. The proceedings were varied by some excellent singing and reciting by a glee party and several friends, and altogether the event was marked by a hearty enthusiasm which evidenced the full sympathy of all present in the event of the day.

"The series of meetings were held in the large Auction Hall of Mr. William Weatherhead, who very kindly placed it at the disposal of the society free of cost. The above events will be long remembered by all present, and constitute an occasion that will be historical in its relations to the progress of Spiritualism in Great Britain."

None but the pioneer of an unpopular cause can understand the value of the good work effected by Mr. David Weatherhead, or the amount of martyrdom he must have incurred in its performance.

In his time, the publication of a Spiritual journal, and the dissemination of Spiritual literature was only repaid by public odium and social ostracism.

Mr. David Weatherhead, as the first publisher of the first Spiritual journal issued from the English press, undoubtedly courted the martyr's cross that was put upon him ; but who can doubt that he is now reaping the reward of the martyr's crown in the better life to which his brave spirit has attained?

After the *Spiritual Telegraph*, the oldest and most important work of the movement was the London *Spiritual Magazine*, which, during a period of nearly twenty years, sent forth its monthly record of Spiritual work and progress in Great Britain in choice language and scholarly form. This magazine was published by the accomplished writer William Wilkinson, Esq., solicitor, of Lincoln's Inn, a gentleman who contributed his wealth and high social position to the advancement of Spiritualism and the promulgation of its teachings, without fear of or favour from men. Mr. Wilkinson's undertaking was promoted and ably sustained by the literary assistance of Mr. Thomas Shorter, who—under the *nom de plume* of " Brevior "—has written, lectured, and laboured for the cause of Spiritualism, with a devotion and zeal that entitle him to the gratitude of every spiritualist in this generation. Quite early in the history of the modern movement, Mr. Shorter published an admirable and compendious work on the Spiritualism of all ages and times, entitled " The Two Worlds." The production of this lucid, and charmingly written work, would in itself have been sufficient to elevate its author to a high rank in the world of letters had the subject been any other than Spiritualism. Working on unceasingly, Mr. Shorter never paused to enquire whether the sublime truths he promulgated met, or opposed the popular taste. From the first opening of the immortal gates to the eyes of humanity in this century, up to the truly *dark day*, when the irreparable loss of sight fell like a pall across the noble gentleman's way, he has laboured with tongue, pen, and influence, to help to plant the standard of the faith and illuminate the path of others with the radiance of that better world, which alone remains to guide his darkened way on earth.

Even since the affliction of blindness has fallen upon him, Mr. Shorter has not relapsed his efforts to *steady the ark of progress* as it moves on its way. His fearless testimony is ever ready, and his clear voice is heard at every public gathering of Metropolitan Spiritualists. A fine collection of choice poems has lately been issued by him, for the consolation and instruction of those *who can see to read them,*—and Mr. Shorter's career gives promise of closing like that of the good sentinel of Pompeian celebrity who died at his post—"faithful unto death."

In addition to the invaluable services of Messrs. Wilkinson and Shorter, the London *Spiritual Magazine* numbered amongst its staff of contributors the flower of European Spiritual literati.

Pre-eminent above all others, stands out the noble name of William Howitt, an author whose works are the pride of every well-informed English reader; a gentleman whom to know was to love and honour, and a Spiritualist whose fearless advocacy shed lustre on his cause, and became a tower of strength to his co-workers. Happily for the better appreciation of Mr. Howitt and his wonderful literary labours, a faithful transcript of his life is just now passing through the press in a volume entitled "The Pioneers of the Spiritual Reformation." Mr. Howitt's biography forms the opening chapters of this interesting work, and how full of valuable information the volume itself will be, may be gathered from the fact, that it is written by the daughter of Mary and William Howitt, Mrs. Watts,—a lady whose charming contributions to Spiritual literature have already become familiar to admiring readers over the signature of "A. M. H. W." It may not be inappropriate in this place to give an excerpt from the London *Spiritual Magazine* in which Mr. Howitt defines, in his own forcible language, the nature of some of his spiritual experiences. He says :—

"We have seen tables often enough lifted by invisible power from the floor ; seen them give answers to questions by rising and sinking in the air ; we have seen them in the air keep time by their movements to a tune playing on a piano ; seen them slide about the floor of a room, laying themselves down when touched. . . . . We have heard bells ring in the air, and seen them thus ringing move about a room ; seen flowers broken from plants, and carried to different persons, without any visible hand ; seen musical instruments play correct airs apparently of themselves, and even rise up, place themselves on a person's head, and play out a well-known air in fine style. We have heard remarkable predictions given through mediums, and which have come literally to pass ; heard wonderful descriptions of scenes in the invisible world made by persons in clairvoyant trance, which would require the highest imaginative genius to invent or embody in words ; have seen writing done by pencils laid on paper in the middle of the floor, not within reach of any person present, and innumerable such things."

And in speaking of the drawings made by Madam Hauffé under spirit-influence, he takes occasion to make the following statement of his own experience as a spirit-medium :—

"Having myself, who never had a single lesson in drawing, and never could draw in a normal condition, had a great number of circles struck through my hand under spirit-influence, and these filled up by tracery of ever new invention, without a thought of my own, I, at once, recognise the truth of Kerner's statement. The drawings made by my hand have been seen by great numbers of persons, artists as well as others, and remain to be seen, though the power is again gone from me. Giotto, or any pair of compasses, could not strike more perfect circles than I could under this influence, with nothing but a piece

S C HALL

of paper and a pencil. No inventor of tracery or patterns could invent such original ones as were thrown out on the paper day after day, with almost lightning speed, except with long and studious labour, and by instrumental aid. At the same time the sketches given through me are not to be named with the drawings, both in pencil and colours, produced in this manner through others who are well known."

As an example of the logical yet religious tone of Mr. Howitt's philosophical articles on this subject we call the reader's attention to the subjoined passages, taken from the London *Spiritual Magazine* of April, 1863 :—

"And all this time, in England, thousands and tens of thousands were daily sitting down in their families and circles of intimate friends, and quietly and successfully testing those angels under their own mode of advent, and finding them real. And both in America and here, as well as in most of the Continental nations, this has been the great mode of enquiry and convincement. Public mediums have, in reality, only inaugurated the movement : it has been, of necessity, carried on by private and family practice. In this domestic prosecution of Spiritualism, equally inaccessible to the vulgar sorcerer and the interested impostor—where every person was desirous only of truth, and many of them of deep religious truth—the second stage of Spiritual development, the more interior and intellectual, has been reached by a very large community. For there is, indeed, a very large section of society who are sick of empty profession, or disgusted with the dreary cheat of scepticism, and who have been long yearning for some revelation of the immortal hopes of earlier years, in some substantial and unmistakeable form. They have found this in the daily visits of their departed friends, coming to them with all their old identities of soul, taste, or memory of announcements of Christian truth, and of God's promised felicity. They have listened again and again to the words of their beloved ones, bidding them take courage, for there was no death, but that around them walked their so-called departed, ready to aid and comfort them in their earth pilgrimage, and to receive them to immediate and far more glorious existence."

Besides the voluminous mass of historical and descriptive writings for which both Mr. and Mrs. Howitt have attained a world-wide celebrity, Mrs. Howitt has enriched the répertoire of Spiritual literature with a fine translation of Enmemoser's "History of Magic," whilst Mr. Wm. Howitt's "History of the Supernatural," in two volumes, and his splendid magazine articles, are acknowledged to be amongst the best standard works of which the Spiritual cause can boast.

Amongst the many popular and distinguished writers of the day who have fearlessly avowed their interest in Spiritualism and contributed talent and reputation to its advocacy, were Mr. and Mrs. S. C. Hall, the former well-known as the editor of the London *Art Journal*, whilst Mrs. Hall's charming works of fiction, and other writings, have procured for her a world-wide celebrity. It would be difficult to exaggerate the valuable influence exercised by this accomplished couple upon the cause of Spiritualism.

Moving in the highest ranks of European society, their residence was the scene of delightful *reunions*, where gifted Mediums and persons of the highest literary and scientific culture were brought together and combined to send forth an influence which permeated the ranks of the most intellectual classes of Europe. It is but a few short years since the fair form of the talented authoress, Maria S. C. Hall, vanished from her wide circle of admirers and passed to the land of light to which her hand had already pointed so many of earth's weary pilgrims. And thus after fifty years of heart and soul companionship, the noble octogenarian, S. C. Hall, was left alone on earth, at least so far as mortal sight is concerned ; never have the triumphs of Spiritualism become more manifest than in the fortitude with which this truly "Christian" gentleman sustains the temporary separation between the mortal and the immortal. At a crowded reception tendered to the author by the Central Association of Spiritualists, a few months since, on the occasion of her visit to London, Mr. S. C. Hall—then over eighty years of age—made THE SPEECH of the night, and in a strain of glowing eloquence that thrilled every heart, and brought tears to every eye, he declared that the grave had not separated him from his angel wife. Her constant communications cheered his loneliness, he said; guided his mortal footsteps and gave him unceasing assurance that she in heaven and he on earth were now as ever one in heart, life interest, and undying interchange of loving communion. . . . What a triumphant illustration of immortal life over mortal death, and of the value of the much derided facts and philosophy of Spiritualism!

In addition to these eminent writers, many others of scarcely less celebrity assisted in making the London *Spiritual Magazine* a work as valuable in an æsthetic point of view, as it was interesting to the believers in Spirit communion.

One of the first volumes published in the interests of Spiritualism, and still a standard work with those who desire to trace out the movement from its incipiency, is Mrs. De Morgan's excellent sketch of her own experiences, entitled "From Matter to Spirit."

Another valuable and timely compendium of Spiritual facts and philosophy is, "The Natural and Supernatural," written at an early period of the movement in England, by J. Enmore Jones, Esq., of Norwood.

Mr. D. D. Home has published two interesting volumes at different times, the one called "Incidents of My Life," the other "Lights and Shadows of Spiritualism."

Omitting the long list of smaller volumes, tracts, pamphlets, leaflets, &c., &c., which swell the mass of English Spiritual literature, we next call attention to an admirable work—"Miracles and Modern Spiritualism," written by the celebrated author and naturalist, Professor A. R. Wallace. For the unpretentious size of this volume it would be difficult to find any work which presents a more unanswerable array of facts, logic, and scientific deductions; in short, it is in every way worthy to be regarded as a Spiritualistic manual, of equal value to the well-informed Spiritualist, and the earnest investigator.

Besides the intrinsic value of Professor Wallace's admirable work, the public have appreciated it all the more, from the fact that it emanates from the pen of one so highly honoured in the ranks of science and literature as Alfred Russell Wallace. Dividing honours with the alleged founder of the famous doctrine of "evolution"—Charles Darwin—a world-wide traveller, naturalist, and distinguished author, Professor Wallace has never hesitated to contribute his honoured testimony to the much-abused cause of Spiritualism. His clear logical speeches, unanswerable magazine and journalistic articles, and his noble defence and exposition of true Spiritualism, when and wherever opportunity has permitted, all have combined to render Professor Wallace's adherence to the cause of Spiritualism a tower of strength which can never be too gratefully remembered.

Professor Crookes's record of experiments with Mr. D. D. Home, Miss Cook, and other Media; Professor Zöellner's "Transcendental Physics," and the "Report of the Dialectical Society," have been already noticed.

One of the most esteemed and gifted writers in the ranks of Spiritualism is the gentleman known by the *nom de plume* of "M. A., Oxon."

Amongst this truly inspired author's collected writings, the most popular are, the four volumes entitled severally, "Psychography;" "Spirit Identity;" "The Higher Aspects of Spiritualism;" and "Spirit Teachings."

Nothing in the whole realm of occult literature can surpass the deep insight, and profound mastery of Spiritualistic problems, manifested in these works. And yet they are but a small part of " M. A., Oxon's" contributions. His fine magazine and journalistic articles are to be found in most of the high-toned periodicals of the last few years, whilst his well-known signature invariably attracts every thoughtful reader who desires to be instructed, as well as interested.

Three of the most remarkable volumes that have of late issued from the English Spiritual press, are those, circulated chiefly amongst the publisher's personal friends, entitled, " Angelic Revelations." They are a collection of communications given through the Mediumship of a lady in private life, and received by a circle of ladies and gentlemen whose sessions were continued for several years in the city of Manchester. The *séances* were of the most exclusive character, and were only participated in by such persons as the controlling intelligences elected to receive. Each of these favoured individuals was named by the presiding "angels," according to the qualities of mind that distinguished them. To Mr. William Oxley, the well-known and highly-esteemed Spiritualistic author, was assigned the onerous task of recording the communications spoken in trance by the Medium.

Thus the whole of the three volumes above named, have been written out and prepared for the press, and published in the highest form of mechanical art, by Mr. Oxley "the Recorder," with the permission of the controlling intelligences, and under the auspices of the Manchester circle.* No comment can do justice to the ecstatic style or remarkable views of the future life, indicated in these volumes. They must be read to be appreciated, and then they form but one fragment of the innumerable and diverse revealments of the after life, and man's spiritual genesis and exodus, which the trance utterances of the present dispensation have furnished us with. The volumes above mentioned are not the only ones for which the world is indebted to their accomplished publisher.

Mr. William Oxley has written a remarkably fine poetical adaptation of the celebrated Hindoo *Baghavat Gita ;* an excellent metaphysical work entitled " The Philosophy of Spirit ;" and he is now enriching the columns of the *Medium and Daybreak* with a graphic account of the ancient monuments of Egypt, which he describes and comments upon in the progressive spirit of an advanced thinker, and from the standpoint of his own personal knowledge, obtained during a recent visit to the wonderful old land of the Pharaohs. Mr. Oxley's name has become so long familiarized to every reader of the best Spiritual literature, by noble and high-toned articles, that many will rejoice in the opportunity of becoming better acquainted with their favourite author, through the accompanying fine illustrations. The introduction to the facsimiles of the spiritually produced flower and the spirit foot are too graphically recorded in Mr. Oxley's own words to need any other comment than their perusal will suggest.

Mr. Oxley, addressing the author of this volume, says :—

"To Mrs. Britten,—I have the pleasure to furnish you with engravings of a materialised spirit's foot, which represents with perfect exactitude the plaster cast, moulded by a professional artist, from the paraffin wax envelope. Apart from any suggestion of trickery and collusion the cast itself tells its own tale, for it has the cuticle marks in the crucial parts, which it would be impossible to produce *under any circumstances* without a

---

* " Angelic Revelations, concerning the origin, ultimation, and destiny of the Human Spirit, &c., may be had from T. Gaskell, 69, Oldham Road, Manchester.

mould formed of many parts, as any mechanician, or even ordinary person can see at a glance. The cast foot is eight inches long by three inches in the smallest part, and nine inches in the widest part. The opening at the top of the foot is 2¼ inches diameter. And yet through this opening the foot was instantaneously withdrawn. The medium was Mrs. Firman (now deceased). The *modus operandi* was as follows: I prepared the melted hot liquid paraffin, into which the little spirit form dipped her foot several times, so as to make it of sufficient thickness to maintain its figure. After this operation the spirit form—known to us as Bertie—put out her foot *with the wax mould upon it*, and asking me to take hold of it, which I did, the foot was withdrawn (or dissolved, I know not which) and the mould left in my hand. This was at the house of a friend in Manchester, April 11th, 1876, and next morning I took the wax mould to Mr. Bernaditto, who filled it with plaster, and, after melting the wax from the plaster, the result was a beautiful feminine human foot, of which the illustration is a faithful copy. The crucial test of this wondrous phenomenon is seen by reference to Figure II. The ball of the toe (see D C), *half an inch thick*, had to be drawn through an opening only a *quarter-inch deep* (see B A), which of course, under ordinary circumstances, is a physical impossibility, without destroying the fine bridge (see A C), and it is exactly on this bridge that the cuticle marks are delineated as perfectly as on the human foot. Your space will not permit me to give the means employed to eliminate anything like fraudulent action on the part of the medium, neither is it necessary to do so, as the cast itself—still in my possession—leaves its own stamp of genuineness, for there is not a single mark that betokens anything contrary to what it really is, viz., a cast from a whole and perfect mould, without a division; and I challenge the world to produce the like, otherwise than by similar agency. I, myself, made the so-called cabinet, which was the recess of a bay window, into which nothing could get without being seen by ten pairs of watchful eyes (there was a good light all through the *séance*). The medium, who was a woman of great size, went inside, and in the course of some fifteen minutes, the little psychic form of Bertie presented herself, and went through the operations as described above. After the performance she disappeared, and in a moment or two I drew the curtain aside, and there was Mrs. Firman entranced, and the sole occupant. Where was Bertie?

"The other illustration is from a photograph of a plant with flower, produced through the mediumship of Mrs. Esperance, at Newcastle-on-Tyne, August 4th, 1880. The reader must take all accessories for granted, as it is superfluous to enumerate all the precautionary measures to ensure genuine phenomena.

"The cabinet was a plain wooden box, five feet high, closed at top and bottom, with a gauze division in the centre, and a curtain covering the whole front, about six feet wide. The medium sat in one compartment, and the company (about twenty persons) sat round in horse-shoe fashion. In a short time, a little figure, draped in white, known as Yolande, emerged from the other (empty) compartment. That it was not the medium was evident from the fact of the figure being much less in size, and different in outline, and I heard Mrs. E. breathing hard while the figure was outside. Yolande requested my friend, Reimers, to get a glass water-bottle, and some sand and water, which, when mixed, he put into the bottle, and returned to his seat. Yolande then made a few passes over the bottle, and actually *created* a white gauzy cloth before our very eyes. She then retired about a yard from the bottle, and sat down on the floor. Presently we saw—for there was sufficient light to clearly distinguish the operation—the gauze veil gradually rising, as if there was something moving it upwards. In about two minutes, after rising about sixteen inches, Yolande rose to her feet and went to the bottle, from which she removed the covering, and lo! there was a plant with green leaves grown out of the bottle, with its roots in the sand: but there was no flower on it. After we had somewhat recovered from our astonishment, Yolande took it up, bottle and all, and gave it into my hands. She then retired into the cabinet. After the company had inspected it, I placed it at my feet, and waited for what should come next. In a few minutes raps were heard, and then the alphabet was used. 'Look at your plant' was spelt out, and taking it up I found, not only that it had grown very considerably in size, but there was a beautiful flower about four inches diameter on it. *This was produced while it was between my feet.* I took it to my hotel, and next morning had it photographed, of which the engraving is an exact copy. The next night Yolande gave me a *small rosebud* on a short stalk, with not more than two leaves on. This I put in my bosom, and kept it there during the time that the *séance* lasted; but having the impression that something was going on, I put my hand to feel it, and noticing that it felt different I kept my own counsel and did not disturb it. When the *séance* was drawing to a close, I drew forth my rosebud, when, strange to relate, it had developed into a bunch of *three large full-blown roses, with a bud as well!* These I also put away with the plant.

"Extensive as has been my experience—now ranging over many years—with psychic sensitives, there have been no results more satisfactory and pleasing—*i.e.*, on the physical plane—than the above which I have narrated, and curtailed, so as to give only the bald

Le Duc de Medina Pomar.

facts. The top leaves (six inches long), with a part of the stalk and remains of flower plant (preserved under glass), together with the foot—along with other *hand* casts—produced under similar circumstances as told—are before me as I write, and I trust that they may be kept for ages to come as *souvenirs*, or first fruits of that mighty spiritual force and movement—now in its commencement—which is destined to change the face of the whole earth, both as a physical orb, and also the social status of humanity that, from generation to generation, will live and move upon its surface. Without trespassing further on your time and space, allow me to congratulate you on the part which you have been destined to play in this wondrous drama ; and unless I grievously err, the time will come—and at no very distant date—when this new volume, which you are now giving to the world, will be recognised and appreciated at its vastly more than mere money value. Each pioneer has his or her own specific work to perform ; and amongst these, none have laboured more assiduously, and more unselfishly, than the gifted editress of 'Art-Magic' ; 'Ghost Land': and the authoress of the ' History of the Modern Spiritual Movement all over the Earth.' So states

"Your Fellow Workman,

" WILLIAM OXLEY.

"Manchester, August 15th, 1883."

Another of the writers who in any department of human thought rather than that of the " occult," would have achieved a world-wide celebrity, is the noble Countess of Caithness, now Duchesse de Pomar. Besides many fugitive contributions to the journalistic literature of the day, this accomplished authoress has written two remarkable works all too little known ; the one, a volume of nearly 500 pages, entitled " Old Truths in a New Light," the other, "Serious Letters to Serious Friends." These publications are no mere poetical effusions of a high-born lady, but the brilliant, sterling, and philosophic arguments of a master mind, enclosed in one of Nature's fairest and most womanly forms. Soaring far above her compeers in the gay and fashionable world, this truly noble woman maintains her lead in the most aristocratic European *salons*, and yet dares avow herself an "occultist" in the profoundest sense of the term. In the midst of princes and potentates, this brave lady hesitates not to appear in loving companionship with the spirit mediums whom she honours with her friendship, and whilst many of the gay butterflies who crowd her Parisian *fêtes* are spending their time in councilling how to adorn themselves with *modistes* and *friseures*, this high-minded and indefatigable labourer in God's vineyard, is penning sublime lines, which lift the soul up to heaven, and forge the golden links of an universal Brotherhood, for all humanity. Amongst the lesser works that have fallen from the Countess of Caithness's pen, is a charming *brochure* entitled " A Midnight Visit to Holyrood." It is founded upon the singular relations which attach this lady to her much-beloved guardian spirit, the fair and hapless " Marie Stuart, Queen of Scots." At the request of this angelic guide, the Countess paid a midnight visit to Holyrood, there to listen to the spirit voice of her, whose sighs of anguish had been borne on many a wailing breeze through those grim and mournful towers.

We would fain linger on the Countess's thrilling description of her interview with the presiding genius of the scene, did space permit. Failing this, we must still offer a brief extract from this fascinating little work, were it only to give the world—profoundly ignorant of true spiritual ethics—some idea of the tone in which purified spirits commune with mortals, and the character of the advice which the solemn pedagogues of the pulpit so irreverently assure their gaping listeners, proceed from " demons ! "

The modes in which the spirit and the mortal hold communion is thus described by the Countess of Caithness. She says :—

"It is now nearly eight years since I was first made aware of her (Marie Stuart's) connection with me; or rather, perhaps, I should better describe our relations as my connection with her—but only three, since I have enjoyed the happiness of communion with her. I often feel her presence. She makes it known to me in many different ways; and the oral communications I have received from her, and taken down at various times to the best of my ability, have swollen into the size of a small volume. These interviews have generally taken place in the quietude of my own room, and during the calm silence of the midnight hour. But she has also come to me amongst the wild hills of Scotland, or when seated on the high cliffs of Caithness overlooking the stormy Pentland Firth; but only when its wild waves have been comparatively at rest, and reflecting the intense blue of the sky as serene as that which usually overarches the sunny Mediterranean, and when there has been no sign of life around save the white sea-gull sailing majestically overhead between the earth and sky, and the crisp little white crested waves called '*The Merry Men of Mey*' tumbling over one another as if in mad glee at my feet—have I felt her gentle presence, which is ever bright and soothing as a sunbeam, and heard her precious words, which have appeared to me sublime in their beauty, and in their intent, ever urging me onward in the path of truth and progress, and opening out fresh vistas to me of my pathway in the future."

As a specimen of the communication above referred to, we commend the following excerpt from Marie Stuart to Marie Caithness :—

" Go not alone to the Word for life, but also to those who gave it, for they have added knowledge which is more appropriate, and better adapted to the present hour of spiritual growth and unfoldment. Reverently use the Bible for guidance and instruction. Use Nature's great Bible even as reverently, but remember that the passive soul-inspired one will rise even to the beatitudes, gathering new thought-germs, watching the opening bulb and seed of original heaven-inspired ideas ; proving all things, holding fast unto that which will bear all the light which science, art, and reason can bring to bear upon them. You, my child, have a mind capable of grasping truths that are destined to make all nations free and inspired. Aye ! and this is accomplishing even now. Stand out before the world as one who dares think—one who courts the wisdom of the ages, and grasps the light of the universe to guide humanity forward. The sweet, ever-living truths given to the world by its inspired ones are to be revered, but let us not go backward with uncovered heads asking wisdom ; let us rather press forward even into the inner courts of the temple where Deific harmonies lull the soul into conditions of mind that admit of communion with the Builder of all worlds, the Origin of all life, all forms. Let us rise even to the holy altar where a John carried his gifts, and became filled with power."

There is yet another literary work by the Countess of Caithness, to which we only call attention, without attempting in the present historical compendium to analyze its nature, or do justice to its merits. It was during the closing weeks of the year 1880, that the Countess of Caithness contributed a remarkable series of papers to the London *Medium and Daybreak*, on the signs of the times, and the occult prophecies which, from the most remote ages, had pointed to this period. The inspired writer gave an elaborate review of the Cabalistic interpretation of the Biblical writings. She reviewed the Apocalyptic, prophetic, and Pythagorean systems of numbers, and connected them, and the veiled significance of the mediæval mystical writings with the present discoveries which are revealing the occult meanings in Oriental monuments and myths. From all these sources the the learned writer drew the conclusion that the year 1880 completed one of those cycles of time known to, and defined by the ancient prophets, whilst the year 1881 might be regarded as the commencement of an entirely new era, and one which physically, mentally, politically, and religiously, was destined to be regarded by future ages as the opening up of a new dispensation. The Bible, especially the Apocalypse and prophetic writings, was treated of in these remarkable essays, and their mystic meanings interpreted and brought to bear upon the present singularly disturbed condition of human thought, especially in respect to religious opinions.

In testimony of her own implicit faith that a great world dispensation closed in 1880, and another, foretold by seers and prophets, inscribed in the ancient pyramid of Cheops, and manifest in the universal upheaval of human opinions to-day, was inaugurated in 1881, the Countess has adopted the date of the new era together with divers occult emblems on her letter paper, and in not a few of the ornaments which adorn her toilet, and the furniture of her mansion.

When the mists of the new dawn shall have melted into the sunlight of noonday truth, and the *cyclic* progress of the race shall be fully understood, especially in reference to the present transitional and catastrophic period, the essays of Lady Caithness, though they are now "cabala" to the unthinking multitude, will be then recalled and honoured as the advent voice which proclaimed the coming of the new Messiah, the dispensation of peace on earth and goodwill to all men.

Another remarkable addition to the occult, if not the Spiritual literature of the times, has been made by the son of the noble lady of whom we have been writing—formerly the Count, now the Duke de Medina Pomar. This gentleman whilst yet in his teens, became the author of two beautifully written works of fiction designed to illustrate the doctrine of re-incarnation, a belief with which his mind is strongly imbued, and one which finds a more plausible and fascinating illustration in the young Duke de Pomar's writings, than in any of the abstract treatises yet produced on this subject. The names of the works in question are "The Honeymoon" and "Through the Ages." Both these novels are full of exalted sentiment, vivid description, and thrilling interest. Both are designed to present in the form of what in ancient time would have been termed "parables," and in our own age are simply "works of fiction," grand lessons of ideality and Spiritual philosophy. "The Honeymoon" is a veritable dream of beauty; visionary, pathetic, powerful, and enthralling. If not a direct inspiration, it is such a marvellous feat of writing for a mere boy, that it forms to the candid reader a far better proof of an invisible thinker guiding the pen of a mortal scribe than many a voluminous mass of "communications," labelled with the authorship of "the mighty dead." "Through the Ages" is a novel which—as its name implies—traces the progress of a Spirit through all those phases of mortal trial and discipline, which the re-incarnationists affirm to be essential to round out the full perfection of the soul through human experiences.

If ever stern facts could be superseded by the sophistry of undemonstrated theories, it would be through the fascinating influences of a pen so facile, and an imagination so vivid as that of the Duke de Medina Pomar. The pictures are simply perfect, and if ever re-incarnation could be proved, this brilliant writer's "Through the Ages" would be a veritable modern Iliad of the faith.

Since the production of these *chefs d'œuvre*, the Duke de Pomar has published several dashing works of fiction in which his brilliant pen has been more prompt to lash the vices and follies of society, than to renew his earlier and more exalting task of lifting up the unthinking multitude to a higher standard of life and action. Though still a very young man, the Duke has dropped his prolific pen, and to the deep regret of his many admirers, he floats on the surface of society, but writes, *for the present*, no more. Like all subjects of inspiration the fire of his special literary epoch is burnt out, but that it will be rekindled again none who have studied his peculiarly sensitive nature can question. Whatever the future may call forth, none who read the young Duke de Pomar's first literary productions, can hesitate to pronounce them the work of a very talented man, or a phenomenally inspired boy. If years are to decide the question, the latter position is the only solution of which his writings are susceptible.

CHAPTER XXVII.

SPIRITUALISM IN GREAT BRITAIN (CONTINUED.)

STILL MORE CONCERNING THE LITERATURE OF SPIRITUALISM IN ENGLAND.

AMONGST the most important of the contributions that have been made to the literature of English Spiritualism are the writings of Mr. John Farmer, whose name has achieved a wide-spread popularity on both sides of the Atlantic, as the author of "A New Basis of Belief in Immortality," and the admirable pamphlet entitled, "How to Investigate Spiritualism." In both these works Mr. Farmer has dealt with his subjects in an equally scholarly and exhaustive mode. Both have commanded the respectful notice of the secular press, and hold a deservedly high place in the estimation of every reader of Spiritual literature.

It may be remembered that Mr. Farmer's "New Basis of Belief in Immortality," was deemed worthy of being alluded to in terms of warm commendation by one of the great religious dignitaries of the late Ecclesiastical Congress assembled at Newcastle. We do not cite this as praise of any extraordinary value, but simply to show that the religious tone and authoritative character of that work could command the respect of such men as Canon Wilberforce, Dr. Thornton, &c., &c.

One of the most candid and capable critics of the present day, the book reviewer of the *Truthseeker*, says of this volume :—

> "This is an exceedingly thoughtful book ; temperate, earnest, and bright with vivid and intelligent love of truth. Mr. Farmer is no fanatic, if we may judge of him by his book, but a brave seeker after the truth. Incidentally, he conveys a vast amount of information concerning what are called the phenomena of Spiritualism—what these phenomena are, under what conditions they are obtained, and to what they lead ; but his main purpose is to show how Spiritualism explains the Bible, supplies the key to not a little that is mysterious in 'historical Christianity,' and furnishes, as he says, 'a new basis of belief.' We commend his book to the attention of all who are prepared to give serious attention to a very serious subject."

To the above-quoted opinions every intelligent reader, whether Spiritualist or opponent, must say *Amen*.

In noticing the two most popular works that have emanated from Mr. Farmer's pen, it must not be supposed that these are his only contributions to the realm of Spiritual literature.

Mr. Farmer is the author of a fine metaphysical essay on " Present Day Problems," and a work on Mesmerism, the modest title of which—"Hints on Mesmerism "—bears no proportion to the valuable, and truly practical matter it contains. It was to the zeal and enterprise of this gentleman also, that the excellent monthly periodical entitled *The Psychological Review,* after an interregnum of many months, was revived in July, 1881, and carried forward to the current year of 1883.

Since the suspension of this magazine became inevitable, Mr. Farmer has given time and indomitable effort to the editorial management of the fine journal so often referred to in this volume, called *Light*.

Mr. Farmer's devoted and untiring services in the cause of Spiritualism have been rendered in so quiet and unostentatious a manner, and his name has obtained so little prominence, except as the author of the popular works above referred to, that the reader may be surprised to learn how largely the present literary standing of the movement is indebted to him; indeed it is with the view of "rendering honour where honour is due," that the author tenders this brief but well-merited tribute of acknowledgment to one of the best and most philosophic writers, as well as one of the most efficient and faithful workers in the ranks of Spiritualism.

Of the other periodicals connected with the movement, it is only necessary to say, the first metropolitan journal that was issued as a weekly organ was published by Mr. Robert Cooper, and called *The Spiritual Times*.

The unfortunate prosecution incurred by Mr. Coleman, involving in its results the publisher of this paper, occasioned its suspension after a short-lived existence. About 1870, Mr. James Burns commenced the publication of an able, well written weekly paper entitled *The Medium and Daybreak*. Still later the enterprising editor started a fine monthly magazine called *Human Nature*.

This periodical—although filled with the articles of able contributors—maintained only an ephemeral existence compared to its cotemporary *The Medium*, which has continued through a period of thirteen years, and still holds its own against the claims of younger rivals. Its editor, like many of the prominent workers in the divided ranks of Spiritualism, has incurred some amount of both ban and blessing from his fellow labourers. Amongst his most determined antagonists however, none will deny him the credit of indomitable energy, perseverance, and a determination to uphold his paper, and all that he conceives to be his special work in connection with the cause of Spiritualism, at any sacrifice. Mr. Burns is a clever, lucid, and interesting speaker, besides being an expert phrenologist. His lectures on phrenology, temperance, vegetarianism, hygiene, &c., &c., are as creditable to his advanced thought as a practical reformer, as they have been instrumental in lifting up humanity to higher motives of life and action throughout Great Britain. In an excellent speech made at the anniversary celebration of the 31st of March, 1882, Mr. Burns gives the following graphic account of his first attempt at Spiritual journalism :—

"Twelve years ago the Movement was expectant of a change—a widening out of its sphere of action. Some autumn seed had been sown to prepare for the harvest of the year just closed. *Daybreak* had been in existence as a monthly paper, and the *Spiritualist* had been commenced fortnightly. To our great regret it was not weekly, as we shrank from the task of taking up the burden of a weekly paper, and hoped the *Spiritualist* would step in and save us. Sunday services had been started at Cavendish Rooms by Mr. Peebles, and a penny hymn book had been printed. The Spiritual Institution was at work, and means for bringing the phenomena before the public were in operation. There was at that time no public movement; but the elements of such a thing were in a state of combination and development.

"The experienced journalist will smile when told that when we set about the first number of the *Medium* we had no contributors, no means, no experience, no ambition, no end to serve. The spirit world required a 'medium' of the press, and we gave it one, by the aid of a kind lady, now in the spirit-world, who came in and laid a £5 note on the counter. Like a little stream at its fountain head, our first number was insignificant, and contained no specious promises for the future. We felt the shadow of years of suffering and toil enveloping us, and moved in our work, as the hands do on the face of the clock, with no purpose of their own, but obedient to the unseen power within."

Through good and evil report, Mr. Burns has carried his enterprise forward with unflagging energy, and with the exception of the London *Spiritual Magazine* no other English periodical has bravely weathered so many storms, or maintained the flag of the movement it advocates for so long a period, and that under the pressure of the severest trials.

The *Spiritualist* newspaper mentioned by Mr. Burns, and often referred to in these pages, was a very scholarly journal representing the scientific aspect of Spiritualism, and for several years was ably conducted by Mr. Wm. Harrison.

Notwithstanding the unbounded generosity with which Charles Blackburn, Esq., of Didsbury, Manchester, contributed to the support of this paper, it was quite recently suspended, and perhaps forms another evidence, that when the purposes of the Spirit world are accomplished, the instruments are laid aside, and a fresh set of influences are brought to bear upon the progress of a movement—of unmistakably supra-mundane power and purpose.

At the time when this volume was commenced, there were, unfortunately for the best interests of each individual enterprise, four Spiritual journals put before the English public, namely, the two already mentioned, *The Herald of Progress*, published at Newcastle-on-Tyne, and the latest and one of the finest of the Spiritual journals, called *Light*, formerly conducted by Mr. Dawson Rogers, and now under the editorship of Mr. John Farmer. Like the *Spiritualist; Light* represents the scientific and metaphysical phases of the Spiritual movement, and its articles—especially those contributed by " M. A., Oxon," and Mrs. A. H. M. Watts, are of the highest interest and value.

With such a *corps* of contributors as " M. A., Oxon," Hon. Roden Noel, Mr. Spicer, Hensleigh Wedgwood, Prof. Barratt, Dr. Wylde, and many other writers of no less ability, but above all, with Mr. John Farmer in the editorial chair, *Light*, like its veteran cotemporary, *The Medium*, ought to be as nobly sustained as it deserves, and compensate for many of the evanescent ephemera of past years, by an unquenchable and permanent existence. Since this volume was commenced, another monthly journal entitled *The Spiritual Record*, has been issued by the indefatigable veteran publisher of Glasgow, Mr. Hay Nesbit. Report speaks highly of this new venture, and Mr. Nesbit's long and gallant services in the cause of Spiritualism, should alone be sufficient to recommend any publication to which his honoured name and skilful directorship is attached. The mention of Mr. Nesbit's much respected name will necessarily call forth the desire to know how the movement progresses in the city where his valuable services are so faithfully rendered.

Although Spiritualism in its two well-defined phases of religious belief, and phenomenal demonstration, has permeated every part of the United Kingdom and found acceptance from all classes, from the palace to the hut, it has made little or no distinctive mark anywhere *as a public movement* except in England. The following notices concerning the status of the cause in Glasgow may furnish some evidence of exception to this rule, hence their introduction in this place.

In the year 1867, the few believers in spirit intercourse resident in Glasgow, solicited the author to pay them a visit in her capacity of a

Spiritual lecturer. It was represented to her that the unusual phenomenon of a lady speaking on religious subjects *in the city of John Knox,* might awaken popular sentiments of an antagonistic character, especially as Spirit communion was to be the theme; one which, though well known and practised largely in private circles, had hitherto borne but an evil name in the censorship of Glasgow public opinion. Altogether the prospects were not very encouraging, but as the author had ever been accustomed to make choice of such scenes for her public efforts, as her wise and far-seeing Spirit Guides advised, she yielded to their persuasions, and proceeded to fulfil the proposed engagement.

The visit was made; more lectures were demanded than had been covenanted for ; and a far more satisfactory impression was produced than could have been anticipated.

Several curious phenomenal occurrences marked this visit, which neither time nor place now permit us to notice.

At the risk of incurring the charge of egotism however, we deem it necessary to the progress of the history, to give the following excerpt from the London *Spiritual Magazine,* of December, 1867, as it records the commencement of an era in Glasgow Spiritualism which our next quotation will bring down to the present day.

The first notice is headed :—

"EMMA HARDINGE IN SCOTLAND.

"Mrs. Hardinge has been delivering a course of lectures at Glasgow, under the auspices of the Association of Spiritualists in that city, and she seems to have created quite a sensation in Glasgow, and to have won the hearts of all who heard her. The newspapers, to their credit, whilst asserting that they do not agree with all she said, have not published, I believe, a word in derogation of the subjects of her discourses, and in some instances they commend her eloquence in unstinted terms of praise. The *Christian News* says :— . . . ."

[Then follows a series of highly eulogistic personal notices, of no moment in the present record.]

"At the close of her course of lectures, the members of the Glasgow Association of Spiritualists presented Mrs. Hardinge with a *souvenir* as an additional mark of their respect, and as Mrs. Hardinge has found a new field by this visit to Scotland for the exercise of her great gifts, I feel sure it will be improved on a future occasion, and will lead to a more general understanding of the truths of Spiritualism."

Since the author's first and only visit to Glasgow, Mr. J. J. Morse, one of the most brilliant and eloquent trance speakers of the new dispensation, and Mr. Wallis, another very able and interesting Spiritual lecturer, have from time to time filled the rostrum most acceptably. The sensationalism awakened by the first public acts of propagandism—especially in consideration of the propagandist being *a lady*—has of course died away, but a steady and healthful growth of public sentiment in favour of the noble philosophy enunciated from the Spiritual rostrum has manifested itself in Glasgow, and still maintains its hold upon the hearts of a large number of the population.

The indefatigable efforts of Mr. Hay Nesbit, the well known printer and publisher, and the sterling work of a large number of brave men and women who have formed and held circles, organized public meetings, and given platform addresses, have kept the lamps which light poor blind mortals to the higher life, well trimmed and burning. And this has been done too, at much disadvantage, the distance of Glasgow from the English metropolis and the places where Mediumistic effort is most rife, rendering the expenses of transit very heavy, and the time consumed in making the journey an obstacle not easily overcome. The following communication to the *Religio-Philosophical Journal of America*, by one of its most esteemed contributors, will give some interesting facts concerning the progress of Spiritualism in Glasgow :—

"A Lyceum was started here last year, and is continued each Sunday afternoon under the supervision of the present writer. The library of the society is well stocked with the literature of the movement, both English and American, and is largely taken advantage of. . . . Through the kindness of one of our most enthusiastic and generous members, Mr. James Bowman, the public library in our city has also been supplied with many volumes bearing on the subject. . . . Meetings are held in the room on several of the week nights, Friday evening being devoted to Mr. David Duguid, so well known for his varied forms of mediumship so ably set down by Hay Nisbet, in his introduction to the volume "Hafid, Prince of Persia." . . . Mr. Duguid is one of the most retiring of men, working every day at his business of a photographer, and giving largely of his spare moments to those who are in earnest to investigate the subject. Numbers come from all parts of the world, who carry with them mementos of their visit in the shape of those marvellous productions, the little direct paintings which are sent forth as missionaries over the world.   .   .   .

"Only lately we had a visit from Irving Bishop, a conjuror of some note from your side, and this gentleman was taken in hand by all the professors of the Universities of Glasgow and Edinburgh, who presented him with an elaborate address, because he had exposed Spiritualism. Exposures have been most prolific in directing men and women to the subject, and Mr. Irving Bishop's visit was no exception to this.

"Mr. Alexander Duguid, of Kirkcaldy, and a brother of Mr. David Duguid, the trance painting medium, is among the more recent platform workers, and does yeoman's service. In his private sittings, which have extended over many of the towns in Scotland, his clairvoyant powers have been most successful in bringing the fact of Spirit communion home to many hearts. He is largely sought after, and appreciated for his quiet, unassuming manners and hopeful, manly life ; recently he has been in London for the first time, where he met with warm reception from the friends there, speaking at Gospel Hall services, with 'M. A., Oxon' in the chair.

"Professor James Coates, who has resided in Glasgow for over eighteen months, has been quite a tower of strength to the movement since his arrival, ably filling this platform on many occasions, acting as secretary and energetically promoting the progress of the movement in many ways. Mr. Coates is a phrenologist and mesmerist, who has worked up a great reputation in circles outside the spiritual.

"In Dundee the cause has taken firm root among a great number of families.   .   .   . The Secretary of the Glasgow Association is Mr. John Munro, 12, Govanhill-street, Glasgow; the president, James Walker, a veteran in the cause.   "J. R."

"Glasgow, Scotland."

It has often been questioned why Glasgow, a merely commercial centre and by no means remarkable for its tendencies to metaphysical speculations, should have taken the palm over Edinburgh, the *reputed* seat of science, learning, and as might be expected from such a reputation, of *good breeding* also. Whether the above-named desirable elements are peculiar to University men in their *presence or absence*, the following excerpts written by Mr. J. Greenwell, now of London, a well known and reliable correspondent of the *Medium*, and a gentleman incapable of falsehood or exaggeration, will sufficiently prove. Mr. Greenwell, writing to the *Medium* about 1878, says :

"Some time ago, Mr. Morse lectured at Edinburgh, and his merits were recognised by one eminent gentleman, whose words of commendation we quoted from the newspapers. As the gentleman in question contrasted Mr. Morse's abilities in the trance with those of men who are public teachers of the fashionable stamp, it might be imagined that revenge would be taken sooner or later. Reports in the *Review* and *Scotsman* have reached us of the meeting held in Upper Oddfellows' Hall, Forrest Road, Edinburgh, on Friday, June 6, at which Mr. Morse was advertised to speak on a subject to be chosen by the audience. A botanical term was voted for by the students, and they would have no other.   .   .   .

Faithfully Yours
S. J. Morse.

" As a supplement to the report, I must say that it was the most disgraceful meeting of any description that it has been my lot to attend. About a quarter of an hour before the lecture was to commence, 100 students, at the very least, came trooping into the hall, with the avowed intention of breaking up the meeting, for as soon as they gained admission, they began their ungentlemanly operations of throwing peas, singing songs, and performing on tin whistles, &c. Thinking they would probably quiet down when the lecturer appeared, Mr. Morse, with Mr. J. T. Rhodes as chairman, made their way on to the platform ; when, instead of abating, the noise was resumed with increased vigour, and neither the chairman nor Mr. Morse were allowed to speak, owing to the unearthly yells issuing from the very refined students. Mr. Morse, in the trance state, was then proceeding to deliver his lecture on ' Is Man Material or Spiritual after Death?' when the interruption broke out afresh, and continued for two hours, Mr. Morse under control all the time. The guides then declined to proceed further, and left the medium.

"The meeting was then declared closed, when the students in a body made for the platform, and commenced to hustle Messrs. Morse, Rhodes, and myself most unmercifully, throwing the table from the platform, and smashing a form. Some one then got Mr. Morse into the ante-room, where I found him a few minutes afterwards quite overcome and in violent convulsions, which continued for almost an hour. It is really difficult to realise such a state of things in a free and *Christian* country in the nineteenth century, but such is the case ; and I feel more fully persuaded than ever that the power is only wanted to put the existing will in force, and we should soon see the ancient stake, or something more torturing, revived for the benefit of Spiritualists and Free-thinkers.

"I know full well the feelings of indignation that will be evoked from the many friends of Mr. Morse, owing to the cruel treatment he has suffered here ; consequently I need not remind those friends that increased sympathy towards him is necessary on this occasion, the first instalment of which I feel sure would be accorded to him when he arrived in Glasgow. . . . .

" I am, yours in the cause of truth,

"JOS. N. GREENWELL.

" Edinburgh, June 7."

It is satisfactory to remember that the scenes described above took place some six years ago—since when, the general tides of progress may have even had a contagious influence upon the *gentlemen* of the Edinburgh University, and inspired them with a higher tone, both in the realm of morals and manners.

In the British metropolis, many of the well-known Mediums of past years have retired from public life, Mrs. Mary Marshall, the well-known test and rapping Medium, being almost the only one remaining. Mr. Cecil Husk, a new Medium for the production of materialized forms, is highly reported of ; and Mr. Towns, a veteran seer, still astonishes the strangers who visit him with revelations of their most secret thoughts.

Miss Lottie Fowler, the inimitable clairvoyant, trance and test Medium from America, and Mrs. Kate Jencken (*née* Katy Fox)—a name inscribed on the warmest spot of every true Spiritualist's heart—are also ministering most successfully to the investigators who seek for test facts of Spirit communion. It is much to be regretted that the cause of phenomenal Spiritualism has suffered a great loss, in the retirement into private life of Mr. Eglinton, a young gentleman who, though not classed as a professional Medium, was the subject—a few years since—of manifestations, the marvel of which has resounded through many countries of the earth.

The Calcutta *Indian Daily News* publishes in its issue of January 28th, 1882, the following striking communication concerning Mr. Eglinton's Mediumship :—

" To the Editor of the Indian Daily News.

"SIR,—In your issue of the 13th January, I stated that I should be glad of an opportunity of participating in a *séance* with a view of giving an unbiased opinion as to whether, in my capacity of a professional Prestidigitateur, I could give a natural explanation of effects said to be produced by spiritual aid.

"I am indebted to the courtesy of Mr. Eglinton, the Spiritualistic Medium now in Calcutta, and of his host, Mr. J. Meugens, for affording me the opportunity I craved.

"It is needless to say I went as a sceptic; but I must own that I have come away utterly unable to explain, by any natural means, the phenomena that I witnessed on Tuesday evening. I will give a brief description of what took place:—

"I was seated in a brilliantly-lighted room with Mr. Eglinton and Mr. Meugens. We took our places round a common teak-wood table, and after a few minutes the table began to sway violently backwards and forwards, and I heard noises such as might be produced by some one thumping under the table. I tried to discover the cause of this movement, but was unable to do so. After this Mr. Eglinton produced two common school slates, which I sponged, cleaned, and rubbed dry with a towel myself. Mr. Eglinton then handed me a box containing small crumbs of slate-pencil. I selected one of these and in accordance with Mr. Eglinton's directions, placed it on the surface of one of the slates, placing the other slate over it. I then firmly grasped the two slates at one of the corners. Mr. Eglinton then held the other corner, our two free hands being clasped together. The slates were then lowered below the edge of the table, but remained in full view (the room remaining lighted all the time). Instantaneously I heard a scratching noise, as might be produced by writing on a slate. In about fifteen seconds I heard three distinct knocks on the slates, and I then opened them and found the following writing:

"'My name is Geary. Don't you remember me? We used to talk of this matter at the St. George's. I know better now.'

"Having read the above, I remarked that I knew of no one by the name of Geary.

"We then placed our hands on the table, and Mr. Eglinton commenced repeating the alphabet until he came to the letter 'G,' when the table began to shake violently. This process was repeated till the name of Geary was spelt.

"After this Mr. Eglinton took a piece of paper and a pencil, and with a convulsive movement, difficult to describe, he wrote very indistinctly the following words:

"'I am Alfred Geary, of the *Lantern;* you know me and St. Ledger.'

"Having read this, I suddenly remembered having met both Mr. Geary and Mr. St. Ledger at Cape Town, South Africa, about four years ago, and the St. George's Hotel is the one I lived at there. Mr. Geary was the editor of the *Cape Lantern.* I believe he died some three years ago. Mr. St. Ledger was the editor of the *Cape Times,* and I believe is so still. Without going into details, I may mention that subsequently a number of other messages were written on the slates, which I was allowed to clean each time before they were used.

"In respect to the above manifestations I can only say that I do not expect my account of them to gain general credence. Forty-eight hours before, I should not have believed any one who had described such manifestations under similar circumstances. I still remain a sceptic as regards Spiritualism, but I repeat my inability to explain or account for what must have been an intelligent force, that produced the writing on the slate, which, if my senses are to be relied on, was in no way the result of trickery or sleight-of-hand.—Yours, &c.,   "HARRY KELLAR.

"Calcutta, January 25th, 1882."

Without commenting on the illogical position assumed, not alone by Mr. Kellar, but by hundreds of others who are compelled to admit both the supra-mundane character of the phenomena and intelligence displayed, and then wind up by denying emphatically that "either can be Spirits," it is enough to say that Mr. Kellar, the professional conjurer, duplicates the assurance of his Italian *confrère,* Signor Bellachini, in respect to Mr. Slade's manifestations at Leipzig. When two thoroughly skilled professional jugglers acknowledge that they cannot simulate by trickery, the demonstrations performed through Media without any trickery, is it not time that the flimsy pretence of Spiritual phenomena being ALL trickery and fraud, should be abandoned by travelling exposers, even though the petty set of shams they exhibit, of which any tenth rate juggler would be ashamed, were patronized by Scottish Lord Provosts and English Right Reverend Lord Bishops?

Another remarkably-endowed Medium for physical manifestations who has till recently exercised her Mediumship successfully in many parts of England is Miss Wood, a young lady who was developed in private circles at Newcastle-on-Tyne, and subsequently became professionally engaged by the "Newcastle Spiritual Evidence Society," to give *séances* at their rooms for "form materializations." During her sittings with the Newcastle Society, Miss Wood cheerfully submitted to the most exacting tests, and amongst the numerous testimonials that were rendered to the integrity of her Mediumship, are the following—the first being from Mr. H. Kersey, then Secretary to the Society, and the other from the well-known scientist, Mr. T. P. Barkas, F.G.S.

Mr. Kersey says, in writing to the *Medium*, Oct. 25th, 1878 :—

"This morning, Oct. 20, I had the pleasure of witnessing some very convincing form manifestations through the medial power of Miss C. E. Wood, at the Newcastle society's rooms. I will spare unnecessary detail, and shortly say that the cabinet, which consisted of a curtain suspended across the corner of the room, was inspected by myself and others, both previous to and after the *séance*. The medium sat *outside* the cabinet in full view of all the sitters, numbering nineteen, the whole of the time, and was never once out of their sight. Three forms successively appeared, the first a woman, who, after several efforts, walked out of the cabinet and passed around the medium, and re-entered the cabinet on the other side of her. At the solicitation of the sitters she repeated this. The next form was a child, who came out of the cabinet, and succeeded in getting about two feet clear of the medium, but could not get around her. The last form was a large one, that of a man, but did not succeed in getting far out.

"'Pocka' controlled and spoke through the medium whilst the last two forms were out. Now the value of this to me, Sir, is that I never lost sight of the medium from first to last, and I am certain none of the sitters left their seats and went into the cabinet.

I am, Sir, yours truly,

"Newcastle-on-Tyne.   "H. A. KERSEY.

" We, the undersigned, testify to the correctness of the above report :—

> "John Hare, Chester Crescent.
> "Martha Hare,   „
> "Nellie Hare,   „
> "H. Norris, 59, Newgate Street.
> "E. Sanderson,   „
> "Jane Hammarbon, Northumberland Street.
> "Jno. Mould, 12, St. Thomas Crescent.
> "James Cameron, Gallowgate Steam Mills.
> "W. C. Robson, 8, Brandling Place."

Mr. Barkas, writing to the same paper about a year previously, gives a slight account of Spiritualism in Newcastle and the formation of the first society there. He says :—

"Spiritualism had been investigated in Newcastle-on-Tyne for twenty-five years. Prior to 1872 the manifestations had taken place in private houses and before select circles. In that year a society was formed for the investigation of the phenomena, and in a few months several members of the society became developed as mediums. In the year 1873 it was discovered that two young ladies had very great mediumistic power. The one, Miss Wood, was at that time eighteen years of age, and the other, Miss Fairlamb, was about a year younger. For some trifling remuneration as a compensation for much time spent in the interests of the society, the young women devoted themselves to the work, and soon there were not only trance controls, but extraordinary movements of tables, chairs, bells, and other articles of furniture and musical instruments took place in the dark, under test conditions. In 1874 spectral forms of human faces and hands presented themselves at the openings of the cabinet in which the mediums were enclosed. Then fully developed forms ; and, to make certain of the genuineness of these phenomena, private *séances* were organised in the houses of well known gentlemen. Rigid but friendly tests of many kinds were tried, and the result was that materialisations took place, which nothing but a stubborn prejudice, perfectly inaccessible to the logic of facts, could resist or gainsay.

"I have seen through the mediumship of Miss Wood, in a private house, living forms walk from the curtained recess, which it was utterly impossible for her to simulate. I have seen children, women, and men of various ages, walk forth under her mediumship.

I have seen a materialised form and the medium at the same time. I have had through her mediumship a child-like form standing beside me for about half an hour together; the child has placed its arms around my neck, and permitted me at the same time to place my arm around her neck, and has laid its cheek against mine, breathed upon my face, and, in fact, caressed me precisely as a child would do its parent or guardian. This was not in darkness, but in light, and in the presence of professors and fellows of one of the leading universities in the kingdom. I have, under these conditions, and after having handled the psychic form, seen it gradually vanish or dematerialise, and become invisible in the middle of the room."

A full and elaborate account of Miss Wood and the phenomena occurring in her presence has been published in pamphlet form by W. P. Adshead, Esq., of Belper, a wealthy and intelligent gentleman, who sent for Miss Wood to his own house, wherein he set up a *wire cage*, constructed for the purpose, in which the Medium, firmly secured, was placed, during a given number of experimental *séances*.

The marvellous phenomena of many different materialized forms appearing under these circumstances, is fully detailed by Mr. Adshead, but as the manifestations present little or no variety in effect from those already alluded to, it would be unnecessary to describe them any further. We would commend Mr. Adshead's methods, however, to the attention of the various contending parties who now make the subject of "tests" the theme of warfare—the one side alleging that tests "degrade the Medium," and "ruin the conditions under which spirits manifest;" the other equally pertinaciously insisting that no Medium should claim credence for extraordinary or unusual occurrences without tests of the most crucial and convincing character. Miss Wood was Mr. Adshead's guest for some time. The manifestations were given in his own house, in the presence of scores of the most inveterate sceptics, and under the extraordinary conditions stated above.

Yet Miss Wood felt no degradation in submitting to the tests imposed, and often invited them, nor did they spoil or even interfere with the manifestations, numerous attestations to that effect being given and signed by the parties who attended the *séances*. The following paragraph, taken from page 24 of Mr. Adshead's pamphlet, offers perhaps what the world would deem one of the most striking proofs that can be rendered of Mr. Adshead's unassailable position in reference to these manifestations. He says :—

"For the medium to liberate herself from her bondage, and place herself in such a position that, had she the necessary skill and appliances, she could represent the different forms we had looked upon, and then return to the condition in which we left her—the cage, tapes, and seals being found as when the *séance* commenced—would, to me, be almost as great a marvel as anything else which could be done. Indeed, so profoundly impressed am I with the impossibility of this being done, that unless those who have boasted that it is their mission to stamp out the 'imposture of Spiritualism,' of 'their great charity,' are moved to take the scales from our eyes, I have to say, I am prepared to write a cheque for two hundred and fifty guineas, and my friend, Mr. A. Smedley, will write one for a similar amount, and the FIVE HUNDRED GUINEAS shall at once be paid to any person who will, under similar conditions to those described above, produce phenomena which shall in all respects be like those of which I have just spoken, and so distinctly explain the method by which they are produced that the person to whom the method is made known, or any other person or persons to whom, in turn, the said method may be made known, will be able at any time, or in any place, to produce exactly the same kind of phenomena as those which appeared when Miss Wood was screwed up in the cage. If, as is claimed, the marvels are simply clever conjuring, the above conditions will not be regarded as too stringent. It is also to be understood that those who accept this challenge forfeit a like sum in the event of failing to produce the phenomena under the conditions named above."

Despite all the blatant pretensions of conjurers and their clerical supporters, Mr. Adshead's cheque so freely proffered, still remains unclaimed.

In Cardiff, South Wales, for several years past, circles have been held by a party of earnest Spiritualists, amongst whom was developed Mr. Spriggs, a non-professional Medium for the production of "form materializations." As Mr. Spriggs is now in Australia, placing his phenomenal powers at the service of the "Victorian Association of Spiritualists," we reserve all further accounts of his demonstrations for our Australian section.

In the direction of healing, there are still a much larger number of excellent phenomenal individuals engaged, than we have space to particularize. Not one of the least remarkable, is Mrs. Illingworth, the celebrated seeress and medical trance Medium of Bradford, Yorkshire. Although entirely uneducated, and the wife of a plain Yorkshire mechanic, this wonderful clairvoyant can trace—even by a lock of hair taken from the head of strangers at any distance—the most obscure diseases, prescribing under the influence of medical Spirits the most effective remedies for all complaints of a curable nature. And good Mrs Illingworth is only cited as a representative of many others whose beneficent labours are carried forward with eminent success throughout the North of England. Another of these highly gifted seers practises in the immediate vicinity of the author's residence near Manchester, and scores of Nicodemuses who would treat the openly avowed claim of Spiritual influence with holy horror or scornful derision, resort privately to Mr. Edward Gallagher* to be treated for complaints that baffle all the skill of the faculty—even to trace out— much less to cure. Many are the laudations that the author hears passed upon this quiet unassuming gentleman, who as a "clairvoyant" is permitted to describe hidden diseases and cure them by *occult* power, until his fame fills the country round and attracts even the sacred presence of the very "divines" who devote their next Sabbath's sermons to unsparing diatribes against the impious practices of Spiritualism.

In the metropolis, Dr. Mack, the renowned Spiritual healer; Mr. Younger, the fine mesmerist; Mr. and Mrs. Hagon, Mr. Omerin, and Mr. Hawkins, all pursue their beneficent work with many a secret blessing, and many a public ban, as the reward of their services. These are all professional healers and their services are offered, and their addresses registered in the *Medium*, and that, much to the scandal of those who would cheerfully pay their twenty guineas to a solemn-visaged physician who gives a rough guess, and often an erroneous one, at the seat of their disease, and yet shrink with horror at the idea of paying a modest fee to the clairvoyant and healer because the truths they tell, and the relief they impart, are "the gifts of God, and should not be made the subject of mercenary traffic." And thus it is, that when capable Mediums, and highly gifted seers and seeresses are starved out of their spheres of usefulness, and the sound of their good report is hushed, and for very sordid need of bread they are driven to abandon their Mediumistic calling, the world cries "See how this delusion of Spiritualism has died out," and the Pharisees rejoice that they have succeeded in "crushing out professional Mediumship."

---

* Mr. E. Gallagher, Greenfield Villa, Bloomfield Road, Heaton Chapel, Manchester.

In Cardiff, South Wales, for several years past, circles have been held by a party of earnest Spiritualists, amongst whom was developed Mr. Spriggs, a non-professional Medium for the production of " form materializations." As Mr. Spriggs is now in Australia, placing his phenomenal powers at the service of the " Victorian Association of Spiritualists," we reserve all further accounts of his demonstrations for our Australian section.

In the direction of healing, there are still a much larger number of excellent phenomenal individuals engaged, than we have space to particularize. Not one of the least remarkable, is Mrs. Illingworth, the celebrated seeress and medical trance Medium of Bradford, Yorkshire. Although entirely uneducated, and the wife of a plain Yorkshire mechanic, this wonderful clairvoyant can trace—even by a lock of hair taken from the head of strangers at any distance—the most obscure diseases, prescribing under the influence of medical Spirits the most effective remedies for all complaints of a curable nature. And good Mrs Illingworth is only cited as a representative of many others whose beneficent labours are carried forward with eminent success throughout the North of England. Another of these highly gifted seers practises in the immediate vicinity of the author's residence near Manchester, and scores of Nicodemuses who would treat the openly avowed claim of Spiritual influence with holy horror or scornful derision, resort privately to Mr. Edward Gallagher* to be treated for complaints that baffle all the skill of the faculty—even to trace out— much less to cure. Many are the laudations that the author hears passed upon this quiet unassuming gentleman, who as a " clairvoyant" is permitted to describe hidden diseases and cure them by *occult* power, until his fame fills the country round and attracts even the sacred presence of the very " divines" who devote their next Sabbath's sermons to unsparing diatribes against the impious practices of Spiritualism.

In the metropolis, Dr. Mack, the renowned Spiritual healer ; Mr. Younger, the fine mesmerist ; Mr. and Mrs. Hagon, Mr. Omerin, and Mr. Hawkins, all pursue their beneficent work with many a secret blessing, and many a public ban, as the reward of their services. These are all professional healers and their services are offered, and their addresses registered in the *Medium*, and that, much to the scandal of those who would cheerfully pay their twenty guineas to a solemn-visaged physician who gives a rough guess, and often an erroneous one, at the seat of their disease, and yet shrink with horror at the idea of paying a modest fee to the clairvoyant and healer because the truths they tell, and the relief they impart, are " the gifts of God, and should not be made the subject of mercenary traffic." And thus it is, that when capable Mediums, and highly gifted seers and seeresses are starved out of their spheres of usefulness, and the sound of their good report is hushed, and for very sordid need of bread they are driven to abandon their Mediumistic calling, the world cries " See how this delusion of Spiritualism has died out," and the Pharisees rejoice that they have succeeded in " crushing out professional Mediumship.'

---

* Mr. E. Gallagher, Greenfield Villa, Bloomfield Road, Heaton Chapel, Manchester.

CHAPTER XXVIII.

SPIRITUALISM IN GREAT BRITAIN (CONCLUDED).

IN THE PROVINCES.

SINCE it has been the custom to create an aristocracy of places as well as of classes; to talk of London as the geographical apex from whence the traveller goes *down* to every part of England, whether to the *north* or south; it has also followed, that prestige in every direction must originate in the metropolis, in order to fall into line with the subservience of public opinion.

Whether the immense growth of many of the large provincial towns justifies this traditional reverence for metropolitan lead, we do not care to enquire.   Certain it is, that Spiritualism is one of the iconoclasts, that has boldly defied this proscriptive deference to "the hub" of the British kingdom, for it has taken a far deeper hold on the common sense and intelligence of thoughtful minds, and exercised a far wider influence on the masses in the provinces, than it has done in the great Modern Babylon.

Whether this may be considered matter of praise or blame, the Modern Babylonians themselves may determine; the fact remains nevertheless, and we are now about to speak in illustration of this position, by citing the experiences of individuals as well as societies, who have only as yet attained to the distinction of being classified as provincial Spiritualists.

At the beautiful estate of Parkfield, Didsbury, near Manchester, till quite recently, resided Mr. Charles Blackburn, a gentleman who by his unnumbered acts of private and public munificence, has exerted a widespread influence upon the growth of English Spiritualism.   Whilst there are but few of the leading Spiritualists who have not become familiar with the lineaments of his kind cheery face, and exchanged pleasant greetings with him in circles, social gatherings, and beneath his own hospitable roof, there are not many who know as well as the author, how much the cause of Spiritualism is indebted to Mr. Blackburn for timely aid in periods of trial.

Mr. Blackburn's generous contributions were the chief support of the excellent periodical entitled *The London Spiritualist*.   Professor Crookes in the closing lines of his authoritative work, entitled "Phenomena of Spiritualism," when writing of his experiences with the celebrated Medium, Miss Florence Cook, says:—

"My thanks, and those of all Spiritualists, are also due to Mr. Charles Blackburn, for the generous manner in which he has made it possible for Miss Cook to devote her whole time to the development of these manifestations, and latterly to their scientific examination."

Few and simple as these words are, their significance is immense to those who follow out in detail, experiments which have obtained a world-wide celebrity, and are still of the highest authority as scientific testimony.

Had Mr. Charles Blackburn's munificence taken no other shape than that of upholding the usefulness of a fine Spiritual journal, and enabling

Professor Crookes, and through him, the entire generation, to profit by the wonderful Mediumship of a young lady in limited circumstances, this Manchester gentleman has done enough. But the waymarks of Mr. Blackburn's good services are to be found in many other directions—amongst scores of poor Mediums, and struggling societies whom he has aided. The investigator will remember him for the ingenious machines for weighing "materialized" Spirits which he has had constructed; in the famous Newcastle "Blackburn Cabinet," and all the associative efforts to which his name has been given, and on which his benefactions have been bestowed.

Family cares and bereavements have thickened around this worthy gentleman's path of late, and compelled his withdrawal from the scenes in which he has so long and faithfully laboured, but he carries with him into his retirement, a philosophy which will be a quenchless light in the darkest hour of trial, whilst he leaves behind him "on the sands of time" footprints of good, that can never be erased from the grateful memories of men or the imperishable records of eternity.

Another of the brave "provincial" Spiritualists, whose fearless advocacy has "helped to shake the world," is Mr. John Fowler, of St. Ann's, Sefton Park, Liverpool, a gentleman whose wealth, and influence, have been freely devoted to the advancement of the Spiritual cause.

Mr. Fowler's name became memorable in the first instance, by the uncompromising faith in Spirit power which led him to stake the sum of one thousand pounds, against the ability of one Cumberland—an itinerant conjurer and "exposer of Spiritualism"—to imitate by trickery, the manifestations which are produced by Spirit power alone, through Mediums. It need hardly be stated, that Cumberland, like the rest of his craft, had taken ample care to make his appearance as an "exposer," just at the time when there were no public Mediums at hand to compete with him. As it is well known that very few Mediums are so peculiarly endowed as to be able to meet large heterogeneous audiences, or furnish the force necessary for Spirits to produce phenomena requiring the most finely balanced psychological conditions in the rude arenas of public antagonism, so Cumberland could safely retort Mr. Fowler's challenge, with the counter demand to place his Mediums and Spiritual manifestations on the same platform with his (Cumberland's) alleged exposures.

As this very indifferent trickster was actually supported by the Lord Bishop of Liverpool, and, besides a right reverend chairman, claimed and advertised the "moral support" of hosts of other clergymen and church dignitaries, who, it thereby appeared, had been unable to find any other means of putting down the *bête noir* of their cloth—Spiritualism—so Mr. Fowler, perhaps moved to a higher concern for the honour of his "Diocesan," than that right reverend gentleman manifested for himself, addressed a letter to his Lordship through the public journals, advising him that he was only being made a tool of by an indifferent conjurer, and that the petty tricks Cumberland could display, bore no sort of relation to the manifold and inimitable phenomena produced by Spirits.

Encouraged by the rich harvest which the poorest tricksters can reap from the "moral support" of English bishops and clergy when they come before the public under the pretence of destroying that cause which a whole bench of bishops could not otherwise assail, soon after Cumberland's disappearance from the scene, still another "exposer" hastened to Liverpool to secure its clerical patronage and pocket the coin of its gullible citizens.

The new "exposer" was Irving Bishop, of American notoriety. Once again Mr. Fowler tried by the offer of the thousand pounds bait to tempt this adventurer into exposing anything that Spirits *could do, under precisely similar conditions.* This time the trickster's chairman and "moral supporter" was the Rev. J. H. Skewes, a clergyman of the Church of England, who after Bishop had utterly failed to expose anything but the credulity of his audiences, changed the base of his attack to his pulpit, where he treated his congregation to a succession of sermons on the demoniac character of Spiritual manifestations in the nineteenth century, and their angelic nature thousands of years ago, in illustration of which, amongst other notable instances of divine power, he cited the case of Jonah's living in the " cold, damp, and uncomfortable habitation of the whale's interior for three days and three nights."

Although there were few platform orators of any standing in the ranks of Spiritualism, who would not have desired to measure swords with an antagonist of a somewhat different description to the Rev. J. H. Skewes, Mr. Fowler's determination to put clerical assumptions to the test, was indomitable, and as the author of this volume was engaged periodically to lecture for the Spiritualists of Liverpool, Mr. Fowler caused answers to Mr. Skewes to be announced, for two successive Sunday evenings, by Mrs. Britten. Mr. Fowler then, by a series of letters published in the Liverpool papers, endeavoured to induce the reverend opponent to meet Mrs. Britten in public debate. Finding all his attempts in this direction only met with repeated evasions, Mr. Fowler requested Mrs. Britten to write out the replies given to Mr Skewes, the authenticity of which could be easily tested by the witness of the immense audiences assembled to hear them.

These replies were subsequently published in several papers, and by the liberality of Mr. Fowler, thousands of copies were scattered broadcast through various English-speaking countries.

The special circumstances which called forth these lectures, were stated in an introductory note which is republished below, as the final conclusion of the whole matter :—

"MRS. HARDINGE BRITTEN AND THE REV. J. H. SKEWES.

"By information received from my Spiritualistic friends in Liverpool, I learn that the faith they profess, and of which I am one of the public exponents, has been repeatedly attacked by certain members of the clergy of that city, in sermons denunciatory of Spiritualism, and by the openly avowed 'moral support' rendered to those travelling conjurers who profess by the exhibition of a few clumsy tricks to imitate and explain the *modus operandi* of Spiritual phenomena. The last, and, as I understand, the most pertinacious of the clerical assailants above named, is a 'Rev. J. H. Skewes.'

"Within the last few weeks, two sermons have been delivered by this gentleman, reported in a paper called the *Protestant Standard*, under the several (editorial) titles of 'Death-Blow to Spiritualism,' and 'Spiritualism in its Coffin!—Nailing Down the Lid ! !' It being the desire of my committee in Liverpool that I should answer these discourses, I proceeded to do so in two lectures, given at Rodney Hall, on the Sunday evenings of February 18th and March 4th, 1883.

"As Mr. Skewes stated in his second sermon that there were still many points in Spiritualism that he had not noticed, my committee followed up my lectures by challenging him to debate the subject with me on a public platform, on conditions honourable to him and beneficial to the charities of Liverpool. In answer to the repeated invitations to accept this challenge, addressed to Mr. Skewes both by public and private correspondence, the reverend gentleman declines, on the ground that he has had no fair report of my Answers to his Sermons.

"As the only report that has been given of my lectures is a series of paragraphs, headed 'Howlings from the Pit,' put forth by the *Protestant Standard*, a report which is not only interpolated by rude and unworthy personal remarks, but is most imperfect, and scarcely touches on half the matter contained in my first lectures, my committee have urged Mr. Skewes to debate the subject of Spiritualism either from the stand-points assumed in his sermons, or any fresh ones he might be able to allege against the Spiritual movement. As Mr. Skewes continues to base his refusal upon the absence of any authentic report of my Answer to his Sermons, I deem it my duty to the cause I represent, to place my Answer to Mr. Skewes's attack on record, and in such a form as cannot be mistaken. It is with this view that I put the annexed statements before the tribunal of public opinion.

"Before entering upon my task, I wish it distinctly understood that I make no profession to repeat, except in general terms, the lectures given by me at Rodney Hall, in answer to Mr. Skewes's sermons. I am not ashamed to avow that I speak in public under the inspiration of those whom I deem to be good spirits, whose wisdom supplies me with the ideas most appropriate to the occasion, and whose power far transcends my own to meet the demands which the spiritual rostrum makes upon me. Under these conditions I find it impossible to recall my lectures by memory, or to transcribe them, as they were originally delivered.

"The following Answer will, however, embody the sum of the arguments before used, and I have only to add, that, for any further elucidation of the question at issue, I still hold myself ready to meet Mr. Skewes in public discussion, under such conditions as may be agreed upon between him and my Liverpool Committee of Spiritualists.

"EMMA HARDINGE BRITTEN."

It must be added that the lectures referred to, being a complete exposition of what Spiritualism is—and what it is *not*, Mr. Skewes's action, supplemented by Mr. John Fowler's indomitable enterprise, has undoubtedly aided in bringing Spiritualism to the notice of vast numbers of the community who would otherwise have remained in profound ignorance of its verities.

Mr. Fowler also was the only individual, outside the ranks of the clergy, privileged to bear testimony to the faith of Spiritualism, before the English Church Congress, held in 1881, at Newcastle-on-Tyne. On this occasion, one or two of the clerical speakers present bore witness to the tone and temper of the times, by speaking unreservedly in favour of Spiritualism, whilst others exhibited the rancour and bitterness which this all too popular element had excited, by vituperation of a *high ecclesiastical order*.

Whilst we could wish that Mr. Fowler's necessarily brief but compendious paper could be read by thinkers of every shade of faith, we can only find space for the following excerpts from his brave utterances :—

"Every man must observe the present indifferent state of the intelligent public to the service and doctrines of the Church. Those who have had opportunities of observing the intellectual state of the country say that infidelity is on the increase. Now, what does the Church propose to do in this matter? Of its seriousness proof is offered by the fact of this discussion. Until the facts of spiritual existence have been demonstrated, like Peter, who denied his Master, we want evidence, and, like Thomas, we want to put our fingers into the prints of the nails. If demonstration was needed to establish the faith in the hearts of the disciples, demonstration is as much needed to-day, to establish its claims in the experience of the present generation. The fabric cannot be maintained. It will fall to pieces without the interior leavening power of the Spirit. Narrow creeds and ceremonies cannot impose on and influence for ever the minds of men. Therefore, Modern Spiritualism has appeared as a Divine necessity of the times. It does not come to destroy the law and the prophets, but to establish that which came aforetime, and to make the possibilities of spiritual growth and strength in the heart of man more possible. . . .

"Therefore we say that a case has been made out on behalf of Modern Spiritualism to be recognised and utilised by the Church itself, that it may become strong to defeat its own doubts, and, in the full reliance of its hope, do battle with the hard foes who deny the immortality of the soul. If Spiritualists do not universally retain their allegiance to the doctrines of the Church of England, it matters but very little. The Church, by fairly and squarely investigating the alleged facts, will bring together into one focus philosophers and thinkers who otherwise might have remained outside the pale of the Church. To shelve the question by saying that Spiritualism is an imposition displays either presumption or ignorance." . . .

The example above given of Mr. Fowler's address, is sufficient to demonstrate its admirable lines of argument. The effect produced upon the community has been marked and healthful. A far more respectful sentiment has been manifested towards Spiritualism by the thinking classes, since the Church Congress was in session, whilst the impulse given to the cause in Liverpool, is sufficiently proved by the large numbers who gather together each Sunday to attend the Spiritualists' services. For the present these meetings are held in Rodney Hall, under the management of an efficient committee, and the presidency of John Lamont, Esq., a gentleman held in the highest estimation by all classes of his fellow-citizens, besides being a seer and inspirational speaker of remarkable power. Mrs. Hardinge Britten is the regular lecturer of the Society for two Sundays in each month during the present season; Mr. W. J. Colville, from America, Mr. and Mrs. Wallis, Mrs. Groom and other speakers of pronounced excellence filling the rostrum on alternate Sundays.

In Belper, Derbyshire, the Spiritualists enjoy the privilege of holding their Sunday services in the pleasant and commodious hall built, and generously placed at the disposal of his Spiritualist friends and associates, by Mr. W. P. Adshead, the gentleman before mentioned in connection with Miss Wood's *séances.*

The kindly sentiments which prevail amongst the Spiritualists of Belper, and the many acts of beneficence towards the poor which are practised in their hall, fill the place with a high and holy influence, and fittingly consecrate it to the ministry of angels, on earth as in heaven.

In Bradford, Yorkshire, a large and zealous society of working men and women have combined to hire a good hall, which they entitle the Walton Street Church, and here, as in Belper, the exalting influence of a specially-consecrated place, and the effect of well conducted and orderly services is felt by every sensitive who visits the meetings. Two other well attended meetings are held every Sunday in Bradford, besides what may be emphatically called "mass meetings" in one of the largest halls in the town, when the author, or other speakers from a distance, are engaged, by the energetic and self-sacrificing Bradford Spiritualists.

A special hall has also been built and devoted to the Spiritual Sunday services, at Sowerby Bridge, Yorkshire, where a fine and well-trained choir of young people adds the charm of excellent singing to the elevating influences which pervade the place.

Those who, like the author, have realised with painful sensibility the injurious or favourable effects produced by the different places where Spiritual services are conducted, will be ready to join with her in the fervent wish that wealthy Spiritualists would emulate the example of good Mr. Adshead, and provide in every town and hamlet of Great Britain a true Spiritual home for the people, and a fitting scene in which to invite the angels to come and participate in holy Spiritual exercises. If there be any truth in Spiritual revelations at all, those who would make such an use of the means committed to their stewardship on earth, would certainly find that they had been

"Fitting up a mansion
Which eternally will stand."

In Leeds, Halifax, Keighley, Bradford, and nearly all the principal towns and villages of Yorkshire, well conducted Sunday meetings are held, some- times aided by renowned speakers from a distance, but in general ministered to by resident Mediums, most of whom—under trance conditions—give discourses far beyond the average of their normal capacity. The speakers are for the most part such devoted men and women as good faithful Joseph Armitage of Batley Carr ; Mrs. Dobson, Mrs. Illingworth ; Misses Hance, Shipley, and Harrison ; Mrs. Wilson, Mrs. Greig ; Messrs. Wilson Oliffe, Blackburn, and many others too numerous to mention. All these are working people, toiling during the week in their several vocations, but giving cheerfully, without stint, and often at the cost of labour and fatigue to themselves, their best service every Sunday to platform utterances, and that most commonly with little or no remuneration.

In the meantime, such noble gentlemen as Mr. John Culpan of Halifax, a Spiritual veteran who for thirty years has given means, untiring service, and an honoured name to the advancement of the cause. Mr. B. Lees, Mr. John Illingworth, Mr. Etchells, of Huddersfield, David Richmond, the veteran Spiritualist of Darlington, Dr. Brown, of Burnley, Mr. Foster, of Preston, good John Harwood, of Littleborough, and Peter Lee, of Rochdale, splendid representatives of Yorkshire and Lancashire Spiritualism—these, and hosts of others, with not a few faithful and zealous ladies, devote themselves by purse and person to the best interests of humanity through the noble cause of Spiritualism.

In a crowded record of this character, many a good and honoured name must necessarily be omitted, but none can doubt that they are all engraved in the imperishable types of the higher life to which their noble services so effectually point the way.

In Newcastle-on-Tyne, the residence of the esteemed scientist T. P. Barkas, a " Spiritual Evidence Society " has been formed, which has done good service by maintaining Sunday meetings, and promoting *séances* for the culture of Spiritual gifts, and the investigation of phenomena.

It was at these circles that Miss Wood—the celebrated physical medium mentioned in a former chapter—was developed.

The Newcastle Society has moreover exercised a fostering influence upon that large section of country in the vicinity, devoted to the industries of coal mining. Here, as in Yorkshire, local Mediums and trance speakers keep alive the interest of their various districts, with addresses which produce a deep and favourable impression on their listeners.

The author has herself visited two or three of these collieries, and was deeply moved by the sight of the earnest-looking sons of toil massed in serried groups around her. When no strangers visit them, they are addressed by some of the inspirational speakers who abound in these districts. One of the most eloquent, sincere, and popular lecturers of the Northumberland meetings is Mr. Henry Burton, a good and true man, whose life and preaching are both well calculated to demonstrate the exalting influence of Spirit teachings.

The large manufacturing county of Lancashire, though by no means as thickly studded with zealous Spiritual communities as Yorkshire or Northumberland, is nevertheless a stronghold of the faith. Liverpool has already been noticed ; meantime Rochdale, Oldham, Manchester, Burnley, Blackburn, and numerous other places of importance maintain Sunday meetings, where vast multitudes listen with profound interest to the consoling doctrines of Spiritualism, taught by the zealous local Mediums who are to be found in those districts.

In the last named place, Blackburn, a large and busy manufacturing town, the author was instrumental in forming the excellent " Psychological Society," which now holds regular Sunday meetings there.

After the occasion of Mrs. Britten's first visit, the secretary of the Society sent a report to the *Medium* which is reprinted for the sake of the *declaration of principles* it contains—one which might be profitably adopted by other religious societies besides the Spiritualists of Blackburn. Our correspondent says :—

" Spiritualism is looking up at present in Blackburn. During the last few months we have had Mrs. Britten two Sundays occupying the platform of the Exchange : afternoon and evening each visit. The room will hold from 1,200 to 1,800 people, and was packed at each of the four lectures. . . .

" We have also opened rooms for Sunday evening lectures, at the School of Science. There seem to be plenty of fresh faces every Sunday come to listen to what is said. We have a very nice meeting room, and best of all is, that everything is paid for ; we mind that, whatever comes or goes not to run in debt. We are very strong Trinitarians, but the Trinity we believe in is, ' One God ; no Devil, and twenty shillings to the pound.'

" We feel confident if we only had real good speakers like Mrs. Britten, we could without any fear take the Exchange every Sunday. We make no charge for tickets or admission, but trust to the voluntary offerings of the people, and strange to say that although not making much more than bare expenses, we have never come short of meeting the expenses. The people are thirsting for more knowledge on the subject ; the pity is we have no one to give them the knowledge.—Yours, etc.,

"R. WOLSTENHOLME."

In Macclesfield, an earnest and united Society of believers in Spiritualism have hired and furnished a pleasant little hall, where services are generally conducted by the Rev. Adam Rushton, an estimable gentleman, formerly a Unitarian Minister, but one who gave up sect, and even the goodwill of friends and kindred, to throw in his lot with those who believed in the faith of which he became convinced, and to which, in his modest and unostentatious way, he gives his life and able services.

A similarly self-sacrificing profession of the Spiritual faith has been made by the Rev. Mr. Stoddart of Middlesboro', near Stockton-on-Tees. This gentleman was also an Unitarian Minister, but one whose persecutions for the sake of his faith have not as yet, been attended with a settlement as peaceful as that which Mr. Rushton finds in his little Macclesfield Society. Mr. Stoddart however is bound to make his mark, and the good angels he serves have obviously not forgotten their charge over their faithful soldier.

In Nottingham, Mr. Wm. Yates, a gentleman of fine culture, and indomitable energy, together with a few ladies and gentlemen of superior intellectual attainments, have struggled bravely to sustain an unsectarian representation of Spiritualism. Mr. Yates has also commenced the practice of medical electricity combined with magnetism, under the direction of beneficent healing Spirits, and report speaks in enthusiastic terms of the brilliant conquests he is effecting over otherwise incurable forms of disease.

In Birmingham, resides Mrs. Groom, an indefatigable trance speaker, healer, and seeress, who adds to her interesting Sunday lectures, the faculty of seeing and describing the spirit friends of persons in her audience. The labours of this excellent Medium have effected an immense amount of good in the places she visits.

In Birmingham, Walsall, Leicester, and other Midland towns and villages, small Sunday meetings are held, which promise, with good speakers and good management, to swell to large gatherings.

In the West and South of England, less public evidence of progress is demonstrable, although there are many places where it is generally known that good Spiritual meetings have been held, and large numbers of private circles are in session.

One of the most prosperous Spiritual societies in the South-west of England, is that established at Plymouth, where many private circles are held, and regular Sunday services are at present conducted with great acceptance by Mr. Clarke, an excellent inspirational speaker.

The formation of the Plymouth Society, as well as much of the good work which it has achieved, is due to the labours of the Rev. C. Ware, but as this gentleman's experience is modestly narrated in his own statement recently published in the Society's report of their first anniversary celebration, we cannot do better than give the account which we find printed in a recent issue of *Light*, and which is to the following effect :—

"PLYMOUTH.—THE FREE SPIRITUAL SOCIETY.

"The Free Spiritual Society of Plymouth last evening celebrated its anniversary at Richmond Hall, Richmond Street, it being exactly twelve months since its origin. The Rev. C. Ware, having laboured for two years in this town as a minister of one of the Methodist bodies, was suspended in January of last year on account of his belief in Spiritualism ; but a number of persons holding similar views having formed themselves into a Society, invited him to become their minister, in which capacity he has since acted. The Society during the year has considerably increased its membership and extended its operations, and now claims to enjoy the patronage, sympathy, and support of many influential friends beyond its formal membership. The proceedings last evening afforded a fair indication that the community is in a flourishing condition ; about eighty sat down to tea, and at the public meeting that followed, presided over by Mr. W. T. Rossiter, of Torquay, addresses were delivered by several gentlemen from the town and neighbourhood. Several mediums also took part in the meeting.

"The Rev. C. Ware, after making reference to the general aspects of Spiritualism, said it was pretty well known that he had laboured in this town for two years as a minister of one of the Methodist bodies. During that time he became acquainted with Spiritualism, and at the outset it presented itself to him as an astounding and glorious reality. Because he would not deny what he knew to be the truth, and forego the study of the profoundest subject that could occupy the mind of man, he was suspended from the denominational pulpit. There were those, however, who refused to submit to ecclesiastical tyranny and mental slavery, and these formed themselves into a Free Spiritual Society, and invited him to become their minister. The Society was formed twelve months ago in the house of one of their friends ; a few days afterwards they secured a room at the Octagon, and took their stand as a religious body. Soon after this they removed to their present hall. They had had to encounter great difficulties and various forms of opposition. In September, a conjurer, called Irving Bishop, came to Plymouth to give the ' death blow to Spiritualism.' For a time the subject was in everybody's mouth, and of course ' everybody' went to hear him ; for a time Spiritualists seemed to be objects of commiseration until Irving Bishop proved himself a cheat, by failing to exhibit a single phase of Spiritualism. A correspondence thereupon commenced in the *Western Daily Mercury*, in which a whole galaxy of writers took part ; for a time the battle was tremendous, but he thought they could say without boasting that they poured into the enemy's ranks such a fire of stubborn facts as to leave their opponents ' without a leg to stand upon.' It was impossible for him to give them an idea of the advantage their cause derived from this controversy ; it was certainly the best work ever done for it. Since the year commenced they had placed a splendid harmonium in the hall, and he was pleased to tell them that the past week was a worthy climax to the year's work, for he had not seen such vitality manifested at any time during the year. The fact was, that no cause ever had a brighter outlook than theirs. They had no creed, except the Fatherhood of God and the brotherhood of humanity ; and they enjoyed perfect liberty, their motto being to think and allow others to think ; their aim being simply the natural development of each individual human soul. They could reckon amongst their company that evening some ten mediums, and ere the meeting closed they would, no doubt, hear some of them speak in the trance state, expressing the thoughts of their invisible friends."

Of the few professional speakers who are from time to time engaged in the work of Spiritual revivalism, the limitations of space will only allow us to make very brief mention.

15

Mr. and Mrs. Wallis of Walsall are both highly gifted trance speakers, and their eloquent ministrations are warmly appreciated wherever they go. Of unblemished character and moral worth, the very lives of this noble couple form a sermon, of which any religious denomination might be proud. Mrs. Groom has already been noticed. Several other acceptable speakers of the Spiritual rostrum might take exception to being classified as professionals, consequently, in addition to the author of this volume, it only remains to notice Mr. J. J. Morse, a most admirable lecturer, and a gentleman who has rendered himself worthy of that designation, by Spiritual culture alone.

When the author first knew Mr. Morse, he had risen from an obscure position of drudgery, to one but little better, as the shopman at Mr. Burn's Spiritual Institution. Here his marvellous powers as a trance Medium became unfolded, until at length, by virtue of being made the instrument of exalted and philosophic Spirits, he grew nearer to their level; became one with them instead of simply their automatic mouthpiece, and finally, by force of these educational processes, and his own indomitable perseverance, Mr. Morse has risen to a position of honourable eminence in the realm of Spiritual literature, and occupies the rank of one of the most attractive trance speakers of the day.

In a cause which is still *in transitu*, and amongst a vast number of moving forms who are still *making history*, it would be as unwise to find fault with methods, and criticize the action of individuals, as to complain of the variable clouds which may disappear to-morrow, or the oppressive sunshine which may be modified in the course of a single hour. Every movement in Spiritualism is at present transitional; nearly all the efforts at propagandism now conducted by Spiritualists, are expedients of the hour, whilst to-morrow may call for a widely different course of action. It need be no matter of surprise therefore, that the traditional grumbler finds ample food for his discontent to prey upon, whilst the enthusiast hails every gleam of sunshine that glances across his path, as the advent of the long looked for millennium. On the mountain top, or in the valley, still we repeat we are but *in transitu*, and whilst we pause to criticize, dogmatize, or even attempt to organize, the occasion which seemed to call for our special line of conduct will have passed away, and sweep us along with the current to meet a new emergency of the times.

It is under these ever-changing aspects of the Spiritual cause, that the author's pen has been again and again suspended by an invisible but ever present monitor, when she would have applied in her human blindness, words of censure in one direction, and urgent counsels in another. "God understands," murmurs the angel of guidance in the ear of the scribe. "Write—Behold I make all things new!" cries another angelic teacher. Satisfied that the movement which seems so confused and heterogeneous in the dazzled eyes of humanity, is dictated by divine wisdom, ruled by Almighty power, and working together for supreme good, our part is to keep our lamps trimmed and burning and wait for the coming of the Heavenly Bridegroom whose name is—Divine Order.

This is the end of this publication.

Any remaining blank pages are for our book binding
requirements and are blank on purpose.

To search thousands of interesting publications like this one,
please remember to visit our website at:

http://www.kessinger.net

CPSIA information can be obtained
at www.ICGtesting.com
Printed in the USA
BVHW011734271218
536529BV00003B/43/P